Informal Learning and Digital Media

Informal Learning and Digital Media

Edited by

Kirsten Drotner, Hans Siggaard Jensen
and Kim Christian Schrøder

Cambridge Scholars Publishing

Informal Learning and Digital Media,
Edited by Kirsten Drotner, Hans Siggaard Jensen and Kim Christian Schrøder

This book first published 2008 by

Cambridge Scholars Publishing

15 Angerton Gardens, Newcastle, NE5 2JA, UK

British Library Cataloguing in Publication Data
A catalogue record for this book is available from the British Library

ISBN (10): 1-84718-551-7, ISBN (13): 9781847185518

TABLE OF CONTENTS

LIST OF FIGURES

LIST OF TABLES

INTRODUCTION

CONCEPTUAL AND RELATIONAL VAGARIES OF LEARNING AND MEDIA

KIRSTEN DROTNER, HANS SIGGAARD JENSEN AND KIM CHRISTIAN SCHRØDER

Learning holds a paradoxical position in contemporary societies. The widespread discourse that we live in knowledge economies, or knowledge societies, has propelled policies and practices of education and learning to the center of public attention unknown a few decades ago. Yet, at the same time the conceptual boundaries of learning and education are contested and transmuting.

The present volume cuts into that paradox by exploring answers to the simple question: in what ways, if any, do digital media play a role in the formation and possible handlings of this paradox? The overarching perspective framing the following contributions is to analyse and attempting to understand the current relations between digital media and learning in order to advance the possible benefits that may be reaped from their interaction. These benefits may range from conceptual synergy through empirical practices on to policy implications, and the volume is structured so as to cover all three dimensions.

Contributors also approach these dimensions from different fields such as media studies, ICT studies and education studies. But indicative of the intensified collaboration between these fields, the contributors share an interest in what may be termed a relational approach to digital media and to learning. In terms of media, this means an approach which acknowledges that digitization facilitates a joint technological platform for text and image, sound and numbers, and a blurring of boundaries between media that are born digital, so to speak, such as the personal computer, the internet, games consoles and mobile devices, and media that may be, or already are, digitized such as books and newspapers, television, film and radio. *Digital media*, in the this perspective, encompass information and communication technologies, or ICTs, as well as print and broadcast media. Importantly, such a perspective serves to transform scholarly interest from technology to substance and uses, to textual and social relations.

The relational perspective equally informs our understanding of learning. The increasing scholarly and practical interest in learning as much as education not only signals the contested nature of the boundaries between the two. It does. But, more important to this volume, it signals an increased interest in the social processes of knowledge formation, irrespective of the means, sites and objectives of these processes. The term *informal learning*, in this perspective, highlights this relational take on learning in two capacities. It defines *learning* as socially situated processes of knowledge formation; and it acknowledges that these processes can be thought about and take shape within a number of boundaries that mutually help define one another, as in the case of the term *informal* which immediately invites its opposite *formal*.

Both digital media and informal learning are conflictual terms, and their respective transmutations are taken up in several contributions. Still, the key interest rests with the relations between the two. One need not buy into the rhetoric, often of a celebratory or concerned nature, about the knowledge society in order to realise that digital media do hold a potential to transform learning in a number of important ways. Online games, social networking websites such as the videosharing site YouTube and community-generated encyclopedias such as wikipedia all offer new means of communication, collaboration and creation for their users. Equally, it seems beyond doubt that school no longer holds a monopoly as a site for learning experiences that are deemed relevant by learners. Notably the internet and mobile devices have been instrumental for a dispersion of sites for potential learning. In terms of physical place, the advanced mobile technologies now available in many areas of the world facilitate location-based learning options as users may generate and share images, surf the internet and use socalled satellite maps, or sat maps. In terms of virtual space, the internet facilitates an immediacy of exchange and interaction whose full potentials are still to be explored.

When the dispersion of physical and virtual settings for learning is matched by the ever-increasing storage capacities of computing, it seems obvious that both digital media and learning are transmuting phenomena, whose relation merits closer inspection. Still, technological change often outpaces socio-cultural practices. A relational research perspective, therefore, fundamentally involves that we pay close attention to the particulars of just how learning processes and digital media interact -

under which cirumstances, through which practices, and with what outcomes and implications. Questions of inclusion and exclusion immediately spring to mind, just as do questions of the economic ramifications within which digital media are explored for learning.

In terms of digital media, questions of inclusion and exclusion are debated as questions of socalled digital divides (Warschauer 2004). These divides are often tackled as problems of access, while their most drastic implications are possibly to do with inequalities of use – of children having very pronounced differences in terms of learning and knowing how to handle the complexities of media in ways that are relevant to their current lives and future situation. Digital divides demonstrate an intimate connection to familiar fault lines in terms of class, gender, ethnicity, age and region (Fox 2005, Peter & Valkenburg 2006). Questions need to be asked about the ways in which we must structure and develop learning in order to minimise such divides, and several contributors offer theory-based empirical answers.

The economic ramifications, within which relations between digital media and learning are currently explored, equally merit close inspection. While education in many countries upholds democratic ideals of access based on personal, not financial, abilities, learning processes hold no such promises, since, in principle, they may take place anywhere. When learning takes shape through the appropriation of digital media, economic considerations loom even larger. It may be argued that internet technology is free for the end user, but access is not, or only rarely so. Equally, most other digital media are developed as commercial enterprises, both in terms of hardware and software. Use comes at a price, and often a substantial one. However, the commercial nature of most processes of digital learning is easily downplayed in favour of more visible aspects of appropriation and policy-making - a structural bias which is taken up most directly by Julian Sefton-Green in the book's concluding chapter.

The organization of the book

The chapters which make up this book originate in the conference *Informal learning and digital media: Constructions, contexts, consequences*, organized by the Danish Research Centre on Education and Advanced Media Materials (DREAM) in September 2006 (http://www.sdu.dk/Om_SDU/Institutter_centre/Dream.aspx), and are organized in three parts. Part One, *Practices of Production*, is opened by Kirsten Drotner's chapter "Informal learning and digital media: Perceptions, practices and perspectives", which lays out the relations between informal learning and digital media in conceptual as well as policy terms. Her claim, in brief, is that the increasing interest in this relation is based on conflictual remappings of competence formation that the pervasive discourses on the knowledge society have brought about, and she argues for an inclusive and critical definition of digital literacy as a key competence that may help bridge boundaries between informal and formal takes on learning.

In Chapter Two, "Googling movies: Digital media production and the 'culture of apropriation'", Øystein Gilje argues that the digitization of media makes it much easier to appropriate, combine and remix semiotic material than ever before. The chapter presents both quantitative and qualitative data from a new media and communication subject in the curriculum of the upper secondary school in Norway. Gilje argues that digital software and an internet connection, as *cultural tools*, provide the learner with new affordances in the process of editing video, and discusses *literacy practices* that evolve in the 'culture of appropriation'.

In Chapter Three, "Acting and learning with avatars: Sense-making strategies of reflection in the virtual world of a massively multi-user online role-playing game', Sisse Siggaard Jensen reports from an ongoing research project on actors and avatars communicating in virtual worlds. She suggests that we should study the informal learning processes of massively multi-user online role-playing games (MMORPGs) in order to help us inform a designing strategy for virtual framings aimed for acts of reflection. Using video-interviewing to follow the actors while they are playing the role-playing game of EverQuest, Jensen explores whether such framings may support informal learning and show new directions for organizational learning.

Part Two, *Contexts of Use*, opens with Glynda Hull and Nora Kenney's chapter, "Hopeful children, hybrid spaces: Learning with media after school," in which they focus on a case study of a digitally very proficient young boy and his experience in an informal, non-scholastic, after-school learning environment. This environment was established in order to give new learning opportunities and forms of learning experience to young people in a city area close to UC Berkeley, thus making it possible to study media and digital learning in a multimodal context. Based both on close case studies and theoretical reflection, the chapter contributes to our understanding of learning, popular culture and digital literacy in today's society.

Sarita Yardi's chapter, "From multimedia to multiple voices: Conflicts in collaborative learning cultures," discusses the role of collaboration in formal and informal learning environments and the challenges posed by the use, reuse, and appropriation of different types of media. Like the previous chapter, it is based on an after-school program in which students participated in collaborative digital story telling activities, and it applies Mikhail Bakhtin's theory of dialogism to describe the factors that contribute to students' ideas about ways in which they can collaborate in classroom activities. The study thus explores how the collaborative tensions can be transformed into a positive learning environment in the classroom.

In Chapter Six, "(Student) life's a game: Personal development planning as an interactive simulation," Kirkpatrick, Lancaster and Wilson describe an on-line game which has been developed for first year undergraduate students at the University of Manchester in the U.K. The purpose of the project was to develop a computer game to support the students' Personal Development Planning (PDP). It focuses on the experience of actually playing the game, and discusses game play as a particular repertoire of learning in the digital domain.

In the last chapter in Part Two, "When all else fails: The internet and adolescent-immigrants' informal learning," Nelly Elias and Dafna Lemish look into the roles of the internet in the lives of immigrant adolescents, whose social situation is characterized on the one hand by social isolation and the weakening of traditional socializing agents, and distrust of the local socializing agents, on the other. They find that for these adolescents the internet serves as a central agent of socialization, a source of information about their new society, its mores, norms, and culture, as well as an important resource to teach peers about their homeland and to build self esteem.

Part Three includes five insightful contributions that illuminate *Perspectives for Education*. The first, Chapter Eight, "Learning theory, video games, and popular culture," by James Paul Gee is based on the basic – and new – assumption that the best current model of the mind is a video game. The astonishing successes of video games have significant implications for learning theory and the design of learning processes. Various aspects of video games, both connected to their character as simulations and as games, are explored. The fact that the player is both inside and outside the game - has a proxy in the game - is significant, and so is the experience of seeing the world from different and new perspectives through playing the game, and being forced to make important decisions. Finally the potential for taking the learning principles of video games – not made for learning explicitly – into design of games made explicitly for learning is explored for a game of urban planning.

In Chapter Ten, "Literacy on a social networking site," Håvard Skaar presents an ethnographic study of a group of 6th graders' (aged 11-12) literacy on a social networking site called Piczo, where the users present themselves not only through written text, but also by the use of photos, animations, sounds, music, video clips, and other kinds of semiotic resources. Skaar develops a typology of literacy types and subsequently discusses the commercial aspects of the pupils' literacy on the Piczo site in contrast to the normative aspects of literacy in the school environment.

Moving to internet terrain that is perhaps more familiar to international readers, Dan Perkel in the chapter titled "Copy and paste literacy? Literacy practices in the production of a Myspace profile" argues that MySpace is an environment that fosters the development of new literacies. Drawing on examples from fieldwork and his own use of the site, the analysis is based on a model that tries to reconcile social and technical perspectives on literacy. The expressive power found in the creation of a MySpace profile concerns a technically simple but socially complex practice: the copying and pasting of *code* as a way to appropriate and reuse other people's media products. By integrating theories of appropriation and reuse of media with theories of literacy, a new way of thinking about this practice emerges in which "participation" and "remix" are important concepts to describe the social and technical aspects of these new literacy practices.

In chapter Eleven, "Creating media literacy in Japan: Initiatives for new Citizenship," Yosuke Morimoto discusses the challenges facing Japanese students in the advanced media society, and the need for systematic media literacy education in Japanese schools, on the basis of the Takatsuki Media Literacy Project, a three year research project being conducted by the Japan Media Literacy Research Institute (JMLRI). In Japan, Media Literacy Education has not been integrated into the curriculum of the formal educational system, and no government initiatives currently exist to promote media literacy, so it is up to centres like the Tonda Youth Center to actively foster new citizenship, which includes media literacy. The chapter includes a survey mapping the current media environment of young people in Japan 2006 and the influence of the mainstream media on students' life styles and values.

In the final chapter on "Informal learning: A solution in search of a problem?", Julian Sefton-Green self-critically examines the notion of informal learning and its close association with commercial media uses in out-of-school contexts. Bringing a much-needed historical perspective to the ongoing and conflictual discussions on informal learning, Sefton-Green critiques applications of the term for a general analytical disregard of the political economy involved in informal learning practices with digital media, and thus tacitly assuming an empowering potential that may not be empirically substantiated.

As this brief appetizer to the work collected in this volume has hopefully demonstrated, the contributions are diverse in their varying emphases on and mixtures of theoretical, methodological and empirical perspectives on mediatised learning along the continuum from informal to formal learning environments. Moreover, the authors represent a wide international range of scholarly experience and expertise, a range that not only documents important, empirical variations, but equally testifies to the deep interest across sites and settings in exploring the relations between informal learning and digital media. However, all contributors share a commitment to explore the ways in which the media/learning nexus is creatively played out by young people in our more and more pervasively digital age. And in the course of their explorations they manage to challenge their readers to reflect imaginatively on what precisely we mean by 'digital literacies', on the ways to research these, and the measures to be adopted if we want to promote them.

References

Fox, S. 2005. *Digital divisions: The Pew Internet and American Life Project*, http//www.pewinternet.org (retrieved August 14, 2007).

Peter, J., and P. M. Valkenburg. 2006. Adolescents' internet use: Testing the "Disappearing Digital Divide" versus the "Emerging Differentiation" Approach. *Poetics* 34(4-5): 293-305.

Warschauer, M. 2004. *Technology and social inclusion: Rethinking the digital divide.* Cambridge, MA: MIT Press.

PART I:

PRACTICES OF PRODUCTION

CHAPTER ONE

INFORMAL LEARNING AND DIGITAL MEDIA: PERCEPTIONS, PRACTICES AND PERSPECTIVES

KIRSTEN DROTNER

Informal learning is a much used, some would say misused, term in educational theory and debate. Indications of the wide interest in sustaining organised, professional dialogue around informal learning and related terms are, for example, the emergence of the *Informal Learning Review*, *Journal of Informal Science Education*, *The Handbook of implicit learning* (Stadler and Frensch 1998) and the not-for-profit internet sites www.infed.org, which hosts an encyclopedia and archive, and www.informalscience.org, which resources research on learning at science centres and museums.

How may informal learning be defined? How is it applied and developed? What is its intellectual and pedagogical heritage? The many answers given to questions such as these have primarily focused on conceptual characteristics and pedagogical applications, with rather less offered in the way of intellectual discourses and historical contextualisation of the term. In order to help balance our understanding of the term, I will first address its discursive positionings before discussing some of the key attempts to define its substance and ramifications as these pertain to digital media. For, the basic claim underlying the present chapter, is that digital media serve to transform our understanding and appropriations of informal learning, not only in conceptual terms, but in policy and practical terms, as well.

Informal learning as supplement: Liberal discourses

The term informal learning immediately conjures up its opposite, namely formal learning. Whoever applies the term informal learning does so with a view to what lies beyond, evades or is neglected by formal learning policies and practices. In discursive terms, informal learning invariably carries on a tacit or explict dialogue with current understandings of formal learning, which is most often defined as the educational system or schooling. Naturally, this system involves a number of dimensions, legal, organisational, physical and pedagogical, and in the second part of this chapter I return to the ways in which these dimensions impinge upon our substantive definitions of informal learning. At this stage, the important point to be made is that different discourses on informal learning tell us as much about different conceptions of educational systems as they do about informal learning itself. With this caveat in mind, we may distinguish between three discourses on informal learning, namely a liberal, a critical and a functional discourse. Each of these maps on to similar discursive distinctions of formal learning, and they may partly be linked to different aims, spatial settings and temporal cycles of what learning is for, and where and when it takes place.

The liberal discourse takes informal learning to be an important, even necessary, supplement to what school has to offer both in terms of aims and processes of learning. The German term *Bildung*, dating from the late 18th century, neatly sums up the ideal of a rounded character formation which school may not always attain in its attempts to inculcate more concrete skills and competences. And while the actual term informal was not used to define the many music schools, drama societies and sports clubs emerging during the late 19th and early 20th centuries in newly urbanised and industrialised areas of Europe and North America, their rationale and pedagogical focus speak centrally to a liberal understanding of informal learning which still informs current trends. The individual is at the core of attention, and the arts offer important topics of interest.

The liberal discourse unfolds at a time when industrial societies develop mass schooling that trains pupils within demarcated parts of their lives in well-defined skills based on the three Rs, reading, writing and arithmetic. In tandem with these organisational developments, and informing their aims, psychology develops a view upon the formation of the human mind as a gradual progression in ages and stages, thus lending credibility to the individualist view upon learning. Today, such views are reflected when educationalists argue for self-paced progression as an important asset of informal learning, and when it is claimed that learning needs no organisational underpinnings but may result from unplanned, everyday interactions.

Informal learning as alternative: Critical discourses

Informal learning is defined as an alternative to formal learning within discourses that take a critical view on schooling. The Brazilian educationalist Paulo Freire's approach is exemplary of this tradition in its insistence upon the inherently social and dialogical character of learning and in its sustained linking of knowledge, power and social change (Freire 1972, 1995). Also, Austrian-born Ivan Illich has influenced the critical discourse with his insistence that the very organisational framework of schooling is a key constraint on learning (Illich 1971). The critical approach has particular resonance in societies that demonstrate stark social divides in the access to formal schooling and in societies struggling to develop educational structures. Thus, from its inception UNESCO has strongly supported informal learning as a democratising force and as a means of social inclusion (*Fundamental Education* 1947, Faure et al. 1972, Singh 2005).

Unlike the liberal discourse, the critical discourse on informal learning extends its focus of interest to include adults in addition to the younger generations. Bearing in mind the political economy of most societies, this extended focus offers new possibilities to address the power implications resulting from unequal distribution of resources for learning. Critical educational policies advancing informal learning structures in opposition to school follow in the ideological footsteps of Britain's socalled working-men's institutes flourishing in the 19th century. These self-organised institutions were based on a claim that knowledge is power and a belief in learning as a joint practice. Still, learning was defined in relation to the type of knowledge-formation generated through schooling rather than through the learning practices that many participants would be familiar with from their daily work in the workshop or the mine. However, the hands-on learning processes of the workplace, or in direct preparation for a job, have assumed increasing professional interest since the 1980s, not least with community groups and non-governmental organisations (see overview in Colley et al. 2003). Informal aspects of vocational training have since been taken up in a big way by more functional discourses on informal learning.

Informal learning as extension: Functionalist discourses

Today, it is difficult to conceive of learning as a process neatly confined to specific physical and organisational domains or to particular phases of the human biography. In some sense, the concept of lifelong learning, which has assumed a key policy importance in many parts of the world, harks back to age-old ways of learning in terms of apprentices and helping-hands. Research on lifelong learning ranges from critical to more celebratory positions (Knowles 1970, Bentley 1998, McGivney 1999). But most researchers and policy-makers associate lifelong learning with vocational work and with ongoing training that may take different degrees of planning, organisation and validation – from work interactions and in-house training to longer spells of certified competence development. Informal learning is defined as a key element in these processes, and a central point of debate is whether or not to develop systems of outcome validation (Bjørnåvold 2000).

Particularly in education policy, informal learning is seen in functional terms as an ongoing and flexible means through which the workforce may update specific skills necessary to operate successfully in dynamic societies. For example, the European Union has pushed for integration of informal learning schemes into the general education provision in its member states as a critical element in fulfilling the Union's vision of making Europe one of the leading knowledge-based economies of the world (European Commission 2001, Edwards and Boreham 2003). Similar efforts are made in countries such as Australia and Canada (Misko et al. 2007, Livingstone 2001, *Unlocking* 2007).

Informal learning and knowledge societies

Indeed, the functionalist discourse on informal learning is nurtured by even more pervasive discourses, namely that current societies are information societies, knowledge societies, learning societies or network societies (Castells 1996, Hutchins 1968, Husén 1974, Ransom 1994, Stehr 1994). Irrespective of terminology and scientific tradition, these discourses claim that we have witnessed a qualititative transformation from material to immaterial forms of production, distribution and consumption. What is more, it is claimed that the crucial drivers of this transformation are digital technologies including the internet, the personal computer and mobile forms of communication. While the technological optimism underlying such claims has been severely criticised (Robins and Webster 1999, Garnham 2000), the discourses have nevertheless had what Roland Barthes in another context called a "reality effect." For, in tandem with these discursive developments, and indicative of their surmised implications, have been intensive economic, technological and political initiatives and interventions on a national as well as an international scale to help further what is perceived as a massive transformation in competence formation.

Two aspects of this transformation are crucial to note in order to understand the complex interlocking of informal learning and digital media. First, it is assumed that the vital tenets of knowledge societies, to use a shorthand for the numerous terms applied, are the storage, formation, processing and increasingly global communication of signs – be they numbers, text, sound or images. A key competence is therefore semiotic competence, that is the ability to give shape to and handle an increasingly complex constellation of signs as part of everyday collaboration, communication and participation. Second, since the internet and mobile devices facilitate access to these complex, semiotic learning processes at different spatial and temporal locations, school is seen as no longer holding a monopoly on resourcing literacies that are deemed necessary for the 21st century (Drotner 2007). More and more social practices are defined as learning processes, and more and more aspects of identity are enrolled as potential competences. For example, online and mobile forms of communication involve (unsolicited) encounters with distant others, and successful communication during these encounters involves participants' ability to deal with such "semiotic othernesses" by drawing on a range of situated personal capacities.

As is evident, the reality effect following from the discourse on the knowledge society and similar terms serves to renew discussions about informal learning, and, I would claim, to transform our understanding of the relations between formal and informal dimensions of learning. In order to substantiate these claims to be unfolded below, I will first revisit some of the key attempts to define informal learning and its associated terms.

Defining informal learning: A nexus of family resemblances

There is no dearth in offers of defining informal learning and its properties. For example, Daniel Schugurensky specifies it as "learning that is not organized as a pedagogical activity by an educational institution, and it can happen both outside and within educational institutions" (Schugurensky 2006, 166). David Livingstone details informal learning as "any activity involving the pursuit of understanding, knowledge or skill which occurs without the presence of externally imposed curricular criteria (…) in any context outside the pre-established curricula of educative institutions' (Livingstone 2001, 4). Other researchers, reviewing the diverse attempts of definition, second the conclusion drawn by Helen

Colley and her colleagues that "either the boundaries between formal, non-formal and informal learning or education, or the relationships between them, can only be understood within particular contexts" (Colley et al. 2003, 6). More explicit criticism of the concept is leveled by Gerald Straka who notes that "'informal learning' is a metaphor with a severe problem, namely the lack of systematically and empirically grounded valid evidence on why, where, when, how and what is learned under 'informal conditions'" (Straka 2004, 2).

Informal learning is, indeed, a fuzzy term and one which competes for scientific currency with a range of related terms. These include implicit learning (Reber 1993), non-formal learning (Eraut 2000), situated learning (Lave and Wenger 1991), self-directed learning (Knowles 1975), incidental learning (Marsick and Watkins 1990), informal education (Jeffs and Smith 1996), non-formal education (Simkins 1977) and tacit knowledge (Polanyi 1967). Over the years, a gradual terminological change may be observed in that learning gradually ousts education as the prevalent term in definitions of the organisations and activities beyond curricular frameworks, just as non-formal and informal juggle for priority of use. These transformations indicate a shift of professional focus from institutions and outcomes on to processes and people, a shift that mirrors wider transformations of scholarly knowledge interests in parts of the humanities and social sciences from structural to more relational takes on research topics.

However, there is persistent diversity in researchers' theoretical approach and in the detail with which they break down their definitions – ranging from two properties (Eraut 2000) to 20 properties (Colley et al. 2003). Many also acknowledge the relational character of any definitional endeavour. However, as indicated by the examples above, all definitions of informal learning and its related terms include two key dimensions, namely the degree to which the context of learning is structured and planned and the degree to which the learner defines, or is aware of, the process going on as an act of learning. It follows from these dimensions that it makes no sense to describe learning itself as more or less formal; and so, in a literal sense, informal learning is an empty term.

Rather than contributing to the ongoing debates over the correct terminology, I would argue that scholars would do well to focus interest on the very fuzziness of the term. Perhaps it is the semantic interlacings between related terms that should merit closer inspection. According to Ludwig Wittgenstein's famous dictum in his *Philosophical Investigations* some definitions are best made through what he terms family resemblances (*Familienähnlichkeit*). Family members do not all look the same but share some traits that together define them as belonging to that particular family. In the same vein, the overlaps and criss-crossings between different terms help delineate the topical hotspots of scholarly interest. These hotspots circle around the two key dimensions, mentioned above, namely contexts and subjects of learning. Both of these dimensions of learning are currently undergoing substantial transformations; and formative to these transformations are the divergent socio-cultural embeddings of digital forms of communication.

Digital media as transformative resources of learning

Digital media is a catch phrase for an ensemble of technologies. Some of these are "born" digital, such as the personal computer, the internet, games consoles and mobile devices; others can be made digital, such as print media, radio and television, because of the technical possibilities to digitize all signs so that text, image, sound and numbers can be brought on to the same technological platform and begin to "speak together" in multi-faceted ways. Fundamentally, the increasing range of communication channels available and the complexity of their uses help push spatial, temporal and social boundaries of learning and knowledge formation. Terms such as distance learning and e-learning are indicative of the possible dispersion of learning sites just as m-learning is gaining ground as an indication that learning is, in very concrete terms, an ongoing activity. Moreover, social sites of learning are being distributed across different online communities; across broadcast, web-based and interpersonal forms of communication; and across ad-hoc networks and established organisations. One result of this redistribution is a renewed contestation of what counts as legitimate forms of knowledge and which institutional frameworks best promote relevant forms of knowledge. The conceptual flourishing of informal learning and its family resemblances are both symptoms of, and suggested answers to, these contestations of knowledge formation, its pace and the sites of learning. Both contexts, learners and the substance of learning are brought into play here.

While cultural-historical education theorists may rightly claim that new technologies merely highlight what was always the case, namely that learning is socially situated and integral to everyday interactions (Säljö 2000, Wertsch 1985), we nevertheless need to specify in what ways digital media serve to transform these processes. The key here is the meaning-making across time and place. Media are particular technologies that facilitate the storage and modification, articulation and exchange of signs, be they text, images, numbers or sound. Signs are tools of meaning-making, and so media may be defined as meaning-making technologies. Media are material tools, and mostly commercial tools (books, television sets, mobile phones), and as such media are like many other tools such as cars, toothbrushes and saucepans. But, unlike such object-like tools, media are also immaterial tools of signification, of meaning-making. This dual definition of media as both material and immaterial tools (Carey 1989) places them at a particular cultural vantage point.

Unlike interpersonal forms of meaning-making, such as dinner conversation, the forms of meaning-making taking shape through media may be preserved and handed down through time, and they may cross boundaries of place. Media are also selective cultural resources, in that they mostly require a bit of money, some free time and sometimes also some formal knowledge of the semiotic codes (reading, writing, numeracy) as prerequisites of use. In short, media are means through which we may express ourselves and reflect upon the world; and they are means through which we may connect to other people, times and places beyond our immediate spheres of interaction.

In terms of *the immaterial aspects of media* then, users' relations to media may be defined as means through which they can connect to and encounter other realities and as means of engaging with other people beyond their physical reach – what I defined above as "semiotic othernesses". In terms of *the material aspects of media*, these encounters and relations may be regulated through institutional arrangements or personal rules of access and use such as broadband availability at school, work or home and organisational limitations on gaming or texting; through structural or economic shortcomings such as lack of books, computers or money; or through insufficient skills to break the codes of expression, understanding and use such as illiteracy, ignorance of internet distribution networks or sparse insights into the handling of texts and images.

Digital media latch on to existing media cultures which serve to modify the introduction of mobile media, computer games and the internet, just as these digital media serve to relocate existing media cultures both in terms of discourses, legal frameworks and social uses. Crucially, media that are digital from their inception, are all commerical products whose survival is largely dependent upon their success on globalised markets. Unlike some radio and television channels that belong to a public-service, and often a national, domain, most digital media access depends on potential users' economic acumen and priorities. Since economic divides and socio-cultural patterns of production and use change at a much slower pace than do technologies, the transformations brought about by digital media should not be overstated. Still, four characteristics of digital media serve as catalysts of qualitative changes in relation to uses and to learning practices, namely:

Semiotic codes	digital media invite more seamless forms of multimodal (co-)production and interactivity
Time	digital media allow immediate exchange of mediatized forms of communication and, for mobile media, ad-hoc coordination
Place	digital media widen options of mediatized communication virtually everywhere
Social relations	digital media intensify meaning-making practices as forms of action, participation, collaboration, and reflexivity.

As for the multimodality of *semiotic codes*, it should be noted that this is not particular to digital media. Even the earliest books display a mixture of text and images, so the novelty of digital media is rather the ease with which different sign systems may be brought on to the same platform and manipulated there. Moreover, this manipulation of signs is also well-known from other media – writing letters or modifying photo negatives through special forms of development. Again, it is the immediacy and relative ease with which such manipulations may be carried out that are particular to digital media and are unknown to analogue media apart from the telephone. Young people in particular also (co-)produce new mixtures of visuals, graphics and sound, and these processes involve often complex handlings of a range of semiotic codes and conventions (Gilje this volume, Perkel this volume). Several studies demonstrate that young people's out-of-school uses of digital resources are more varied, more advanced and less task-oriented than are their uses at school (Livingstone and Bovill, 2001; Levin and Arafeh 2002, Erstad 2005, Arnseth et al. 2007). A key, and contested, issue is whether or not such activities are learning processes of relevance for future competence formation or are, indeed, competences. I will discuss this issue in the final part of the chapter.

That media help orchestrate users' *time* is well known from studies of television for example, especially prior to the introduction of the VCR, and this still holds true for young children and special programmes such as Disney animated cartoons in some countries (Lemish 1987, Drotner 2004). Exchanging communication across time through media is also known to many earlier generations who have treasured letters to distant friends and relatives; who have coordinated social arrangements on the family landline phone; and who may have written to the socalled agony columns of magazines in search of advice on looks, friendship or fashion. But mobile phones, internet messaging and social networking sites on the internet allow synchronous, continuous and easy exchanges. Moreover, these forms of communication serve to integrate what we may term "distant intimacies" as mundane, and increasingly mobile, elements of people's everyday lives in many parts of the world (Drotner 2005, Ito et al. 2005, Ling and Haddon 2008).

Notably, mobile devices and the internet impact on social relations in that they serve to widen users' options of creation, communication and participation *across space*, and these options become increasingly globalized (Harasim 1993, Holloway and Valentine 2003). Since the 1980s, satellites in the sky, cables under the sea and corporate mergers and acquisitions have brought about an intensified media globalization and commodification, so that today most people around the world, irrespective of their actual options of taking up and engaging with globalized media, know about their existence and relate to perceived assumptions about mediatized forms of otherness (Block and Buckingham 2007, Feilitzen and Carlsson 2002). Digital and increasingly globalized media, then, are both symptoms of and possible solutions to the demands made on many people in late-modern societies to exert temporal coordination, spatial flexibility, and personal identity performance. As such, they have attained a central importance, not accorded to media with former generations.

Digital media also impact on *social relations* and practices. Because of the ease with which signs may be manipulated and modified, digital media offer more, and more advanced, possibilities than other media technologies of semiotic production, such as is evident when users make their own profiles on social networking websites such as Facebook or MySpace. Moreover, because of their flexible and often mobile nature of joint meaning-making, digital media intensify modes of virtual co-production and collaboration, as when friends edit images and circulate them via their mobile, discuss work tasks or do homework together on the internet. In particular, the socalled second-generation services on the internet, called web 2.0 - such as social networking sites, free, user-generated encyclopedias (wikipedia or wikis) and internet diaries (weblogs or blogs) - offer more and easier ways of social participation and networking, of shaping and sharing content. The rapid takeup of these services by the younger generation in many parts of the world has meant an enormous expansion of informal communication, participation and play.

Even if the research literature is still limited and inconclusive, several studies indicate that these virtual social sites offer a good many young people new ways both of expressing intimacies and of reflecting upon the reactions brought about by their articulations (Brake 2007). Some of the most advanced digital experiences are brought about through gaming, since these processes both assume and advance virtual action – to be a gamer one has to *do* something in a very concrete sense, such as manipulating objects or figures, and thereby one helps create and sustain universes of practice (see Gee this volume, Jensen this volume). These universes offer spaces of articulation, collaborative experimentation and playful action, to which are sometimes added options for reflection if the gamer joins one of the many game communities.

Digital media, then, do impact on temporal, spatial and socio-cultural arrangements of relevance to the boundaries drawn up between formal and informal definitions of learning. A key question, of course, is whether or not this pushing of boundaries has, or could have, any bearing on the ways in which learning is understood and practiced; and, similarly, on the ways in which media environments are developing.

Digital divides: A challenge to informality?

Much has been made of the potentials inherent in the rapid take-up of digital devices, not least by young people, and the embedding of complex media environments into people's daily lives. Still, recent studies of digital divides note the intimate connection to familiar fault lines in terms of class, gender, ethnicity, age and region (Fox 2005, Peter and Valkenburg 2006). Broadly speaking, the digital elites are young, Caucasian people from middle-class backgrounds with women having a slight critical advantage in terms of digital forms of communication such as phoning and blogging while their male counterparts are more avid gamers. These results confirm previous studies of the diffusion of new media technologies, and in three important ways: technological availability does not guarantee equal access; access to a particular media technology does not guarantee equitable use; and, most important in the present context, use of particular media resources does not equal competence (Rogers 1962, Buckingham 2000, Livingstone and Bovill 2001).

So, is anything new under the sun when it comes to the current situation in terms of the media environment? The answer is yes in so far as my argument made above is accepted that the reality effect following from the pervasive discourse on the knowledge society and similar terms implies a change in the demands made on learning and its outcome in terms of competence formation. A fundamental form of infrastructure in globalised knowledge societies are interconnected networks and these increasingly hinge on the handling of interlocking media environments. So, future competence formation fundamentally concerns advanced handling of digital semiotic resources, be they numbers, text, images or sound – or intricate mixtures of all. Therefore, the digital divides of today may be regarded as economic, social and political divides of tomorrow.

Several studies note how the current media environment serves to reframe articulations of inequality both within and between societies so that symbolic exclusion for some segments becomes as important as material exploitation. For example, Scott Lash speaks about an "underclass" which is excluded in both material and symbolic terms, and in a similar vein Zygmunt Bauman speaks about first and second world inhabitants, defined not in terms of positions of place but of symbolic space and resources of articulation and action (Lash 1994, Bauman 1998). Manuel Castells extends this mode of reasoning to also include areas of cities and entire regions into what he terms a "fourth world" (Castells 1998). However, in noting that digital divides are basically social divides, Castells also stresses that education plays a key role both in the formation and the potential dissolution of these divides.

Education systems in democratic societies serve a dual function in that they operate as primary means of social selection while at the same time holding the possibility of being one of the only social sites of sustained learning that may cross boundaries of age, class and gender. The ways in which competences are defined and deployed by education systems are therefore of vital importance to schools' abilities to minimise the digital divides that pupils bring to the classroom. How do schools today sustain and advance pupils' competences in handling the meaning-making resources offered by an increasingly complex and interlaced media environment, so that they may be competent participants of tomorrow's knowledge socities? Answers to this question basically follow the three discourses on informal learning outlined above, and this is not very surprising. Because, as already noted, informal and formal understandings of learning are discursive twins, and so the discourses on informal learning mirror, indeed are part of, the discourses on formal learning either as their supplement, alternative or extension.

Transforming informal learning?

According to the liberal discourse on informal learning, digital competences formation is already well served through users' voluntary and often entertaining engagements in out-of-school contexts. Within this context, we find arguments to the effect that users already know what is best for them and are in a position to exercise their own choices. The education system should not enter the wider field of informal learning, including out-of-school digital practices, but should keep to well-trodden paths of training basic skills, possibly followed by voluntary parental advice on self-regulation or co-regulation of children's and young people's media uses. In its emphasis on individual choice and voice, the liberal discourse on informal learning may act as an endorsement of assertions made by commercial stakeholders who define users as already savvy and sophisticated consumers, particularly when it comes to the younger generation. Statutory training would be seen as a means of top-down regulation of use that is ill-suited to the liberal arguments for consumers' self-regulation or stakeholders' co-regulation.

Critical discourses on informal learning define learning as an embedded social practice and informal learning as an alternative to what is perceived as curriculum-driven and evidence-based school environments. Crucially, informal learning is seen as a lever of possible change in these educational priorities, and such notions find particular resonance with advocates of digital litearcy as a competence that should be systematically exercised within the curriculum. Skeptical of the commercial and individualised nature of out-of-school learning in the digital domain, they define digital literacy as a critical social resource for citizenship as much as for vocational work or consumer society (Buckingham 2007, Sefton-Green this volume). While liberal discourses focus on individual choice and digital practices as personal resources in everyday life, critical discourses take their perspective more from political economy in their insistence on institutional and commercial constraints. While both take a normative approach to digital learning, the liberalists tend to assume their knowledge interests unlike the critics most of whom spell out their wish to minimise social inequalities.

According to the functionalist discourse, informal learning with digital media is first and foremost defined in relation to work with information and communication technologies (ICTs), that is primarily computers and the internet. E-learning, computer literacy (Turner, Sweany and Husman 2000) and information literacy (Bruce 1997) are among the "hyphenated literacies" that are advocated with the aim of furthering efficient online collaboration and solution of well-defined problems. Unlike both the liberal and critical takes on informal learning and digital media, the functionalist approach tends to see ICTs as stand-alone and transparent tools applied in order to reach specific goals. Advocates see these tools as important levers of more efficient competence formation and on-the-job collaboration, and hence they want these tools integrated into formal education and into all subjects. In tune with liberalist discourses, the functionalist approach to digital media focuses on the means for personalised and self-paced learning but few would follow the liberal thinking in terms of digital meaning-making as an important supplement to a rounded character formation. Despite its apparent neutrality, the funtionalist discourse harbours a technological optimism that is rarely made explicit, perhaps because its focus on the lofty ends to be reached easily sidetracks any deliberations on their more mundane means.

Together, the three discourses on informal learning and digital media reflect back on some of the key tensions involved in current educational priorities, policies and practices. Few would dispute that the complex media environment and the interlacing of new and old media do impact on learning. Yet, in answering just how priorities, policies and practices should be defined and developed a variety of stakeholders mobilise wider tensions about the aims of education and its socio-cultural contexts. Unlike educational scholars who see an ever-increasing rationalisation and restless monitoring of education, I would note the contested nature of the discourses and the conflictual routes taken by educational policymakers. For example, Singapore is currently reforming its school system to allow for more child-centred and creative work processes stimulated by virtual forms of collaboration and participation; while in the USA and most of Europe, the pendulum is swinging in the opposite direction: here policy-makers put increasing emphasis on national tests and on evidence-based learning along well-defined steps in order to counter what is perceived as over permissive frameworks of education.

Neither discourses nor practices are uniform or unilateral. Key oppositions and tensions, some of which have been discussed in this chapter, offer ways of mapping out tasks in terms of scholarship, collaboration and practice. As I see it, in many parts of the world school is still the most important institution in the formation and validation of competences for all. One of the urgent challenges facing educational policy-makers and practioners is therefore to specify more precisely how literacy as a technologially mediated meaning-making competence should be defined and developed so as to minimise digital and social divides (Drotner 2007). Furthermore, this challenge must be handled in a situation where sites and settings of learning are dispersing alongside the appearance of an intensified discourse on knowledge economies and knowledge societies. In short, rarely have societies been so obsessed with learning and knowledge formation, and rarely has it been so difficult to define the whats, hows and wheres of these processes. Illuminating the conflictual relationship between informal learning and digital media is one way of trying to handle this paradox. To this end, the authors in the present volume may inspire other scholars by offering theory-driven empirical studies of the ways in which particularly young users handle the underlying dilemmas and divergences.

References

Arnseth, H. C., O. Hatlevik, V. Kløvstad, T. Kristiansen, and G. Ottestad. 2007. *ITU monitor 2007: skolens digitale tilstand 2007* [ITU monitor 2007: the digital state of education 2007]. Oslo: University Press.

Bauman, Z. 1998. *Globalization: The human consequences*. Cambridge: Polity.

Bentley, T. 1998. *Learning beyond the classroom: Education for a changing world*. London: Routledge.

Bjørnåvold, J. 2000. *Making learning visible: Identification, assessment and recognition of non-formal learning in Europe*. Thessaloniki: European Centre for the Development of Vocational Training (Cedefop).

Block, L. de, and D. Buckingham eds. 2007. *Global children, global media: Migration, media and childhood*. Basingstoke: Palgrave.

Brake, D. 2007. Examining my life or just "about me"? In the shallows of the digital self. Paper presented at the International Communication Conference, May 24-28, in San Fransisco, USA.

Bruce, C. 1997. *The seven faces of information literacy*. Blackwood: Auslib Press.

Buckingham, D. (2000). *After the death of childhood: Growing up in the age of electronic media*. Cambridge: Polity.

—. 2007. *Beyond technology: Children's learning in the age of digital culture*. Cambridge: Polity Press.

Carey, J. W. 1989. *Communication as culture: Essays on media and society*. Boston, MA: Unwin Hyman.

Castells, M. 1996. *The rise of the network society. Vol. 1: The Information age: Economy, society and culture*. Oxford: Blackwell.

—. 1998. *The end of the millennium. Vol. III: The information age: Economy, society and culture*. Oxford: Blackwell.

Coffield, F. ed. 2000. *The necessity of informal learning*. Bristol: The Policy Press.

Colley, H., P. Hodkinson, and J. Malcolm. 2003. *Informality and formality in learning: A report for the Learning and Skills Research Centre*. Leeds: University of Leeds.

Drotner, K. 2004. Disney dilemmas: Audience negotiations of media globalization. *Nordicom Review* 25 1-2): 137-48. Special issue, ed. U. Carlsson, 16th Nordic Conference on Media and Communication Research, http://www.nordicom.gu.se/common/publ_pdf/157_137-148.pdf (retrieved August 14, 2007).

—. 2005. Media on the move: Personalised media and the transformation of publicness. In *Audiences and publics: When cultural engagement matters for the public sphere,* ed. S. Livingstone, 187-211. Bristol: Intellect Books.

—. 2007. Leisure is hard work: Digital practices and future competences. In *Youth, identity and digital media*, ed. D. Buckingham. Cambridge, MA: MIT Press. The McArthur Foundation series on Digital Media and Learning, http//:www.mitpressjournals.org/toc/dmal/-/6 (retrieved December 11, 2007).

Edwards, R., and N. Boreham. 2003. 'The centre cannot hold': Complexity and difference in Euopean Union policy toward a learning society. *Journal of Education Policy* 18(4): 407-21.

Eraut, M. 2000. Non-formal learning, implicit learning and tacit knowledge in professional work. In *The necessity of informal learning*, ed. F. Coffield, 12-31. Bristol: The Policy Press.

Erstad, O. 2005. *Digital kompetanse i skolen: en innføring* [Digital competence at school: An introduction]. Oslo: University Press.

European Commission. 2001. *Making a European area of lifelong learning a reality*. Brussels: Commission of the European Communities, SEC (2001), 678 final.

Faure, E. et al. 1972. *Learning to be: The world of education today and tomorrow*. Paris: UNESCO.

Feilitzen, C. von and U. Carlsson, eds. 2002. *Children, young people and media globalization*. Gothenburg: Nordicom.

Fox, S. 2005. *Digital divisions. The Pew Internet and American Life Project*, http// www.pewinternet.org/PPF/r/165/report_display.asp (retrieved August 14, 2007).

Freire, P. 1972. *Pedagogy of the oppressed*. Harmondsworth: Penguin.

—. 1995. *Pedagogy of hope: Reliving pedagogy of the oppressed*. New York: Continuum.

Fundamental education: Common ground for all peoples. Paris: UNESCO.

Garnham, N. 2000. Information society as theory or ideology. *Information, Communication and Society* 3(2): 139-152.

Harasim, L. M., ed. 1993. *Global networks: Computers and international communication*. Cambridge, MA: MIT Press.

Holloway, S. L., and G. Valentine. 2003. *Cyberkids: Children in the information age*. London: Routledge Falmer.

Husén, T. 1974. *The learning society*. London: Methuen.

Hutchins, R. M. 1968. *The learning society*. Harmondsworth: Penguin.

Illich, I. 1971. *Deschooling society*. New York: Harper and Row.

Ito, M., D. Okabe, and M. Matsuda. 2005. *Personal, portable, pedestrian: Mobile phones in Japanese life*. Cambridge, MA: MIT Press.

Jeffs, T., and M. K. Smith. 1996. *Informal education: Conversation, democracy and learning*. Ticknall: Education Now.

Knowles, M. S. 1970. *The modern practice of adult education: Andragogy versus pedagogy*. Chicago, IL: Follett.

—. 1975 *Self-directed learning: A guide for learners and teachers*. Englewood Cliffs: Prentice Hall/Cambridge University Press.

Lash S. 1994. Reflexivity and its doubles: Structure, aesthetics, community. In *Reflexive modernization*, ed. U. Beck, A. Giddens, and S. Lash, 110-73. Cambridge: Polity.

Lave, J., and E. Wenger. 1991. *Situated learning: Legitimate peripheral participation*. Cambridge: Cambridge University Press.

Lemish, D. 1987. Viewers in diapers: The early development of television viewing. In *Natural Audiences: Qualitative Research of Media Uses and Effects*, ed. Thomas R. Lindlof, 33-57. Norwood, NJ: Ablex.

Levin, D., and S. Arafeh. 2002. *The digital disconnect: The widening gap between internet-savvy students and their schools. The Pew Internet and American Life Project,* http//www.pewinternet.org (retrieved August 9, 2007).

Ling, R., and L. Haddon. 2008. Children, youth and the mobile phone. In *The international handbook of children, media and culture*, ed. K. Drotner and S. Livingstone, 137-51. London: Sage.

Livingstone, D. W. 2001. *Adults' informal learning: Definitions, findings, gaps, and future research. NALL working paper no. 21*. Ontario: New Approaches to Lifelong Learning (NALL), Ontario Institute for Studies in Education, University of Toronto, www.oise.utoronto.ca/depts/sese/csew/nall/res/21adultsifnormallearning.htm (retrieved August 9, 2007).

Livingstone, S., and M. Bovill, eds. 2001. *Children and their changing media environment: A European comparative study*. New York: Lawrence Erlbaum.

McGivney, V. 1999. *Informal learning in the community: A trigger for change and development.* Leicester: NIACE.

Marsick, V. J., and K. E. Watkins. 1990. *Informal and incidental learning in the workplace.* London: Routledge.

Masuda, Y. 1980. *The information society.* Tokyo: Institute for the Information Society.

Misko J., F. Beddie, and L. Smith. 2007. *The recognition of non-formal and informal learning in Australia: Country background report prepared for the OECD activity on recognition of non-formal and informal learning.* Canberra: Department of Education, Science and Training, http//:www.dest.gov.au/sectors/training_skills/publications_resources/profiles/The_Recognition_of_Non_formal_Informal_Learning_Aus.htm (retrieved August 9, 2007).

Peter, J., and P. M. Valkenburg. 2006. Adolescents' internet use: Testing the "disappearing digital divide" versus the "emerging differentiation" approach. *Poetics* 34(4-5): 293-305.

Ransom, S. 1994. *Towards the learning society.* London: Cassell.

Polanyi, M. 1967. *The Tacit Dimension.* New York: Doubleday.

Reber, A. S. 1993. *Implicit learning and tacit knowledge: An essay on the cognitive unconscious.* Oxford: Oxford University Press.

Robins, K., and F. Webster. 1999. *Times of the technoculture.* London: Routledge.

Rogers, E. 1962. *Diffusion of innovations.* New York, NY: The Free Press.

Schugurensky, D. 2006. "This is Our School of Citizenship": Informal learning in local democracy. In *Learning in places: The informal education reader*, ed. Zvi Bekerman, Nickolas C. Burbules, and Diana Silberman-Keller, 163-82. New York: Peter Lang.

Simkins, T. 1977. *Non-formal education and development: Some critical issues.* Manchester: Department of Adult and Higher Education, University of Manchester.

Singh, M. 2005. *Meeting basic learning needs in the informal sector: Integrating education and training for decent work, empowerment and citizenship.* Berlin: Springer.

Stadler, M. A., and P. A. Frensch, ed. 1998. *The handbook of implicit learning.* Thousand Oaks, CA: Sage.

Stehr, N. 1994. *Knowledge societies.* London: Sage.

Straka, G. A. 2004. *Informal learning: Genealogy, concepts, antagonisms and questions.* Bremen: Institute of Technologies and Education, University of Bremen.

Säljö, R. 2000. *Lärande i praktiken: ett sociokulturellt perspektiv*

[Learning in practice: A socio-cultural perspective]. Stockholm: Prisma.

Turner, G. M., N. W. Sweany, and J. Husman, N. 2000. Development of the computer interface literacy measure. *Journal of Educational Computing Research* 22(1): 37-54.

Unlocking Canada's potential: The state of workplace and adult learning in Canada. Report on learning in Canada 2007. Ottawa: Canadian Council on Learning, www.cclcca.ca/CCL/Reports/StateofLearning/UnlockingCanadasPotential.htm (retrieved August 9, 2007).

Wertsch, J. V. 1985. *Mind as action.* New York: Oxford University Press.

CHAPTER TWO

GOOGLING MOVIES: DIGITAL MEDIA PRODUCTION AND THE "CULTURE OF APPROPRIATION"[1]

ØYSTEIN GILJE

The term "Napster-generation" has frequently been used to describe how young people download music, film clips and images from the Internet and use these in their own media productions, which they to a large extent share on the Internet (Jenkins 2006). The Pew study (Lenhart and Madden 2005) showed that almost one-quarter of American teens had remixed existing media content. This "remix culture" is powered by an increasing number of websites that offer space for publishing. It is a "culture of appropriation" (Jenkins 2006) where young people create multimodal texts by remixing authored and copied semiotic material[2] in a meaning making process. This chapter investigates how media and communication students take part in this culture of appropriation in the process of editing video. The students google on the Internet to find semiotic materials for producing their own movies; they google movies.[3]

According to recent classroom-research from a socio-cultural perspective on learning, students also use copy and paste practices in general with information and communication technologies (ICT) in schools (Facer et al. 2003, Arnseth 2004, Rasmussen 2005). When it comes to education and schooling this practice is not high valued as a learning process. A common claim is that the students plagiarize other people' s work and that copying is a sign of laziness that does not involve any kind of learning (Collins 2001).

This chapter investigates the remixing and editing process by looking at ways in which these copy and paste practices evolve in a digital production task within the subject Media Education. By integrating terms from socio-cultural theory (Vygotsky 1978, 1986; Wertsch 1991, 1998) with terms from social semiotics (Kress 2003, Van Leeuwen 2005), the media and communication student is understood as a "designer" (van Leeuwen 2005, Jewitt 2005). In other words: An agent who uses a wide range of different semiotic resources in an editing process that includes digital editing software. Following a social semiotic approach the term *literacy practice* and *literacy event* (Barton 2007) is explored by arguing that the designer works not only with words and letters, as the English linguist David Barton defines these terms. The notions *mastery* and *appropriation* (Wertsch 1998) are discussed both in relation to the culture of appropriation (Jenkins 2006) and as key terms in socio-cultural theory understood as *mediated action* (Wertsch 1991, 1998, 2002).

The chapter is arranged in two parts. In the first part a theoretical framework for approaching the "culture of appropriation" is established and there is a review of research on editing digital video. Terms to distinguish "found" material (googled) from recorded (authored) material are also suggested, and the process of selecting semiotic material (google) compared to traditional recording with a camcorder is also discussed. Drawing both on quantitative and qualitative data, the last part of the chapter investigates what kind of semiotic material media and communication students download and how they interpret and select music and pictures in the editing process of a short TV feature.

Video production and editing software

Studying the practical and creative aspects of media production by students in media education is becoming widely accepted by media educators both in its own right (Burn and Parker 2003a, 2003b, Buckingham 2003), and as a means of promoting self-expression (Drotner 1991, Sefton-Green and Buckingham 1998, Hull and Nelson 2005). In the Ofcom review on media literacy, the British media educator David Buckingham stresses that media production provides "a more participatory, 'hands-on' approach to pedagogy, which students generally find more motivating than approaches based solely on discussion and writing" (Buckingham et al. 2005, 44).

In the last ten years there is a growing body of research that deals with young people and digital production (Sefton-Green 2004, 2005). Some work points out the advantages that digital editing software gives the students when they want to revise their work (Buckingham et al. 1995, Sefton-Green and Buckingham 1998, Burn and Durran 2006). The *Evaluation Report of the Becta Digital Video Pilot Project* emphasises that there is a clear distinction between the recording process and the editing process when it comes to working with digital video (Reid et al. 2002, 14).

The report also suggests that DV–editing can be used to explore moving image language by editing material "found" elsewhere, effectively "re-purposing it". Burn and Durran confirm this with findings from a project where eight students (aged 12-13) re-edited a piece taken from Baz Luhrmann's film *Romeo and Juliet* (Burn and Durran 2006). By approaching moving images as an assemblage of different communicative modes, which they term the *kineikonic* mode (Burn and Parker 2003a), Burn and Durran (2006) stress the meaning the students are reaching for at certain moments in the editing process. Drawing on social semiotics and socio-cultural theory I define these moments in the digital editing process as *literacy events* (Barton 2007). I will develop this argument in the next two sections.

The main characteristic of editing software is the ability to handle different kinds of semiotic material. Furthermore software for editing video includes features for importing picture, music and other semiotic modes. Unlike analogue editing equipment, digital editing software shows all these modes on the screen, and afford editing modes along a horizontal timeline. In other words, digital technology makes the editing process visible in an interface which is relatively easy to learn, as the educational researcher Roger Säljö has emphasised related to other digital devices (Säljö 2007). Julian Sefton-Green stresses that the affordances the software offers need to be integrated into any discussion about pedagogy (Sefton-Green 2005, 100). However there is little or no research on how students learn by downloading material from the Internet and remix such modes using editing software in an educational context.

Culture of appropriation: taking culture apart?

According to Henry Jenkins appropriation is the process whereby students "*learn* by taking culture apart and putting it back together" (Jenkins 2006, 32 – my italics). With a broad cultural approach, Jenkins' argument is built on the assumption that the digital remixing *makes visible* how all cultural expression builds on what has come before. This has never been truer than in the case of editing software. The digital technologies give the opportunity to copy and paste these "cultural expressions" and visualize them on a timeline in the editing software. For that reason literacy practices which involve new digital tools are different from practices where analogue cultural tools are used.

I propose that rather than a definition of being literate, as reading and writing (with the aid of analogue tools), digital technologies give the opportunity to merge this process into one: copy and paste. This copy and paste process, as a literacy practice, is fundamental in many social niches outside of school, but in traditional schooling "to copy and paste is to plagiarize, unless there is careful attribution of source" (Dan Perkel, this volume). Perkel argues that copy and paste, which means re-using code, is a core competency in making a MySpace profile. I suggest that in the production of a video, the processes of editing are even more complex than just copying and re-contextualizing code. Editing video is a chain of literacy events involving different cultural tools in an assembly process as pointed out in the book *Analyzing media texts*:

> This means that the whole business of designing and producing a text is of interest, as each stage involves a transformation, adaptation and reworking of the semiotic material available. Each transformation adds another layer, leaves another trace. Each move in the process uses tools of inscription, maybe different tools at each stage, all with their own possibilities and constraints. This has never been more true than it is today of digital media, where the appropriation, transformation and synthesis of earlier signs is, perhaps, the defining characteristic of the medium (Burn and Parker 2003a, 78).

As Burn and Parker stress, the defining character of the video editing software is the affordance it gives to copy and paste in the process of editing. This copy and paste process is fundamental in the culture of appropriation, but is not highly valued in the social niche of schooling.

One way to discuss these different social niches on a theoretical level is to distinguish between *meaning making* and *learning.* A common understanding is that diverse theories raise different questions, and that these two terms are related to different theoretical positions. Gunther Kress stresses this point in his book *Literacy in the new media age*:

> Learning is not a term that belongs in semiotics; sign-making is. However, learning and sign-making are two sides of one sheet of paper as Saussure might have said; which side we choose to look at depends on the perspective from which we are looking. Both learning and sign-making are dynamic processes which change the resources through which the processes take place – whether as concepts in psychology or as signs in semiotics – and change those who are involved in the process (Kress 2003, 40).

My perspective is to analyze how the students take culture apart. This practice is well known as meaning making processes in the culture of appropriation outside school. With social semiotics as the point of departure I will argue that these meaning making processes are literacy events. In schools such literacy events are a question about learning; "but for most literacy events this is not so" (Barton 2007, 35). To understand these practices as influenced by the culture of appropriation within the social niche of schooling I argue that it is necessary to have a perspective *both* on learning and sign-making.

"Culture of appropriation": Taking a theoretical approach

As noted in the previous sections, digital editing software gives the student advantages when it comes to exploring and revising their multimodal work. My contribution is to investigate how editing software serves as new cultural tools that are often quite powerful yet become un-explored and "all too easily escape notice" (Wertsch 1998, 42-43). With respect to learning, digital editing software and the Internet provide affordances that are different from analogue equipment. At the same time these new cultural tools transform literacy practices and raises questions about how to interpret the term literacy.

In socio-cultural theory the task is to explore the relationship between human action and the cultural tools being used within a specific institutional and historical context (Wertsch 1998, 24). The principle for this analytical approach is that human action involves an inherent, irreducible tension between agents and cultural tools (Wertsch 2002, 6). With James Wertsch's term "mediated action" in mind I aim to understand how the media and communication student masters cultural tools like Internet and different kind of software in the editing process: "Analyses of how cultural tools are mastered by individuals in the ontogenesis are often formulated in terms of 'internalization'" (Wertsch 1998, 48).

Because "internalization" is too widely used, Wertsch prefers the terms *mastery* and *appropriation*. These two terms are analytically and in some cases empirically distinct (Wertsch 1998). Mastery is "knowing how" to use a cultural tool, in this case digital devices, Internet and the editing software. The term appropriation is built upon Bakhtins dialogic approach to language (Bakhtin 1981, 1986), which emphasizes that a word always needs to be "populated" by the speaker with her own "semantic and expressive intention" (Bakthin 1981, 293-294). Wertsch interprets appropriation as: "The process of taking something that belongs to others and making it one's own" (Wertsch 1998, 53).[4] These terms offers one way to explain how literacy practices change when new digital tools are introduced for the purpose of finding and selecting images and sounds. While the term "mediated action" highlights how the students master the editing program, I argue that we also need an analytical approach that focuses on the different semiotic material the students work with, like pictures and music. I will argue that social semiotics may be an approach for investigating how the students appropriate semiotic material.

By drawing attention to the sign-making process as a social process, the focal point in social semiotics becomes obvious: "Social semiotics focuses on people's process of meaning making, this being a process in which people make choices from a network of alternatives: selecting one resource (a meaning potential) over another" (Halliday 1978, 1985 in Jewitt 2005). In social semiotics the meaning making process is about giving a certain kind of "knowledge" a shape in the "design-process," the editing of digital video in this case. As the Swedish researcher Fredrik Lindstrand argues, a wide array of modes are used to "create new relations between 'content' and 'form'" in the design process (Lindstrand 2006, 243, English summary). In the following I argue that my informants make meaning with two kinds of semiotic material: material they recorded and material they downloaded from the Internet. When it comes to learning in this process, Lindstrand argues that this is a "process of transformation, which is related to 'difference' in that it describes a change that occurs when new signs are produced internally" (Lindstrand 2006, 243, English summary). Following a social semiotic approach, Lindstrand makes the connection directly between the external and internal sign without paying attention to how the sign is *mediated*. In other words: Social semiotics doesn't pay much attention to the importance of the relationship between the agent and the cultural tool. I will argue that in order to investigate multimodal literacy practices, and especially literacy events when using editing software, we need to understand how semiotic resources (material) are mediated. Perspectives from social semiotics are of importance, but given my approach to learning and literacy socio-cultural theory is crucial to highlight how the semiotic material is mediated in the editing process.

Recently some researchers have argued for a marriage of these theories which combines an approach to text and context (Jewitt 2006, Løvland 2006). In her book *Technology, literacy and learning: A multimodal approach,* Carey Jewitt (2006) aims to understand the relationship between school knowledge, learning and notions of literacy by combining a multimodal approach and activity theory. By investigating different media such as web-sites, CD-ROM and game making applications, Jewitt describes learning as "a process mediated by technologies of the classroom by which students take in and re-make semiotic resources" (Jewitt 2006, 105). Roger Säljö also stressed making new approaches to learning and understanding when he gave his lecture on the occasion of the opening of The Oxford Centre for Socio-cultural Activity Theory Research in March 2007. Addressing Kress, Säljö commented on learning as an issue of "design," arguing for an approach that stresses the importance of the cultural tools within an institutional context: According to Säljö, we learn differently from previous generations. As a consequence of this, we can no longer base our research on traditional notions such as "learning" and "remembering," but have to develop an understanding that is relevant to activities and activity systems (Säljö 2007, 14-15).

By using literacy as a common key-concept, both social semiotics (Kress 2003) and socio-cultural theory (Säljö 2005, Wertsch 1991, 1998) do have the possibility to merge, focusing on the process of learning when the students edit video. Barton's term "literacy event" uses a broad approach: "any activity which involves the written word" (Barton 2007, 35). With the theoretical framework I have established, all signs are a part of the social practice in the literacy event, but an approach like this challenges Barton's definition. For the purpose of understanding this culture of appropriation as a literacy practice, I would like to re-phrase Bakhtin by substituting a few of my own words for his: "Prior to this moment of appropriation, the *semiotic material* [word] does not exist in a neutral and impersonal language, but rather exists on [in] other people's *sites* [contexts], serving other people's intention: it is from there that one must take the *semiotic material* [word], and make it one's own" (Bakhtin 1981, 294 – the original words by Bakhtin are in brackets).[5]

So how can this process of appropriation be interpreted and related to literacy in a digital media age? This re-phrasing of Bakhtin is quite close to Henry Jenkins's definition of appropriation – the ability to meaningfully sample and remix media content (Jenkins 2006, 32). To grasp the textual dimension of making video I argue that we need a social semiotic, and a multimodal approach. But maybe more importantly when it comes to understanding how these modes are mediated (Vygotsky 1978, Wertsch 1991), the terms mastery and appropriation highlight how digital media blur the boundaries between (recorded and downloaded) semiotic material on the one hand and the affordances the digital tools give on the other hand. We may say that "knowing how" to use the cultural tools is the (pre)condition for meaning making in the editing process, but appropriation is more important when it comes to interpreting the semiotic material. My argument is that both these practices, googling and downloading vs. recording, can be covered with the term literacy. In order to research these literacy practices, evolved in the culture of appropriation, in an educational context we both have to theorize *the semiotic material* and *the agent* and their *cultural tools*.

Case study: Gathering data

In this part of the paper I will turn to my empirical data. These are drawn from two different projects: a national survey on media education and qualitative data from the "Greenwood" upper secondary school in Oslo. The qualitative data was gathered first and the preliminary analysis of these data laid the ground for many of the questions in the national survey. Questions about remixing and the use of different software in the editing process was therefore a substantial part of the on-line questionnaire we made (Erstad, Gilje and de Lange 2007b).[6]

The methods used for gathering the qualitative data were inspired by the field of visual ethnography (Banks 2001, Pink 2001, 2006). Compared to other studies of media-production and ICT in Media Education, especially in UK, this method is under-explored and not elaborated, but as Sefton-Green stresses: "It seems that studies with an ethnographic approach to computer culture might be productive for studies of education and learning" (Sefton-Green 2004, 30). In the survey we got answers from 735 media and communication students in over 60 different upper secondary schools in Norway about what kind of semiotic material they used in their most recent video-production at school.[7] More than one out of three students made a short TV feature or a documentary (n=269/735). The production practices reported by these students can be visualized in Table 2-1:

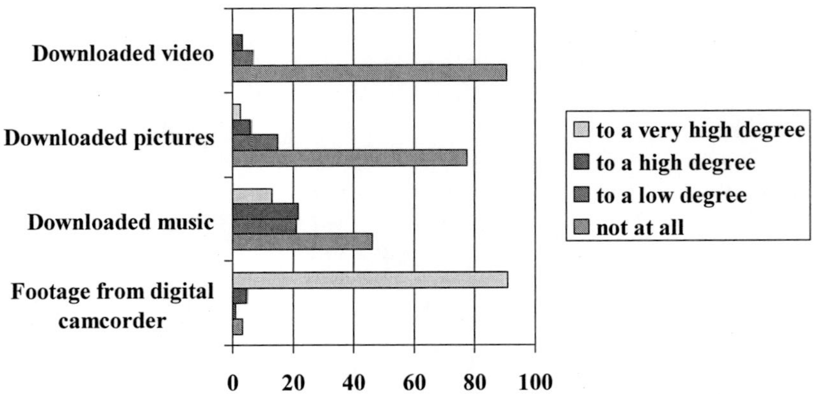

Table 2-1. The percentage of semiotic material used in the documentary, either downloaded or recorded (N=269).

The diagram shows three different kinds of semiotic material. Footage from a digital camcorder was the primary source in the production of documentaries. Also findings from the qualitative study at "Greenwood" indicate that the students largely appropriate self-authored material.

But when it comes to music and pictures, usage changed; nearly 56 per cent of the students said that they had downloaded music from the Internet in the editing process of the movie, and over 23 per cent of the students in the survey had downloaded pictures to a small, high or very high degree as part of the editing process. In other words, the media and communication students use mostly self-authored semiotic material in the production of a short TV feature, but the Internet is a source for finding especially music but also digital pictures in the process.

My claim is that their use of either semiotic material downloaded from the Internet or recorded footage involves *different* literacy practices. The first involves *googling,* selecting and maybe also manipulating existing material, while the latter is a more traditional *recording* method of making more or less conscious choices in a process. Historically, for professional journalists the making of a TV feature has been a process or recording. Footage has usually been made with a camcorder or earlier with a film-camera. However, due to the Internet and digital editing software these journalistic practices are challenged. As a journalist you cannot use other people's material without copyright permission, however young people in general (Lenhart and Madden 2005) and the students in particular do that when they make documentaries and short TV features (Erstad, Gilje and de Lange 2007a). In this case the students were asked to reflect upon the choice of material from the Internet, and I will return to this issue towards the end of the chapter.

To distinguish the material in these two processes (googling versus recording) on an analytical level, the concepts *pre-* and *pro*-filmic are interesting. Drawing on Burn and Parker's adaptation of the French film-theorist Christian Metz (1974), I embed my use of the concepts within a broader understanding of film as text in semiotic terms. Burn and Parker (2003a) use these concepts to distinguish between "found" semiotic material or googling (*pre*-filmic) and "modal assemblies made for the kineikonic" or recording (*pro*-filmic).[8]

The pre-filmic semiotic material is a kind of resource that belongs to our common culture. In a digital media age these semiotic resources can be found, re-shaped and re-contextualized in the literacy practice of digital editing. As the survey shows, it is possible to argue that copy and paste practices that have evolved in the culture of appropriation also take place in the subject media education where the students work with digital technology more or less the whole day (Erstad, Gilje and de Lange 2007b). To analyze the different kinds of semiotic material, the terms pre- and pro filmic may be useful as analytical terms.

Googling music: remixing as a literacy practice

We conducted a qualitative study about film production at "Greenwood" Upper Secondary school near Oslo. The data was gathered during three weeks, as we followed the students (aged 17-18) in the editing process of a documentary. "Greenwood" school is one of the approximately 70 schools that participated in the national survey, as described in the previous section.[9] Like other Norwegian schools that offer this subject, the school is well equipped when it comes to computers and digital camcorders.[10] The qualitative data includes video recordings made during the post-production phase of the three-week project. 28 students at Greenwood participated and made seven films in total. Most of the film groups were mixed-gender, and had three or four participants. In the first phase of the Greenwood film project, the students planned and recorded (shot) video footage with a digital camcorder and downloaded approximately 25 pictures and posters from the Internet. They worked in two groups, one with the two boys and the other with the two girls. The pairs worked on one Macintosh computer together, but with access to a common server where they stored the pre- and pro- filmic material, downloaded from the Internet and uploaded from different devices like the digital camcorders and personal iPods.

Data from "Greenwood" consists of videotaped observations, reflection-notes by students, and the final TV feature made in student groups. We observed and videotaped the student filmmaking groups primarily during their editing process. All of our video observations were subsequently reviewed, and approximately 30 excerpts were chosen for close analysis. Our analytic focus was on how the students negotiated with language and gestures in front of the screen when they edited the digital video. Other data includes the reflection-notes by the students, which were copied after the teacher had commented upon them and given marks (grades). The structure for the reflection notes was made by teachers and consisted of about 20 questions concerning the filmmaking process from idea to final product. Questions cover ethical issues, such as the use of pictures and sounds from the Internet, and copyright issues related to the use of music from the Internet.

One mixed-gender film group with four students (two boys and two girls) was chosen as the primary group for close study. For the purpose of this chapter I call the group the "Blitz group." They wanted to make a short TV feature as the assignment about Blitz. (Blitz is a youth community house started nearly 25 years ago when a group of young people occupied a house in downtown Oslo, to which they now have property rights). Due to the limited space here, I have chosen two extracts showing the Blitz group, one where two boys are finding a piece of music, and the other where two girls are evaluating a picture. These activities were chosen because they are typical, as indicated by our survey data, (i.e. music and pictures are most frequently googled and downloaded).

The first excerpt from the video data comes from a point in the process where one of the two boys in the Blitz group (named Steven here) is searching for a piece of music suitable for the first seconds of their film. Axel, a boy in another group, who occasionally visits the Blitz-house, turns his attention to the computer screen in front of Steven. In this extract they are looking at the official site for Blitz and have been clicking into "files" which gave them a menu to choose from: Stills, drawings, posters and music-files. They chose the latter and were presented to a wide range of different songs presented on the website as files possible to click on:

Excerpt 1

1. Axel: "Police-terror" (addressing a particular piece of music on the site), for example. It is great!
2. Steven: Is it possible to download it?
3. Axel: Yes, That's possible, but listen to it first! In QuickTime. (Listening together).
4. Axel: You can just cut this part, don't you see?
5. Steven: We just cut it into small parts and get what we want from this piece of music.
6. Axel: Yes
   (Listening to the music, sharing a headset with two earplugs).
7. Steven: Yes!, it's a good beat.
8. Axel: It is perfect! You know there has previously been made a documentary about Blitz where they used this piece of music. It does really have a good beat, it is classic punk-rock from the 80's. So that is great.
   There are a lot of different songs to choose from on this site.
9. Steven: Eeh, we have to use something from this site. It is OK, because it has no copyright either.
10. Axel: That is convenient. I'll just move over to my place now.
11. Steven: Hmm. Thank you.

Note that in the second line of the excerpt Steven addresses the possibility of downloading. Axel confirms that it is possible, but recommends listening to the music in a suitable software program (QuickTime), but then addresses the issue of editing. In the dialogue (lines 4-6) they discuss what part of the piece of music fits into their assignment. Steven's utterance in line 5 indicates that he knows how to edit the file and use only suitable parts. This remix is indicated with the utterance: "…and get what we want from it" (line 5). This utterance highlights the core activity in the culture of appropriation: to appropriate and creatively paste the semiotic material into a new multimodal text (the first seconds of the short TV feature) and context (the assignment in the media and communication class). The appropriation of this piece is visible in lines 9-11. Here Axel defines the piece as: "classic punk-rock from the 80s". He also legitimates the use of this piece with the utterance: "there has previously been made a documentary about Blitz, where they used this piece of music."

The second part of the excerpt (lines 12-14) highlights copyright as an issue. From lines 12-14 the two students argue that this is a suitable site for downloading, because they presume that these files are without copyright. This issue is elaborated in the reflection-notes that the students had to write, and I will return to this issue in the last section of this article. In the excerpt above the two boys show authorial voice in evaluating the piece of music as semiotic material, found on the site for Blitz, and Axel explains that the value of the resource is embedded in the punk-rock culture, a core genre closely related to Blitz.

The second extract below shows two girls in the Blitz group (Heidi and Carla) working with pre-filmic material found on the Internet, downloaded and saved on the common server at the school so they can share the material with other students. The activity going on in this excerpt is that the girls are looking at the different pictures, deleting those they don't want to use, and dragging and dropping the other ones to a folder on the desktop to systematize them before the editing process.

Excerpt 2

1. Heidi: Should we use this one, or?
2. (...)
3. Carla: Njaa, I think (..) in the report one issue is about ethics and so on. So ...
4. Heidi: Yes I know.
5. Carla: It is a close up of people. So ...
6. Heidi: Well, I don't know
7. Heidi: And it says "London girl" (on one of the person's T-shirt) so we understand that it is not Blitz.
8. Heidi: So, we should maybe just "drop it".
9. Carla: Yeah (they delete the picture from the folder).

10. Heidi: Or, we could manipulate the picture writing "Blitz" (instead of "London girl").
11. Carla: Yes (laughs).
12. Heidi: That is a very ethical thing to do! (Laughing).

In the above excerpt, Carla refers in line 3 to the report (reflection note) they are supposed to write as part of the work in this project. Because the picture shows three girls composed as a close up, the students find it inappropriate to use. In this case Heidi and Carla don't think primarily of the author's rights, but they find it not right to show these faces (despite the fact that two of them use sunglasses as well). But the argument that settles the case is in the utterance in line 7. The students discuss the photo, how the girl in the middle of the picture uses a black T-shirt with a symbol from the tube in London. On it is written "London girl" on the horizontal bar, in a tube-symbol. These letters and symbols (on the T-shirt) do not fit with Heidi and Carla's understanding of what they are going to make, and the picture as pre-filmic semiotic material is rejected. But after deleting the photo, Heidi (line 10) suggests jocularly manipulating the T-shirt. She suggests that by exchanging the letters with "Blitz" they could use the picture. The last episode (lines 10-12) is first and foremost a joke, but at the same time it indicates that they see this little "semiotic detail" as a closing argument for not using the picture.

Discussion

In the case study, it is apparent to what degree media and communication students download different semiotic material and how this pre-filmic semiotic material is evaluated and dealt with in the editing process. These resources become available because the students master a range of different software in the process of downloading and importing the semiotic material. As previously pointed out, it is a characteristic quality of the computer (and in general digitisation) that it facilitates or affords the easy use of material from different sites on the Internet. Having defined literacy practices as working with different kind of semiotic materials, not only words and letters, it is obvious that these moments when the students evaluate the pre-filmic material are literacy events. I argue that the students not only copy and paste - that is just the technical part of the process of mastering the software. We find that the students also *appropriate* the semiotic material. This appropriation process includes reflections and thought. For instance, by drawing on their knowledge of punk-music and signs (the tube symbol and the words "London girl") the members in the "Blitz group" and Axel show an ability to interpret the meaning of the semiotic material and to make conscious choices on that basis.

We also find that our methodology proves useful for analyzing particular contexts, such as when media and communication students select semiotic material for a particular assignment. The methodology makes it possible to capture the filmmaking process as a literacy practice.

Copy and paste: Ethical implications

Copy and paste implies some ethical questions that are hard to find answers to. The culture of appropriation, understood in the context of the media and communication students, entails obstacles such as copyright rules about downloading materials from the Internet. Various approaches have emerged to solve the problems, for example the organisation Creative Commons seeks to offer a special set of sampling licenses that let artists and authors invite other people to use a part of their work. Founded in 2001 by intellectual and cyber law experts, the Creative Commons organisation provides free tools that let authors, scientists, artists and educators easily mark their creative work with the freedom they want it to carry.[11] The DJ-culture takes a similar approach to copyright. The conceptual artist and DJ Paul Miller argues that digital technology is turning culture into networks:

> The old hierarchies of linear thought, sublime (and sublimated!) engagements with art, poetry, music, science and history are no longer needed to do the ideological work now conducted again along the lines of "current". All-inclusive data networks transform individual creation into a kit of interchangeable parts, Lego building blocks of consciousness in a world that moves under the sign of continuous transformation and atomized perspectives. The machinery of culture acts out in the theatre of mind – how we navigate through the abstract systems we use to maintain meaning. As we say in the DJ world, it's all in the mix. (Miller 2004, 33)

The students use these networks as cultural tools when they edit a video at school, but in this context the issue of copyright becomes important. As stressed earlier, in everyday schooling the students reflect on these issues as well. In this case it is obvious that the students are struggling with making conscious choices when it comes to copyright. As is clear in Excerpt 1, the students argue that it is OK to use anything from the site in an assignment at the school - but they don't write about the copying in the reflection-note. The girls Heidi and Carla, on the other hand, deleted the picture they worked with and chose other pictures from the official Blitz web-site. Without referring to this episode, Carla wrote in particular about copyright in her reflection note:

> Because the pictures in the documentary are downloaded from the Blitz web-page, we assumed that they (the Blitzers) thought it was OK to show these in public. They were also published on the site in such a way that it was possible to download them, and there were no signs of copyright restrictions. Nor was anything written about copyright on the web-site (Reflection-note by the student Carla).

I find that the students at Greenwood take their practice of downloading of pre-filmic material in an assignment for granted. In our case study, the teachers didn't comment on the issues of copyright, but rather they appreciated how these downloaded stills were used in the first part of the final TV feature. In the written assessment it was striking how the Greenwood teachers give the students good comments on the first part with pre-filmic material and assess the more traditional part with pro-filmic material as "looser edited" and not so focused on the issue. According to earlier research in this field (as reviewed in the introduction), it seems, based on this case, that the teachers in media and communication, to a larger degree than teachers in other subjects, are familiar with different kind of semiotic material, both pre- and pre-filmic. The teachers may not give a negative response when students have used material downloaded from the Internet. In the end it is important to consider how the attitudes of teachers impact the attitudes of students.

Conclusions

I have tried to establish a theoretical framework for understanding students as designers in a literacy practice where they google, select, interpret and remix a wide range of semiotic material. My claim is that the use of different kinds of cultural tools plays a crucial role here. Thus, I have highlighted issues of mastery and appropriation. In addition to this I have also pointed to the affordances that the Internet offers the students in terms of pre-filmic material.

As is evident in the Norwegian survey, the media and communication students gather and use various kinds of material in these films as well as the more traditional source of footage on the camcorder. As I have previously argued, human mediated action is dependent on the cultural tools that are developed in different cultures. Digitisation, and in particular digital editing software, *visualize*s the different cultural expressions and is a powerful tool for taking culture apart and putting it together again.

This culture of appropriation is the culture of the Napster-generation. With the opportunity to be online both at school and in their leisure time for several hours each day, the students use pre-filmic material to varying degrees depending on the assignment and the context. These practices challenge the current culture of schooling, but maybe to a lesser degree in media and communication studies than in other subjects. The overall question is how the educational system in general can deal with a culture of appropriation when it comes to issues about learning and literacy in a new media age. Henry Jenkins writes: "Appropriation enters education when learners are encouraged to dissect, transform, sample, or remix existing cultural materials" (Jenkins 2006, 33). Maybe one of the most important literacies in the school of tomorrow is the ability to consciously author multimodal texts by meaningfully googling, selecting and re-mixing pre- and pro filmic semiotic material. The case study described in this chapter provides a limited scope for producing knowledge about how young people engage in processes of digital editing.

What we need is research on the culture of appropriation, both in formal and informal contexts. New literacy practices evolve in this culture, and copy and paste is a central part of these practices. At this time, academic research is exploring the new phenomenon of digital editing practices as it applies to literacy and learning processes. As the educational researcher Roger Säljö has pointed out, we need to re-think learning and remembering in the light of our digital media age.

Notes

[1] Thanks to Ola Erstad, Julian Sefton-Green and Fredrik Lindstrand, Dan Perkel, Andrew Morrison, Lisbeth Frølunde, Kirsten Drotner and Svein Østerud for extensive comments and discussion. Thanks also for inspiration and suggestions from Thomas de Lange and other ph. d. students, as well as from the senior researchers at the doctoral school of the Faculty of Education at the University of Oslo.

[2] I distinguish the term "semiotic material" from the term "semiotic resources" by focusing only on the different modes the students record or download in the process of making digital video. "Semiotic resources" are also features in the software like filters and layers, different fonts and so on.

[3] The term "to google" was included in Webster's dictionary (and others) in July 2006. For that reason the term is used without brackets in the text. The phrase "googling movies" paraphrases the more used phrase "making movies", maybe most known as the title of the famous album by Dire Straits in 1980. Now widely used as a phrase on web-resources for making film (just try google the phrase!).

[4] "Appropriation" is used here as a translation of the Russian verb *prisvoit* which means "one's own" and the noun *prisvoenie* which means "the process of making something one's own" (Wertsch 1998, 53).
[5] The Russian semiotician N.K. Voloshinov (1973), who was also a part of the Bakhtin circle, used much the same dialogic approach to language, but he focused more on sign systems as a whole. By doing that he laid the foundation for social semiotics (Hodge and Kress 1988, Kress and Van Leeuwen 1996, Van Leeuwen 2005) as a theory of sign-making as practice.
[6] The survey was performed over six weeks (November - December 2006), asking students over 70 questions about media use, media production and experiences concerning learning and teaching in the media education classes. It was organized using an online questionnaire that the students used about an hour to answer in one of their ordinary classes at school. The response rate was over 80 per cent.
[7] The original question was: What kind of material (modes of expression) did you use in this production? (In Norwegian: Hvilke elementer (uttrykksformer) var med i denne produksjonen?) .
[8] The terms pre- and pro-filmic can also be related to the French anthropologist Claude Lévi-Strauss, who introduced the terms *le bricoleur* and *l'ingenieur* (Lévi-Strauss 1978).
[9] The school started its first course in Media and Communication in 2000, when the subject was introduced in Norway. During the last six years, the school has increased the number of students, especially in media and communication which now counts 240 students on three different levels.
[10] Every media and communication student has got their own Macintosh with relevant software, and they can borrow a digital camcorder (with accessories) any time they want (and even bring it home at the weekends).
[11] See http://www.creativecommons.org and Lessig (2004).

References

Arnseth, H. C. 2004. *Discourse and artefacts in Learning to Argue: Analysing the practical management of computer supported collaborative learning*. Doctoral diss., University of Oslo.

Bakhtin, M. M. 1981. *The dialogic imagination: Four essays by M.M. Bakhtin*. Ed. M. Holqueist, trans. C. Emerson and M. Holquist. Austin: University of Texas Press.

—. 1986. *Speech genres and other late essays*. Austin: University of Texas Press.

Banks, M. 2001. *Visual methods in social research*. London: Sage.

Barton, D. 2007. *Literacy: An introduction to the ecology of written language.* Oxford: Blackwell. Second edition.

Buckingham, D. 2003. *Media education: Literacy, learning and contemporary culture*. London: Polity press.

Buckingham, D., J. Grahame, and J. Sefton-Green. 1995. *Making media: Practical production in media education.* London: The English and Media Centre.

Buckingham, D., S. Banaji, A. Burn, D. Carr, S. Cranmer, and R. Willett. 2005. *The media literacy of children and young people: A review of the academic research*. London: OfCom.

Burn, A., and D. Parker. 2003a. *Analyzing media texts*. London: Continuum.

Burn, A. and D. Parker. 2003b. Tiger's Big Plan: Multimodality and the moving image. In *Multimodal literacy,* ed. C. Jewitt and G. Kress. New York: Peter Lang.

Burn, A., and J. Durran. 2006. Digital anatomies: Analysis as production in media education. In *Digital generations: Children, young people, and new media,* ed. D. Buckingham and R. Willett, pp. 273-93. Mahwah, NJ: Lawrence Erlbaum.

Collins, A. 2001. Design issues for learning environments. In *Instructional perspectives on the design of technology-supported learning environments*, ed. S. Vosniadou, E. de Corte, R. Glaser, and H. Mandl. Mahwah, NJ: LEA.

Drotner, K. 1991. *At skabe sig – selv: ungdom, æstetik, pædagogik* [Self Creation: Youth, aesthetics, pedagogy]. Copenhagen: Gyldendal.

Erstad, O., Ø. Gilje, and T. de Lange. 2007a. Re-defining media learning: multiliteracies and digital production in Norwegian media education. *Learning, Media and Technology* 32(2): 183-198.

Erstad, O., Ø. Gilje, and T. de Lange. 2007b. *Morgendagens medieprodusenter: Om mediefagselevers produksjonspraksiser i videregående skole. [Media creators of the future: On media education students' production practices in upper secondary school]*. Oslo: report. www.transactions.uio.no (retrieved March 1, 2008)

Facer, K., J. Furlong, R. Furlong, and R. Sutherland. 2003. *ScreenPlay: Children and computing in the home*. London: Routledge Falmer.

Hodge, B., and G. Kress. 1988. *Social semiotics.* London: Polity Press.

Hull, G., and M. E. Nelson. 2005. Locating the semiotic power of multimodality. *Written Communication* 22(2): 224-261.

Jenkins, H. 2006. *White paper: Confronting the challenges of participatory culture: Media education for the 21st century*. Berkeley, CA: MacArthur Foundation. www.digitallearning.macfound.org (retrieved March 1, 2008)

Jewitt, C. 2005. Classrooms and the design of pedagogic discourse: A multimodal approach. *Culture and Psychology* 1(3): 309-320.

—. 2006. *Technology, literacy and learning: A multimodal approach.* London: Routledge.

Kress, G., and T. Van Leeuwen. 1996. *Reading images: The grammar of visual design.* London: Routledge.

Kress, G. 2003. *Literacy in the new media age*. London: Routledge.

Lenhart, A., and M. Madden. 2005. *Teen content creators and consumers: Findings of the Pew Internet and American Life Project*, http://www.pewinternet.org/ (retrieved March 1, 2008).

Lessig, L. 2004. *Free culture: How big media uses technology and the law to lock down culture and control creativity*, http://free-culture.cc/ (retrieved March 1, 2008).

Lévi-Strauss, C. 1978. *Myth and meaning*. London: Routledge.

Lindstrand, F. 2006. *Att göra skillnad: Representation, identitet och lärande i ungdomars arbete och berättande med film* [Making difference: Representation, identity and learning in teenagers' work and communication with film]. Doctal diss., Studies in Educational Science 86. Stockholm: HLS Förlag.

Løvland, A. 2006. *Samansette elevtekstar: Klasserommet som arena for multimodal tekstskaping* [Pupils' multimodal texts: The classroom as an arena for multimodal creation of texts]. Doctoral diss., Agder College, Norway.

Metz, C. 1974. *Film language*. Chicago: University of Chicago Press.

Miller, P. D. 2005. *Rhythm science.* Cambridge: MIT Press.

Pink, S. 2001. *Doing visual ethnography*. London: Sage.

—. 2006. *The future of visual anthropology: Engaging the senses.* London: Routledge.

Rasmussen, I. 2005. *Studying learning as participation trajectories.* Doctoral diss., University of Oslo.

Reid, M., A. Burn, and D. Parker. 2002. *Evaluation report of the BECTA Digital Video Pilot Project.* Bristol: BECTA/BFI, http://www.becta.org.uk/page_documents/research/dvreport_241002.pdf (retrieved March 1, 2008).

Säljö, R. 2005. *Lärande and kulturella redskap: Om lärprocesser och det kollektiva minnet* [Learning and cultural tools: On learning as a process and the collective memory]. Stockholm: Norstedt Academic Press.

—. 2007. *Studying learning and knowing in social practices: Units of analysis and tensions in theorising.* Keynote address on the opening of the Oxford Centre for Sociocultural Activity Theory Research, Department of Education, University of Oxford, http://www.education.ox.ac.uk/ (retrieved March 1, 2008)

Sefton-Green, J., and D. Buckingham. 1998. Digital visions: Children's "creative" uses of multimedia technologies. In *Digital Diversions: Youth culture in the age of multimedia,* ed. J. Sefton-Green. London: Routledge.

Sefton-Green, J. 2004. *Literature review in informal learning with technology outside school.* NESTA futurelab series. Report 7. Bristol: NESTA.

—. 2005. Timelines, timeframes and special effects: Soft and creative media production. *Education, Communication and Information* 5(1): 99-110.

Van Leeuwen, T. 2005. *Introducing social semiotics*. London: Routledge.

Voloshinov, V. N. 1973. *Marxism and the philosophy of language*. Harvard, MA: Harvard University Press.

Vygotsky, L. S. 1978. *Mind and society*. Harvard, MA: Harvard University Press.

—. 1986. *Thought and language*. Cambridge: MA: MIT Press.

Wertsch, J. V. 1991. *Voices of the mind: A sociocultural approach to mediated action.* Cambridge MA: Harvard University Press.

—. 1998. *Mind as action*. Oxford: Oxford University Press.

—. 2002. *Voices of collective remembering*. Cambridge: Cambridge University Press.

CHAPTER THREE

ACTING AND LEARNING WITH AVATARS: SENSE-MAKING STRATEGIES OF REFLECTION IN THE VIRTUAL WORLD OF A MASSIVELY MULTI-USER ONLINE ROLE-PLAYING GAME

SISSE SIGGAARD JENSEN

Millions of actors and players inhabit the so-called Massively Multi-User Online Role-Playing Games (MMORPG),[2] which are some of the advanced virtual worlds of today that facilitate a variety of virtual experiences. The games are different, but they all have one thing in common: the actors will have to *do* something; they will have to act when confronted with danger. Moreover, action is necessary if the actors are to build communities of the game, and, most importantly, to develop the abilities and levels of their chosen avatars.[3] Thus, acting is a predominant feature of the role-playing games. Compared to this, many collaborative virtual learning environments are merely file-sharing and/or exchange systems.

This chapter presents an analysis of some possible starting points for designing virtual framings (Goffman 1986), designs that require mutually coordinated action. The assumption is that such framings may help produce actors' sense-making and informal learning strategies, if the actors are provoked and challenged to reflect on their actions. Furthermore, the presumption is that the prevailing traditions of collaborative learning and knowledge-sharing need to be challenged and complemented, if we are to further develop the diversity of the repertoires of virtual learning activities. Some of the advanced virtual worlds may inspire the design of such provoking and challenging virtual framings. Therefore, the question asked in this chapter is: how do the players of a MMORPG make sense of the many challenges they face while playing the game, and what are the sense-making and informal learning strategies they develop when confronted with such challenges?

However, if we are to learn from the design of role-playing games and from actors playing and surviving in their advanced virtual worlds, then we must be able to conduct empirical research on the actors' activities while they are acting. The current chapter presents some empirical findings from an ongoing research project on actors and avatars communicating in virtual worlds, a project that builds on existing research on avatars and virtual environments (Andersen and Qvortrup 2004, Clemmensen 2007, Damer 1998, Jacobsson 2006a, 2006b; Qvortrup 2001, 2002; Schroeder 2002, 2006; Yee 2004a, 2004b, 2005, 2006, 2007) and incorporates results from a 3D Agora-world project on knowledge-sharing (Jensen 2004, 2007).[4] The empirical findings presented derive from video interviews that combine video recordings of virtual world sessions with in-depth, explorative research interviews with actors while they are acting. The virtual sessions have been undertaken in collaboration between the actor and researcher.

First, the methodological approach, which is based on sense-making ontology (Dervin and Foreman-Wernet 2003) and the concept of a complete act of reflection (Dewey 1933), are briefly introduced, together with the method of video interviewing (Jensen 2001, 2005). Then, some of the findings concerning the actors' choice of avatars and agencies in the virtual world of EverQuest are presented. Finally, the findings are analysed with reference to the sense-making approach and the concept of a complete act of reflection to exemplify the cycle of analysis applied to the empirical findings of research. In order to contextualise the subsequent analysis, some background information about the MMORPGs is first summarized, referring to the research carried out by Nick Yee (Yee 2004a, 2004b, 2005, 2006, 2007) and Michael Jacobsson (2006a, 2006b), and some of the participants of the video interviews are presented.

MMORPGs: Some background

The virtual worlds of the MMORPGs are extensive and complex. Players develop their own avatars, and it is difficult to develop an avatar held in high esteem among other players. EverQuest, which is the virtual world referred to in this chapter, is a typical and classic example of such a MMORPG. It is made up of continents covering more than 400 different zones, ranging from extensive deserts and dangerous mountains to cosy homelands with green pastures, all of which pose increasing levels of difficulty to the players. There is a diversity of avatar classes and characters with given abilities and characteristics to choose among. A vast array of quests, trades, missions, and raids is available to increase the levels and experience points of the avatars and to improve their abilities and competencies. In order to survive in the world of EverQuest, the actors will have to build up knowledge of the many different computer-mediated, non-person characters, each of which poses specific and level-dependent threats to the players' survival. The non-person characters, e.g. in the shape of a multiplicity of monsters, drop a variety of benefits if they are defeated, and the role-players need knowledge of the variety of such "droppings." Also, many different trades and trade skills are necessary to produce high-level and professional avatars. Leadership is required to manage and organize the players of the game into small groups or large-size professional guilds with up to 500 simultaneous avatars and classes fighting monsters in large-scale raids. These make up just some of the parameters that help configure the complexity of the MMORPGs. Such complexity inspires a sense of freedom to act. In a video interview, Martin, an eighteen-year-old and very skilled player of such advanced games, says: "You almost feel as free as is the case in real life, free to choose and decide either alone or in mutual action, without any constraint."

The sense of freedom to act is associated with an experience of realism and authenticity. Acting and communicating as an avatar has a real impact on other players and their avatars, groups and guilds. The amount of time invested to build up knowledge and meet the challenges means that the activities of the virtual world come to matter to players. Profound social relationships may develop; socializing forms part of the organising of activities; managerial and planning skills advance as the activities require leadership similar to real life.

Different levels of play seem to indicate that the experience of playing changes over time. At the beginner's level, the players get adjusted to the virtual world and the role-play. Simple routines, training and guidance are driving forces. Players at the mid-level focus on the building of social relationships in small and flexible groups of players. When playing at the top level, players put a high priority on organising large-size and professional guilds with division of roles and leadership. At the master level, resources of the play are scarce and very often player turns against player, fighting over the resources (Jacobsson 2006b).

Also, Nick Yee's (2005, 2006) studies on MMORPGs illuminate different playing styles and motivational factors. The building of social relationships is a predominant factor with all players, whereas the achievement factor indicates a difference in playing styles among younger and older players. The young players tend to play to obtain achievements, whereas the older players seem to assign priority to the relationship factor.

Yee's survey study also indicates that players spend much time in virtual worlds. On a weekly basis, the average amounts to 22 hours. Surprisingly, it is not only teenagers and young people who spend so much time in the virtual worlds. Only 25 per cent of MMORPG players are teenagers. The average age is 26 years, with ages ranging from 11 to 68 years. During game-play, players regularly get together with retirees, grandmothers, grandchildren and fathers play with their sons and daughters.

The participants of my video interviews exemplify some of Yee's findings and also some of the observations found in Mikael Jacobsson's study of the different levels of play (Jacobsson 2006). The age of the participants ranges from 18 to 30 years at the time of my recordings, and they spend up to 22 hours a week in the world of EverQuest. There is, however, a difference between the playing style of the young player, Martin, aged eighteen, and the older players. Martin's playing style has greater variation over time. Sometimes, all of his leisure time is spent in the virtual worlds, while at other times he spends almost no time there.

The participants have been chosen so as to exemplify different life situations. Martin is a young player and a high school student. Jan is a single male, aged thirty, who receives unemployment benefits, as he is unemployed at the time of recordings. Sia, aged twenty-six, has been awarded a disability pension just prior to the recordings. She is married to Janus, a student teacher, aged twenty-eight, and together they have two children, Bo, who is seven years old, and Alice, an infant. Bo and Alice also have parts to play in the video interviews.

Also, the participants in the video interviews have different playing styles and motivational factors. Martin is a generalist and an expert on many different role-plays. Out of curiosity, he levels-up the avatars in order to experience and study what can be achieved in different games. His primary motivation is the achievement factor. Jan plays a mid-level avatar "grouping" with small and non-permanent groups of virtual friends. His primary motivation is the relationship factor, but also escapism and manipulation of other players seem to influence his playing style. Janus and Sia play a broad range of avatars, some of them at top level. Pursuing a playing style with high ethics, their priority is the development of communities based on collaboration and the sharing of knowledge, wealth and benefits. Sia is the leader of a guild, and her primary motivation is the relationship in combination with the achievement factors. Janus enjoys being immersed in a world of fantasy and in the joint actions of the game, and he is also motivated by the relationship factor.

Ontology and disturbance

The sense-making methodology derives from communication theory (Dervin and Foreman-Wernet 2003), and it is based on an ontology inspired by a phenomenological approach to the understanding of human activity, communication and being. The theory emphasizes the uniqueness of human activity, which is seen as personal, and time-, place-, and space-bound. Conversely, a search for patterns essential to human activity is also seen as a precondition for the more general understanding of human agency and communication. This seeming contradiction is fundamental to the sense-making theory, which acknowledges that discontinuities and contradictions are some of the basic conditions of human activity. These conditions are summarized by the sense-making term gappiness, a term that serves to characterise human movements in time, place and space. From the viewpoint of a sense-making ontology, we continuously move from situation to situation in a world sometimes chaotic and sometimes orderly, but always filled with gappinesses, be they physical or mental, in a "flow" of which we are often not conscious.

However, in many situations we become conscious of our own movements in time and place, in particular if for some reason the movement is stopped. Gaps often cause such stops, and the bridging of gaps is a form of human activity whose purpose is to overcome the gaps or the so-called situation movement stops. Overcoming stops, bridging the gaps, is seen as the source of innovation and creation, even if it is only on a minor scale and as small variations of the ongoing activity. Such movings and stops are the actions and reflections conceived as general patterns of human agency and communication. They apply to unique situations across time, place and space. Situation movement states, whether they are movings or stops, are seen as general patterns essential to the understanding of human activity. Examples of these patterns, identified by Brenda Dervin (2003) in her empirical research, are: DECISION – being at a point where you need to choose between two or more roads that lie ahead; PROBLEMATIC – being dragged down a road not of your own choosing; SPIN OUT – not having a road; WASH OUT – being on a road, suddenly having it disappear; BARRIER- knowing where you want to go but someone or something is blocking the way; BEING LED – following another on the road because he or she knows more and can show you the way (Dervin and Foreman-Wernet 2003, 262).

Travelling around the virtual world of EverQuest, the actors of the game are confronted with many situation movement stops, and continuous action is required as they face many challenges and threats. Being stopped may bring into focus the need for reflection in order to bridge some experienced gappiness. Overcoming the obstacles, the disturbances, and the disorder of complicated situations makes topical the agencies, which John Dewey (1933) conceives of as "complete acts of reflection." In taking this perspective, acting and reflecting is seen as a whole, even if they are very different forms of agency. Acting in the world is a spontaneous and immediate human activity, whereas reflection is only reluctantly adopted as a means through which one may overcome disturbances and problems that would otherwise stop the course of action. Following Dewey, we learn nothing from action alone; only, if for some reason the activity is stopped, are we forced to reflect on the situation in order to resolve the difficulties confronting us. Dewey states:

> Some inhibition of direct action is necessary to the condition of hesitation and delay that is essential to thinking. Thought is, as it were, conduct turned in upon itself and examining its purpose and its conditions, its resources, aids, and difficulties and obstacles (Dewey 1933, 108).

A pre-reflective situation is unsettled and is felt and experienced as such. Moving from a pre-reflective to a post-reflective situation is a process of self-referential reorganising of the felt experience. Together, observation and inference form the acts of reflection, which are the motivating forces of informal as well as formal learning. There is, however, a difference between the two forms of learning in that the objective of the self-referential reorganising of experience differs between informal and formal learning (Dewey 1933). The virtual world of EverQuest provokes certain types of experience that initiate a reorganisation of some of these experiences by acts of reflection. Concurrently, the reorganising of experience is enacted in a process of informal learning framed by the challenges, disturbances and obstacles of the virtual world.

In situ video interviews

As mentioned above, the empirical findings in this study are produced by video interviews (Jensen 2001, 2005). Such interviews are best conceptualised as a hybrid of diverse methodologies, that is field studies inspired by actor-network theory (Latour 2005), visual anthropology and video interaction analysis (Banks 2001, Grimshaw 2001, Jordan and Henderson 1995, Pink 2001), virtual ethnography (Hine 2005), and the in-depth, exploratory research interview of the sense-making approach (Dervin and Foreman-Wernet 2003).

The study of virtual environments with adjacent methods has developed into a relatively independent area of research. Roughly, there are two generations in the development of the area. The early one considers virtual methods to be a "weak" version of existing methods in qualitative research. According to this point of view, virtual interaction is weak in comparison to face-to-face studies (Sproull and Kiesler 1986). The second generation sets out to reinterpret and critically reflect on existing methods used in the exploration of virtual environments. These methods regard virtual environments as a cultural context where ethnographically-inspired methods, in particular, can contribute to the analysis (Baym 2000, Hine 2005, Howard 2002, Williams 2007). This research project about actors and their avatars subscribes to the latter tradition, although with some modifications. In my video interviews, the actors' movements between their life world and their activities in the virtual world are conceived as a whole. If we merely study the virtual activity itself, in isolation from the actors' life world context, it will stand in the way of following the actors through their different forms of agency in the virtual as well as their life world.

Following this approach, recurrent and iterative video interviews with actors while acting have been recorded in situ through field study. This format was chosen for a number of reasons. First, the objective of video-recording the actors' familiar environment is to come as close as possible to the actors' daily practices. Second, focusing on their daily practices also facilitates an illumination of the silent and tacit knowledge of action so important to situated computing. Third, the memory of interviewees, and also often their narratives, are somewhat blurred by the difficulty of imagining, in retrospect, how the computer is handled, and how challenges, forms of collaboration, knowledge-building, and crises are dealt with in action. Finally, recurrent and iterative video interviews serve the purpose of encircling the foci of the recordings when these are viewed together with the participants. These joint viewing sessions inspire the actors' narratives about their experiences as these are seen from an insider's view of being present in the virtual world.

Summing up the approach of video interviewing, the analytical aspiration is not to objectively register activity from a panoptic view; rather, the observer is seen as a part of the observations and conversations, and these are carried out in collaboration between the actor and researcher. The observational stance and the methodological approach may best be characterized as that of a joint voyage of discovery, in the sense that the researcher follows the actors into their world as they together observe, reason, and discuss their mutual experiences.

The video interviews focus on five different themes, namely 1) the actors' conception of the virtual world, 2) their choice of avatars, 3) the diversity of social interactions in joint action, 4) the actors' self-perceptions experienced and expressed, and 5) the interplay between the virtual world and the actors' life world. In the following, some of the findings from the video interviews conducted with Jan, Sia and Janus are presented with reference to these five aspects. It should be emphasized that, due to limitation on space, the findings and thematic aspects chosen serve the purpose of exemplifying a cycle of analysis.

Gnossiz the Gnome: An avatar

The first step an actor must take in order to travel around the virtual world is to choose an avatar from several possible figures and characters that are the preferred means of self-presentation (Goffman 1959). This step is loaded with meaning. Let us follow Jan, one of the actors, while taking this step. Gnossiz the Gnome is his main character and avatar. Jan is present in EverQuest only with this one avatar, as the actor has no other gallery of avatars to choose from. Jan lives in a marginalized zone of society, and his economy clearly constrains his range of possible actions, and with that, the possibility of having a gallery with many avatars. The video interview about Gnossiz takes place in a garage with none of the usual comforts of contemporary society such as, for instance, running water. However, at the very centre of the garage stands a computer, which is configured so as to run the advanced virtual world.

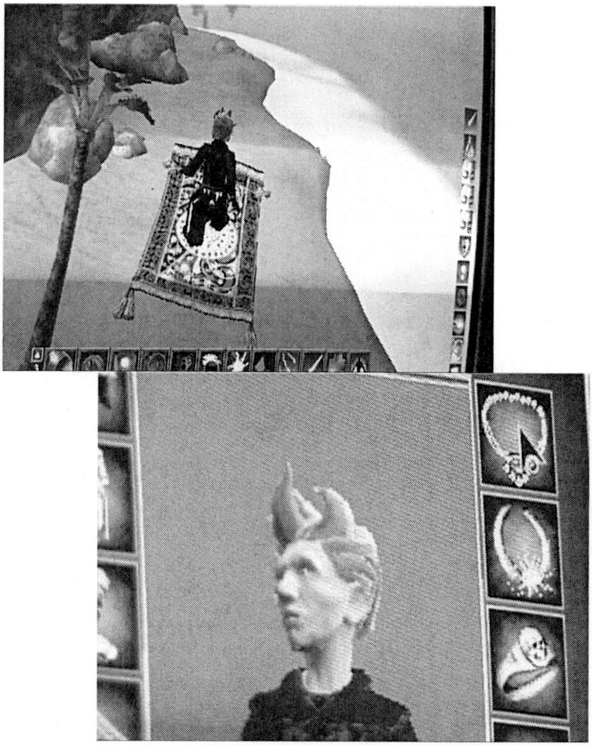

Figure 3-1. Gnossiz the Gnome with his flying carpet is Jan's avatar

Jan has chosen Gnossiz the Gnome because he is good at acting on his own, good at going "solo". He does not have to "balance on the shoulders" of other actors and avatars. Gnossiz can do everything by himself. Actions that would normally require the activity of a group are enacted by this avatar and character. That is possible only because Jan has found ways to get around the design of the world:

> They [the designers of the game] are trying to control and restrict it, so you cannot go solo, but I have found my way round it. If I don't win, then I will just die. My hitpoints will then decrease to only two per cent, and I will have almost no mana. But I will still run the risk. I don't run away. Very often, many players start running, but that is just as if you turned your back to a tiger; you will get seriously wounded. Never run away.

Taking chances, acting bravely and courageously, as opposed to many other actors, and also, acting very cunningly, these are some of the qualities essential to the actor. Gnossiz travels fast on a flying carpet. It took the actor four laborious quests to get hold of his flying carpet. But, it was worthwhile. When travelling on a flying carpet, Gnossiz can easily move around the desert zone of the world. Small, but clever and fast, these are the qualities of Gnossiz the Gnome, as opposed to many other players and their characters, according to Jan.

Gnossiz earns experience points (xps) by solving quests, fighting monsters and averting dangers, and these points enable him to fight ever more dangerous monsters and survive under difficult circumstances. But, most importantly, in this way he can help other players and thus present himself as a knowledgeable avatar. However, having reached level 56 with Gnossiz the Gnome, there is not much fun for Jan anymore. When playing at this level, it is too easy for him to win the fights, to cast his spells, to acquire valuable accessories, and also to survive, as he cannot afford to add on to his world the new zones, which would allow him to further level-up his avatar and face new difficulties. The only challenge left for him is to prove the power of his character by helping other players become as experienced as he is.

The draconic guardians: A virtual guild

Janus and Sia play the game together with their virtual friends and members of the guild, The Draconic Guardians. In this guild, Janus plays Krongh the Troubletroll who is his main character and a medium-level hybrid of different avatar classes. He is the preferred avatar out of several because of the sophisticated skills and abilities it takes to play a complex and compound character. Of course, it is fun to play a high-level character, yet if it involves playing a simple class, such as, for instance, a warrior, then it is of no interest to him. Rather, it is the challenge of playing with refinement that makes sense to Janus. In this way, he can explore and experience how to make the most of his personal abilities and capacity. Janus enjoys the world of fantasy and the building of social relationships with his virtual friends of the guild.

Sia's main character is Gelinu the Shaman. Out of a gallery of 14 avatars, some of which are highly-ranked characters, Sia prefers to play Gelinu because the shaman is an avatar class that is difficult to play. Gelinu is a high-level character who is almost like a goddess to Sia. Playing the high-level Gelinu, she has to master the body of abilities and skills of a shaman. Her role of the game is to assist the other players of the guild while acting and fighting. She must heal, strengthen, and fast-pace the other members of the guild with a wide range of so-called beneficial spells. Also, the shaman is obliged to throw "slow" on the monsters, that is, to slow down their attacks and also to cause widespread damage with spells that help reduce the monsters' ability of resistance. In this way, her avatar class plays the important role of providing the overall conditions for the others when the guild is on missions and raids. She acts in support of their action and offers protection against severe problems and dangerous situations. Gelinu is an almost indispensable character for her avatar colleagues when they are fighting to survive. According to Sia:

> The shaman has so many responsibilities; it is so demanding. Shamans have so many abilities and skills. They can "throw" so many different spells and healings, and it is required. They will *have* to do it! My shaman is so busy. If she fails to take up her role, then seriously the other members of the guild run the risk of getting hard hit and killed in the fight. Her responsibilities are many.

Fig 3-2. Krongh the Troubletroll is Janus' preferred character, and Gelinu is Sia's shaman

To be able to master Gelinu's role and responsibilities, Sia works hard to level-up and become a high-level and professional avatar. To achieve this objective, she has invested much time in the development of Gelinu's trade skills in addition to the level-up effects that come from the other activities of the guild. Thus, her virtual achievements and also the building of the social relationships make sense to Sia.

Mastering and managing the play at the top level with an avatar held in high esteem is essential to Sia, as she is the leader of The Draconic Guardians. The guild has recently been formed, and it is a small-sized and well-organized guild with only ten members from the USA, Denmark, the Netherlands, and Britain. Sia has set an age limit for membership in the Draconic Guardians. Only role-players older than 22 years are allowed in and only if they are approved by Sia. The age limit was introduced because of Sia's experience with what she considers ill-mannered behaviour of some of the younger players.

Before organising The Draconic Guardians, Janus and Sia played the game in a large-sized guild. At that time, Sia was the leader of a guild that had 100-150 members, an assisting co-leader, and a group of officers. It was up to the guild leader to suggest the guidelines, rules and values, and with that, the playing style of the guild, and to help maintain them. As a guild leader of a large-sized guild, her responsibilities were to guide and instruct the guild members how often and how long to play the game, to help maintain the commitments made by the members on how to improve the levels of their avatars, and to keep up with the planning of activities. Also, her responsibilities included the ethics that guide the guild's missions and raids and the mediation in case of conflicts between the role-players.

Thus, playing in a large-size guild with high-level avatars and acting as a guild leader is hard work, and gradually Sia had to accept that she could not cope with the many responsibilities, especially as some of the players of the large-sized guild had arguments over the play. Thus, given their current life situation, Sia and Janus decided to reorganise their playing style and to start a small-sized guild together with some of their virtual friends and family members. Playing the game this way became a necessity, as Sia's situation in particular, seemed untenable with her many responsibilities of the virtual as well as the other-life world. She had to accept the withdrawal from the large-size guild, although clearly she wishes to return as soon as possible as she notes:

> Possibly, we may again become members of another large-sized guild, one of the large raiding guilds, but it involves a different playing style and attitude. It requires that you willingly take part in major raids, for instance

> three times a week, and you are obliged to take an active role in the raids. With family and children that is not possible!

The impact of the virtual leadership on Sia's other life situation became too pervasive, as her husband is also a dedicated player, although with a playing style less demanding than Sia's. As noted above, he plays with the aim of building friendships and relationships, not for the achievements as such. However, he plays the game as often as Sia. With their responsibilities for their two children, they had to reorganise their play. Also, Bo plays Nuser the Troll, a character who looks much the same as his father's main avatar. Bo clearly prefers to play the troll rather than do his homework. In this way, the role-playing game has an impact on his schooling, a fact which Sia and Janus have also to take into consideration.

Getting around constraints

Choosing an avatar is the first move that Jan must make when he enters the virtual world of EverQuest. This step will influence his movements and transformations all through the world and its many different zones. However, it will also connect him to the outside world with regard both to the designers of the worlds and to the virtual friends who are real even if they are acting behind their avatars. Thus, the avatar may be seen as a vehicle by which Jan facilitates the transportation of meaning (Latour 2005) and sense-makings when he decides to move from the outside world in the garage into the virtual world. Moving this way, one of the first gaps facing the actor is the range of avatars to choose among, avatars with different characters and roles to play. The question is how to make the chosen avatar make sense in such a way that he can travel around the world, presenting himself in a particular way. His idea of self-presentation does not necessarily match with what makes sense according to the ideas and plots of the designers. Therefore, Jan has to move to get around the designers' ideas.

Gnossiz the Gnome is the chosen character because he, to some extent, makes sense to the actor in getting around the designers' design. Although the designers of the world may try to delimit the actors from going "solo," promoting instead mutual activity, Jan asserts that he has been very successful in getting around these constraints. The gnome is good at going "solo," or rather; Jan can make his avatar act in such a way as to get around the limitations of going "solo." In this way, his avatar is transformed into a mediator, as it does not only function as a vehicle transporting meaning. Moving around the world with Gnossiz the Gnome acting as a mediator (Latour 2005) enables Jan to take control of the world and to get a feeling of mastering it, controlling it by cheating on the designers, that is, by transforming the input decided by the designers into an unforeseen output serving the purposes of his own sense-makings. Thus, the avatar is transformed to support the actor's movements and activities aimed at developing a highly personal self-presentation and playing style. Not surprisingly, Jan speaks about Gnossiz the Gnome in a compassionate and emotional manner.

Creating an intelligent avatar

In getting around the constraints of the design, Jan's situation movement stops refer to the designers of the world. However, the internal reality of the virtual world also plays an important part in Jan's choice of an avatar. To make the chosen avatar act as a mediator, Jan enacts it by moving around the world from zone to zone, from a cosy homeland with a friendly atmosphere to the dangerous zones and to fighting with monsters. In this way, Gnossiz the Gnome is continually transformed as Jan gradually overcomes the stops and gaps enabling him to raise the levels by increasing the avatar's abilities, skills and intelligence. To become an intelligent avatar is the most important transformation to the actor behind Gnossiz the Gnome. On the one hand, Jan proves to himself that he is capable of raising the level and intelligence, and on the other hand, this capability enables the actor to present himself as a character with the power to share his knowledge with other players of the virtual world. Although he is presenting the avatar as a loner, his endeavour is to be attached to groups of players and thus to transform his avatar into a guide of high esteem, helping the other players; and this transformation is made possible by creating a high-level, experienced, and professional avatar.

The transformation whereby the avatar becomes a mediator in the virtual world is staged in such a way that the actor gets deeply involved with the chosen figure and character. Jan has to go through several transformations to become an avatar of the virtual world, waking up at sea as a refugee, having to choose a zone and homeland, deciding whether to act in service of good or evil, and solving the beginner's quests. These movements are transforming rituals that forge close bonds between the actor and the avatar. It is almost as difficult to part with this presentation of self in the virtual world as it is to suppress aspects of your self-perception and presentation in the other-life world.

Upholding ethics and high standards

Moving from the outside world into the virtual, Sia and Janus also have to choose their avatars. In that process many decisions have to be made and both are confronted with gaps. They work hard at transforming their avatars to be able to present themselves in accordance with their self-perception and self-image. Their aspiration is to communicate to the other role-players the image of serious and responsible role-players and to communicate the playing ethics and the spirit of community which they both hold in high esteem. The spirit of sharing is part of their view of the virtual world values, and it guides their understanding of how to distribute the outcome of the missions, raids and mutual activities. Only in this way does the play make sense to them. In the galleries of their avatars, their preferred characters play this part. In Janus' case, his preferred avatars make sense to him because they are compound characters, which mean that he has to exert himself to the utmost to fully utilize his abilities and skills of the game. As far as Sia is concerned, she moves around the world to transform Gelinu the Shaman so as to become a high-level and professional avatar with far-reaching responsibilities. These are the values of the virtual world that make sense to her. Of course, playing with identity also has a part to play for Sia, Janus and Jan; it is, however, an aspect of minor importance, which even seems to diminish over time.

Maintaining the leadership of a guild

Playing the game in a large-size guild with many responsibilities and with high ethical standards is demanding. Sia, in particular, has been confronted with much gappiness due to the dual responsibilities of her virtual leadership and her responsibilities in the other-life world. Some of the players of her large-size guild had arguments over the play. Because of this, it was difficult for her to plan and organise the activities of the guild, as she never knew which classes and roles were being played, when and by whom. In other words, she lacked the knowledge and information needed to be able to manage and lead the guild and to set up the well-suited configurations of roles and levels in correspondence with the ongoing missions and raids. As a consequence, she was unable to adequately estimate the outcome of the guild's activity and to adhere to her values and ideals of the game.

It is not only Sia who has learned the lessons of the obligations facing large-size guilds in playing the role of a guild leader. Yee (2007) also deals with the question of leadership. From his survey, it appears that 15 per cent of players have been leaders at one point or another, and also they have learned important leadership skills. In particular, the lessons learned of how to mediate conflicts among players seem to have an impact that transfers to other-life world experiences. But playing the guild leader is laborious and demanding almost to a greater extent than is the case in real-life leadership.

In order to deal with the gaps confronting Sia as a leader, and also to uphold their family responsibilities, Janus and Sia have organised the small-size guild together with close virtual friends and family members. In this way, they can now informally deal with a great many leadership responsibilities, and problems of different needs and motivations are more easily solved. Also, turning on the guild's voice chat in the morning in order to start the planning and coordination of the evening's game has become part of the family's daily activities and routines. The voice chat operates almost as turning on the radio in other families, the difference being that the co-ordination undertaken in the voice chat requires Sia's and Janus' active attention and response.

The small-sized, informal and family-like guild is the sense-making strategy developed by Janus and Sia to solve some of the gappinesses that result from the conflicting demands of their guild and other-life situation. The reorganization of the guild allows Sia to maintain the part played by her shaman, and also her role as the leader of a guild. In this way, the playing of the game still makes sense to her. Only in this way can they both go on playing and at the same time keep up with the demands of a family. However, their aspiration is still to play a part in large-sized raids, developing their characters and guild to perform and play the role of professional avatars held in high esteem in the game.

Conclusion

Manipulating the constraints of the design and thus competing with the designers of the game seems to be important to Jan and his avatar, Gnossiz the Gnome. The gappiness of being dragged down a road not of his own choice makes no sense to him. Rather, he conceives of the game as being provoking and challenging. To resist the constraints of the design, he stops his movements and is forced to reflect on his actions. Gradually, he develops a sense-making strategy in order to bridge the gap, a strategy which allows him to circumvent the constraints of the design.

Also, the economic constraints of his life situation do not allow him to follow his virtual friends as they move on when the new zones of the game are launched. Although aspiring to play the game with an avatar that is good at going solo, he has the feeling of being left behind, unable to perform and appear as a professional and intelligent avatar. Once more, he is stopped. The gappiness of knowing where to go, but with someone or something blocking the way, has to be dealt with. Jan is forced to reflect on the situation to be able to continue his movements. To bridge the gap he has to develop a sense-making strategy which will allow him to become once more a recognized and appreciated virtual friend. Thus, he develops the sense-making strategy of knowledge-sharing. In this way, he retains the status of an intelligent avatar, and again Gnossiz the Gnome may be perceived as a professional avatar with the power to help and guide the more inexperienced actors and their avatars.

For Sia and Janus it is essential to be able to uphold the high standards and ethics which are part of their values of the virtual world. Only in this way does the game make sense to them. However, acting as the leader of a large-sized and well-esteemed guild with high ideals Sia has to work very hard in her virtual world. But, high ideals are also part of her other-life world values. Thus, gradually the many responsibilities of the guild leadership surpass her ability. Sia is facing the gap of being on a road towards the high-end leadership of her virtual guild, but gradually having the road disappear as she moves along. Her movement is stopped, and she is forced to reflect on the situation and to reconsider her future actions and obligations together with her husband Janus. Reflecting on her actions, she develops a sense-making strategy that will allow her to realistically assess the scope and style of her leadership and its responsibilities given her current life situation.

So far, this study of the actors of the virtual world of EverQuest has identified a set of gaps and sense-making strategies that may serve as starting points for the design of virtual worlds that may serve to provoke and challenge the actors' complete acts of reflection. The empirical findings presented and analysed have exemplified a cycle of analysis that may help inform a designing strategy for such virtual framings aimed at reflection and informal, as well as formal, learning. By way of concluding the chosen cycle of analysis, I would like to suggest some starting points for the design of action-based virtual framings. The questions of whether to "go solo" or to "group;" how to develop and uphold virtual values and ethics; how to circumvent the constraints of a given design, and the related roles and possible agencies; and the question of how to develop strategies for knowledge-sharing—these are questions that seem to provoke actors' acts of reflection. Furthermore, and very importantly, such a virtual framing should provoke acts of reflection on questions of responsibilities in order to confront actors with the many dilemmas facing them. Thus, the design may help exemplify conflicting responsibilities and along with that, reflection on some different styles of leadership. It seems that the virtual worlds of the MMORPGs may also serve as tools for the informal learning of how to mediate in cases of severe conflicts between actors in order to uphold the high standards and ethics of the game.

In this chapter, some learning processes of a group of actors of the Massively Multi-User Online Role-Playing Game of EverQuest have been followed, identified, and analysed. The study of the existing virtual worlds tentatively reveals a potential for informal learning that may well serve the function of a tool for reflection. However, it is also suggested that the cycles of analysis applied may inform the design of new virtual framings aimed at certain acts of reflection and informal learning, e.g. with new directions of organizational learning and leadership training. Such virtual framings may be termed virtual exploratories, and, as suggested in this chapter, these are key to further develop the diversity of virtual learning environments in the collaborative learning tradition.

Notes

[1] I am grateful to the actors who participated in my research. The research project on actors and avatars is supported by a grant from the Danish Research Council for the Humanities (grant no. 273-05-0312), and I wish to acknowledge the support of the Council.

[2] Virtual worlds and role-playing games such as EverQuest I, II; Lineage I, II; World of Warcraft; Neochron; Anarchy Online.

[3] Avatars, or characters, are the figurative representations of the actor in advanced virtual worlds (Damer 1998, Schroeder 2002, 2006).

[4] The research project: Actors and Avatars Communicating in Virtual Worlds (2006-2007) is supported by the Danish Research Council for the Humanities. The 3D Agora-world in Active Worlds Education was part of the EU EQUEL project on e-quality and e-learning (2002-2004).

References

Andersen, P. B., and L. Qvortrup. 2004. *Virtual applications: Applications with virtual inhabited 3D worlds*. New York: Springer.

Banks, M. 2001. *Visual methods in social research*. Thousand Oaks, CA: Sage.

Baym, N. 2000. *Tune in, log on: Soaps, fandom, and online community*. Thousand Oaks, CA: Sage.

Clemmensen, T. 2007. The psychology of online sociability: Theory and examples. In *Designing for networked communications: Strategies and development*, ed. S. Heilesen and S. S. Jensen, 217-240. Hershey, PA: Idea Group.

Damer, B. 1998. *Avatars: Exploring and building virtual worlds on the Internet*. Berkeley, CA: Peachpit Press.

Dervin, B., and L. Foreman-Wernet. 2003. *Sense-making methodology reader*. New Jersey: Hampton Press.

Dewey, J. 1933. *How we think. A restatement of the relation of reflective thinking to the educative process*. Boston, MA: Heath and Company.

Goffman, E. 1959. *The presentation of self in everyday life*. London: Penguin.

—. 1986. *Frame analysis: An essay on the organization of experience*. New York: Northeastern University Press. Orig. 1974.

Grimshaw, A. 2001. *The ethnographer's eye: Ways of seeing in modern anthropology*. Cambridge: Cambridge University Press.

Hine, C. 2005. *Virtual methods: Issues in social research on the Internet*. Oxford: Berg.

Howard, E. 2002. Network ethnography and hypermedia organization: New organizations, new media, new muths. *New Media and Society* 4(4): 550-574.

Jacobsson, M. 2006a. *Virtual worlds and social interaction design*. Umeå, Sweden: Umeå University.

—. 2006b. Questing for knowledge: Virtual worlds as dynamic processes of social interaction. In *Avatars at work and play: Collaboration and interaction in shared virtual environments*, ed. R. Schroeder, 209-227. Dortrecht: Springer.

Jensen, S. S. 2001. *De digitale delegater: Tekst og tanke i netuddannelse. En afhandling om hyperlinks i refleksiv praksis, der er face-to-interface [Digital delegates: Text and thought in net education. A dissertation on hyperlinks in reflexive face-to-interface practice]*. Copenhagen: Multivers Press.

—. 2004. Knowledge-sharing in the 3d Agora-World. Paper presented at the Networked Learning Conference, Lancaster University.

—. 2005. Videoviews of knowing in action: Analytical views "in situ" in an IT firm's development department. In *Challenges and issues in knowledge management*, ed. A. Buono and F. Poulfelt. Greenwich, CT: Information Age Publishing.

—. 2007. Reflective designing for actors and avatars in virtual worlds. In *Designing for networked communication: Strategies and development*, ed. S. Heilesen and S. S. Jensen, 187-217. Hershey, PA: Idea Group.

Jordan, B., and A. Henderson. 1995. Interaction analysis: Foundations and practice. *The Journal of the Learning Sciences* 4(2): 39-103.

Latour, B. 2005. *Reassembling the social: An introduction to actor-network-theory*. Oxford: Oxford University Press.

Pink, S. 2001. *Doing visual ethnography: Images, media and representation in research*. Thousand Oaks, CA: Sage.

Qvortrup, L., ed. 2001. *Virtual interaction: Interaction in virtual inhabited 3d worlds*. London: Springer.

—. 2002. *Virtual space: Spatiality in virtual inhabited 3d worlds*. London: Springer.

Schroeder, R., ed. 2002. *The social life of avatars: Presence and interaction in shared virtual environments, computer-supported cooperative work.* London: Springer.

Schroeder, R., and A.-S. Axelsson, ed. 2006. *Avatars at work and play: Collaboration and interaction in shared virtual environments, computer-supported cooperative work.* Dordrecht: Springer.

Sproull, L., and S. Kiesler. 1986. Reducing social context cues: Electronic mail in organizational communication. *Management Science* 32(11): 492-512.

Williams, M. 2007. Avatar watching: Participant observation in graphical online environments. *Qualitative Research* 7(1): 5-24.

Yee, N. 2004a. *Dragon slaying 101: Understanding the complexity of raids. The Daedalus Project,* http://www.nickyee.com/daedalus/archives/000859.php (retrieved March 7, 2007).

—. 2004b. *Dragon slaying 102: Unsung heroes.The Daedalus Project,* http://www.nickyee.com/daedalus/archives/000858.php (retrieved March 7, 2007).

—. 2005. *Motivations of play in MMORPGs,* http://www.nickyee.com/daedalus/archives/pdf/3-2.pdf (retrieved February 3, 2007).

—. 2006. The psychology of massively multi-user online role-playing games. In *Avatars at work and play: Collaboration and interaction in shared virtual environments*, ed. R. Schroeder. Dortrecht: Springer.

—. 2007. *Life as a guild leader,* http://www.nickyee.com/daedalus/archives/001516.php (retrieved March 7, 2007).

PART II:

CONTEXTS OF USE

CHAPTER FOUR

HOPEFUL CHILDREN, HYBRID SPACES: LEARNING WITH MEDIA AFTER SCHOOL[1]

GLYNDA A. HULL AND NORA L. KENNEY

We often think of children and youth in today's world as threatened—as at risk in their neighborhoods and the larger society, with uncertain economic, social, and environmental futures, and as poorly served by schools and other institutions charged with their care. No doubt such worry is perennial, the inevitable accompaniment of generational difference and change, but few would debate that at the beginning of the 21st century our lives are challenged in different and difficult ways, or that these challenges weigh quite heavily on young people. McDonald (1999) has written about the fragility of the disenfranchised urban youth with whom he studied and worked in Australia—"their fragile forms of struggle for recognition," as he put it, moving towards adulthoods that don't seem to offer permanent employment or stable relationships. In the United States current worries about young people are frequently voiced in terms of poor academic performance—signaled, for instance, by rates of graduation from secondary school that for some groups hover at 50 per cent and that seem to solidify social, racial, and ethnic inequalities (Greene 2002, Kirsch, Braun, Yamamoto and Sum 2007). When we look elsewhere, to parts of Africa, as well as India and Southeast Asia, not to mention societies newly emerging in Europe (Freedman 2006), threats to the well-being of youth are again numerous and extreme: poverty, disease, trauma, exploitation.

Our times are extreme, to be sure. We argue, therefore, that the need is concomitantly great for hopeful visions, new directions, and immediate opportunities for participation and action. This chapter offers one small example of such a vision, direction, and opportunity, an example that is a piece of a larger fabric, that of informal learning environments for youth taking place after the formal school day ends. Social theorists often mourn the glacial progress of social change, emphasizing the small effects of individual agency, the durability of the habitus, and the unchangeable direction of reproductive forces that both insure social continuity and the maintenance of the status quo. But teachers, visionaries, inventors, social activists, optimists, and children have different dispositions, implicitly realizing the necessity and potentially ennobling effects of struggle and second chances along with the wellspring that is human potential. If the field of this chapter is the unusual and daunting challenges of our current times, confronting all of us but have special import for youth, then the remedies and solutions that must be fashioned are its figure. We are interested, then, in exploring the strategic advantage of opportunities for young people that fall outside conventional schooling and formal learning paradigms associated with the regular school day.

After-school spaces

Over the past ten years in the United States, there has been a flowering of after-school programs accompanied by a growing literature documenting their practices and efficacy, as well as a growing regulatory system of federal policy that has attempted to shape their purposes, especially their relationship to formal schooling. As Halpern (2003) has aptly demonstrated in his history of after-school programs for low-income children in the US, tensions over the roles of after-schools are hardly new. Such programs in the US have struggled for their own identities almost since their beginnings in the last decades of the nineteenth century, needing to define themselves in relation to other institutions, "notably children's families, the schools, and the streets" (Halpern 2003, 5). At various times in their century-long history, after-school programs have sought to "complement, supplement, counter, and even supplant" these other institutions, but they have had an especially rocky history with schools, often characterizing themselves in opposition to school-based practices and values, especially where immigrant or other "at-risk" children were concerned. During the 1990s, due to an infusion of federal aid and substantial support and interest from private foundations, an arranged marriage has occurred between schools and after-school providers, motivated by a determination to improve low-income children's academic achievement. Thus, the pressure has never been greater for after-school programming to mirror and extend the school day. Lines have been drawn in the sand, with some agencies and advocates embracing a union, and others resisting to a greater or lesser extent the imposition of school-based practices onto after-school space, and vice versa (Noam 2004, Hull 2008).

One important tension within the after-school movement has had to do with the control of bodies through the organization of material and social space. Within compulsory schooling children's movements, desires, and forms of participation are generally circumscribed and made to conform to particular institutional rules, culture, and material environments. But after-school programs have traditionally been voluntary, and there has at least been the possibility of organizing children's participation in ways that allow for the exercise of more intellectual and creative agency and freedom of movement. Yet, adults' understandable interest in and responsibility for protecting and also socializing children through control over space has always been with us. In fact, after-school programs originated when the need for child labor decreased, a commitment to compulsory schooling grew, and adults came to view unsupervised after-school time as unsafe—for example, as subject to new dangers such as street traffic (Halpern 2003). Eventually, in response to these concerns and to those of educators and reformers who wanted to "improve" working-class children, there were developed outdoor or playground programs, and these expanded to include indoor activities. In this way, children's freedom to play in the streets was decreased, their playtime increasingly supervised, and their control over space and physical movement constrained. Historical studies report that many youth objected, voting with their feet and spending their time on stoops and streets; they in fact ranked settlement houses as their least favorite places (Wasserman 1991).

Nowadays, worries about the street have if anything intensified, and children are ever more confined to the indoors and to supervision. Kelley (1997), writing about contemporary culture wars and in defense of American Black urban poor, notes that, "for inner city families, the threat of drive-bys has turned porches and front doors, which once spilled out onto sidewalks and streets as extensions of play areas, into fortified entrances with iron 'screen' doors that lock from the inside" (Kelley 1997, 52). As public leisure places disappear and funding for parks and recreation centers wither in the US, as violence and worries about the possibility of violence increase, people are again looking to after-school programs to take youth from the streets, involve them in productive activities, and inculcate particular values related to work and discipline—all of which are reminiscent of the turn-of-the-century Progressive-era practices mentioned above. Kelley warns, however, that "more social control will do little to unleash and develop the creative capacities of black urban youth. Rather than try to change the person through rigid regimentation and supervised play, we need to change the streets themselves, the built environment, the economy, and the racist discourse that dominates popular perceptions of black youth" (Kelley 1997, 76).

What an important and interesting challenge for today's after-school programs—to simultaneously address the desires of parents, school officials, and agents of the federal government to provide safe spaces for academic achievement, and to be cognizant as well of how after-school might be constructed as a social and physical space that also appeals to children's growing needs for increased autonomy and the opportunity to create, embrace, and reinvent popular cultural forms. As we will later illustrate, we were interested in understanding the ways in which one after-school program was able to achieve a balance between being school-connected and being a non-school space where children could flourish even if, and especially if, they were not successful at school. Which of its features resembled school, and which did not? How was it a "liminal" (Bhabha 1994) space, a borderland situated in-between other institutions, in terms of the social and symbolic resources that it provided, and the modes of participation that it fostered?

Digital media, narrative, and agency

As is commonly acknowledged, we live in a media-saturated world where "images, sounds, and spectacles help produce the fabric of everyday life, dominating leisure time, shaping political views and social behavior, and providing the materials out of which people forge their very identities" (Kellner 1995, 1). A media culture includes the creation and distribution of sound, film, image, and print through the traditional mass media means of radio, television, newspapers, and magazines. But with the digital age, those modalities that once inhabited separate spheres are now, more and more often, juxtaposed, blended, and hybridized, as digital spaces such as web pages, blogs, super-phones, and computers provide chances to manipulate, create, and communicate through a range of media and modes. More importantly still, in our view, the opportunity to communicate and compose via multiple modalities and media, once a privilege restricted to the elite and the wealthy, can now be the province of the individual citizen, "ordinary" children and adults who increasingly can have access to cutting-edge digital technologies and the means to share their compositions and viewpoints with large audiences. There are, to be sure, many opposing views about the impact of living in an increasingly "mediatized" world. One stance, long influential and still prevalent, is that the messages to be derived from popular media are apt to corrupt, and consequently that children and young people need protection from their effects. Often embedded in this view is a belief that popular culture is inferior to "high" culture; that images seduce and are inferior to print with its long valued associations with rationality and logic; and that young people are at the mercy of media, almost passively absorbing their messages and ideologies. While these views are most often associated with conservative commentators, it is interesting that they thread through more radical theorizing as well, as scholars across the ideological spectrum similarly privilege print and express concerns about the reproductive potential of the visual (Kellner 1995).

A different stance toward mediatized culture, it too with historical roots but gaining renewed momentum at the current moment, is the view that in addition to protecting youth from media by inoculating them with big doses of critical media literacy, we might well turn over the control of media production to them, urging the examination of the ideologies that inform media close-up, by understanding what it means to communicate and create via a range of modalities. Indeed, the matter is often no longer one of turning something over to youth. In community centers, after-school programs, youth organizations, churches, and schools across the US and the world, young people are claiming new digital media and developing their own products, genres, and distribution networks. To be sure, it would be foolish to assume that simple access to new media will be automatically emancipatory for youth, or that the chance to tell one's story will be necessarily empowering (Soep and Chavez 2005). However, we do endorse the importance of youth being able to produce as well as consume media—there is power to be had in giving body to one's own ideas and setting them forth in the world—and as will become clear, we stress as well the importance of understanding the historical, ideological, institutional, and familial contexts for that production.

Much new research is attempting to capture the nature of youth's cultural productions and educational experiences with new media. Some of this work focuses on the participant structures, pedagogies, and practices that characterize out-of-school educational efforts. Soep and Chavez (2005), for example, have written persuasively about the "pedagogy of collegiality" that characterizes the interactions among young people and adults who take part in Youth Radio, a broadcast training program for students aged 14 to 18. Other work has focused on incorporating a range of digital media into schools and community organizations. In an edited volume of case studies written by practitioners, Sefton-Green (1999) has explored the range of ways that new "digital arts" are impacting the traditional world of schooling. Other researchers have begun to take up long-standing views about media, such as television having direct negative consequences for children's academic and social development, and to interrogate those views, simply by asking what actual uses youth make of media. And thus, Howard (1998) and her colleagues studied how children, youth, and young adults used a panoply of digital media—television, video, video games, and telephones. From such research we are coming to appreciate the kinds of arrangements for learning that characterize out-of-school spaces; we are learning to complicate too simplistic causal models of the intersection of media with learning; and we are beginning to glimpse the array of uses that young people find for new media, uses that suggest their activity as learners and doers in the world.

Our research on digital media shares many of the interests above, especially the importance of media production as well as critical consumption. We have focused particularly on the interfaces among new media, narrative, and identity construction. There is a rich body of research on narrative and the important role that narratives of self—stories about who we have been in the past and who we want to become in the future—can play in the construction of identities (Ochs and Capps 1996, 2001). Our "lives are the pasts we tell ourselves," write Ochs and Capps (1996, 21). This holds for children, too, as Miller and her colleagues demonstrate in their extensive work on the functions of storytelling in early childhood socialization and self-construction (e.g. Miller 1994). Hall (1996) also links identity construction to narrative and self-representation. "Identities," he writes, "are … constituted within, not outside representation" and "they arise from the narrativization of the self" (Hall 1996, 4). To summarize the almost isomorphic relationship of narrative to self, Bruner explains that one's "self is a perpetually rewritten story" (Bruner 1994, 53).

Our particular interest has been to explore the power of "mediatized" (Lundby 2005) narratives, or digital stories, as a potential means for children to construct narratives of self, family, and community. Much attention is currently directed in media studies to the power of narrative, especially in gaming, where theorists have embarked upon enthusiastic considerations of how youth become immersed in video games through the narratives and subject positions that those games allow and promote (e.g. Wardrip-Fruin and Harrigan 2004, Wolf and Perron 2003). Much less attention has been paid, however, to the multimodal, multi-media narratives of self that youth themselves construct, and this is especially true for younger children, some of whom are less likely to have access to such tools (Hull and James 2007, Hull and Katz 2006). Thus, we have wanted to ask, if stories told orally with just words are powerful sites of self-construction, what might be the import of layered modalities—speech, music, images, video—for this process (Hull 2003)? In other research (Hull and Nelson 2005) we have argued that this kind of multimodal composition represents a qualitatively new form of meaning-making and provides a distinctively different experience for readers and viewers than does a print-based text. In the research reported here, we explore the potential of this kind of composing, asking what affordances it offered children for constructing representations of themselves and their social worlds. We were also interested in how, especially within the context of an out-of-school program, youth actively drew upon a wealth of cultural resources, including popular cultural knowledge from media—comic books, music, television, movies—to create digital stories (Brown 1999, Dyson 1997, 2003, Hudak 1999).

Digital narratives and their multimodal affordances have been our window on how the youth enacted a sense of self. They have offered up an array of past, current, and possible selves—as once sickly, but now healthy; as once a trouble-maker but now a student who can follow the rules; as heroes and travelers with adventures to recount; as responsible guardians of pets, fair solvers of disputes, wise social critics, and loyal friends; and as boys and girls on the path to becoming young adults like their moms and dads. In examining the digital stories themselves, and in situating them within the after-school program and children's lives at home and at school, we have been especially interested in noticing whether and how the selves that children enacted were agentive ones. Debates about structure and agency have been hallmarks of much social science research over the last thirty years, as theorists have attempted to reconcile the ways in which individuals and groups reproduce the social order and the extent to which they are able to influence it (De Certeau 1984, Fairclough 1989, Holland, Lachicotte, Skinner, and Cain 1998, Scott 1985, Wenger 1998). Briefly put, most current theorists believe that people can act agentively, even in the most oppressive circumstances, although that ability is in general sharply constrained (Emirbayer and Mische 1998).

It is thereby interesting to think of agency in relation to children, who are the most constrained of all social actors, since parents and caretakers, schools and society regulate their activities, movements, and choices. Yet, children are indeed agents within their own social worlds, and they claim and treasure more and more autonomy as social actors as they grow. We are interested in the role of multimodal learning and expression in this process, as well as the role that an after-school program can play as a space to provide participant structures that allow a different exercise of agency. To what extent, we wondered, do youth represent themselves as agents who could make choices and exercise judgment, who could analyze and influence the world around them, or who could imagine different and better futures? Because most of the children in our programs were people of color and all had experienced, to one degree or another, the kinds of hardships and challenges that accompany life in an inner city and a racist society, we believed that cultivating and enacting a sense of agency was a crucially important part of their childhood (Walker and Snarey 2004). In the words of Curtis-Tweed, "African Americans, like all people of colour, must develop and sustain positive perceptions of themselves, their context and self-in-context to counter the effects of societal marginalization" (Curtis-Tweed 2003, 408).

Context for the study

For five years, 2002-2007, with a range of colleagues, we funded, operated, and researched a community technology center located in the urban neighborhood of West Oakland, California, a local bus ride away from the University of California, Berkeley. Called DUSTY, or Digital Underground Storytelling for Youth, the center was conceived as a mechanism for making available powerful forms of signification—specifically, tools for and practices of digital multimodal composing—to children and adults who didn't otherwise have such access at home or school. A university and community partnership, it drew professors, undergraduates, and graduate students together with youth and children from the community to study, learn, play, and create. West Oakland was known for its high rates of joblessness and crime, a deteriorating infrastructure, and struggling schools; it had few of the ordinary resources that most communities take for granted, like supermarkets, bookstores, restaurants, and banks. Many of its grand old Victorians, once summer homes for the San Francisco wealthy, had been renovated and occupied by outsiders as gentrification marches forward. Yet the citizens in this area—mostly long-time African American residents joined of late, and increasingly, by immigrants from Southeast Asia, Mexico, and Latin America—had found ways to reclaim the community. With a rich history to build on, including a significant role during the Civil Rights Movement in the 60's, as well as memories of a thriving economy related to ship-building and transport around mid-century, residents were alert to and working toward safer, healthier, more equitable and stable futures. DUSTY was but a small piece of this much larger fabric of community growth and change.

DUSTY started as a center to teach digital storytelling, a form of multi-media composing that consists of images and segments of video combined with background music and a "voice-over" narrative. Digital stories are, in effect, brief movies, distinctive in featuring the digitized voice of the author who narrates a personally composed story and an assemblage of visual artifacts–photographs old and new, images found on the Internet, snippets of video, anything that one can convert to digital form. In our experience, digital stories have wide appeal among children, youth, and adults, in part simply because they are multimodal and digital, thereby allowing individuals those compositional means and rights that used to be associated just with the world of mass media. They are often popular, too, because they privilege a personal voice and allow participants to draw on popular culture and local knowledge. Our youth sometimes create stories that feature their own original beats as background music in lieu of commercial hits, drawing on Oakland's distinctive hip-hop sound. A culminating activity at DUSTY was viewing participants' digital stories on the big screen of a local theater or other public venues. On such occasions we invited the young artists to answer questions from the audience at the end of the showing. This is one example of how, in the design of our curriculum and participant structures, we attempted to position digital storytellers as authors, composers, and designers who are expert and powerful communicators, people with things to say that the community and world should hear. Given that many of the youth with whom we worked had not developed a sense of an authorial and agentive self in other settings, including school, the opportunity to do so in an alternative educational site becomes all the more important.

Simultaneous with the creation and operation of DUSTY, we engaged in work broadly within the relatively recent tradition of "design research" (Collins, Joseph, and Bielaczyc 2004), whereby program, curriculum, and tool development is intertwined with ongoing attempts to assess and improve development efforts, to document what participants have learned, and to theorize, in our case, multimodal composing and identity formation. Over the years we collected a range of ethnographic and qualitative data, principally field notes from participant observations and interviews. We also videotaped and audiotaped teaching activities, workshops, and community events, including showings of digital stories. Our data included pre-post inventories and surveys as well, as we attempt to assess not only what kids and adults learn, but how their notions of self as author and communicator develop. Particularly because of the requirements of funding agencies, we also gathered standardized test scores, attendance records, and grades from school, in order to investigate statistically whether participation in after-school appeared to impact school-based achievement. Lastly, we continuously archived the digital stories and other artifacts that participants created.

Data collection and analysis

The case study reported in this chapter is drawn from a larger study of elementary-school-aged boys (Hull, Kenney, Marple, and Forsman-Schneider 2006) who participated in after-school or summer DUSTY programs. In Table 1, we provide demographic data about the focal children in this larger project. Although almost all of these children resided within West Oakland or other low income neighborhoods, simply categorizing them as low SES would camouflage the diversity of children who are similarly labeled at risk. Poverty impacted their lives in different and sometimes intense and complicated ways. Some children brought voracious appetites to snack time at DUSTY and always asked for additional food to eat then or take away, while others ate only if they liked what was being served. Some wore a fresh shirt each day, while others wore the same clothes for many days in a row. Some students had involved stories to tell about their weekend social activities, whereas other students did not. Some lived in subsidized housing, some with parents who paid regular rent, and others bunked with extended family members or were homeless. Some of the children did well in school, while others faired quite poorly, with Taj, our case study child featured here, experiencing extreme difficulty. The children further varied in terms of their status with the other children at DUSTY, with some possessing much social purchase and others having much less cachet, being unpopular and at times ostracized. Available additional support—through church, extended family, and out-of-school resources beyond DUSTY—varied as well. These variations suggest the complexities of circumstance that accompany children to an after-school program, even when they live on the same block or hail from the same neighborhood.

Our data consisted of the children's digital stories and other artifacts (writings, drawings, notes, storyboards); field notes; audio-taped retrospective interviews with the children and sometimes family members. We also collected, long-term, ethnographic data about the West Oakland neighborhood, participating in the life of the larger community center, accompanying children to football games and other sporting events, and paying close attention to happenings that generated conversation and attention in the neighborhood: violence, gentrification, cultural events, housing developments, the openings and closures of schools. We transcribed all audio-tapes and the children's digital stories. For Taj, we created a table in which the narration of his story was paired with the accompanying images he created and a description of his music to facilitate a finer-grained analysis (Hull and Nelson 2005). We then assembled all of our data into loose-leaf notebooks and proceeded with an open coding of the data, reading line-by-line and noting salient patterns, marking these in the margins and keeping a running list of descriptors that we then reorganized and renamed as new categories emerged (Miles 1994). Beginning with analyses of individual children, we next reorganized our data to facilitate comparisons across children, noting cross-cutting themes. As we proceeded, we took note of "key events," those richly textured moments that drew together several thematic threads and that could be used illustratively within and across cases (Dyson and Genishi 2005).

Name of Student	Age	Ethnicity	Living Situation	Place of Residence	Semesters in Dusty
Taj	9	African American/ East Indian	Only child lived with mother	West Oakland	Summer 2004
Leon	10	African American	Only child lived with mother and her boyfriend who took an active parental role	West Oakland	Fall 2003, Spring 2004
Clinton	9	African American	Lived with mother and siblings	West Oakland	Summer 2003, Summer 2004
James	11	African American	Lived with mother and siblings, had regular contact with father	West Oakland	Fall 2003,Spring 2004
Andre	12	African American	Lived with adoptive mother	West Oakland	Fall 2002, Spring 2003

Patrick	10	Cambodian American	Lived with mother, father and sister	West Oakland	Fall 2002
Manuel	10	Mexican American	Lived with father, mother and siblings	West Oakland	Fall 2002, Spring 2003, Summer 2003
Malcolm	11	African American	Lived with mother and father and younger sister	East Oakland	Spring 2004, Summer 2004
Jamal	9	African American	Lived with mother and father, two sisters, and two brothers	East Oakland	Summer 2004

Table 4-1: Demographic information about participants

While our methods for analyzing our qualitative data were inductive, we were also guided by theoretical interests and our readings of related literature. For example, we knew from a wide-ranging literature that boys' predilections for reading and writing often don't match school-based curricula and that they therefore sometimes don't flourish in school. We held out hope, however, that within an alternative out-of-school space—yet a space that provided a structure for engagement in reading and writing activities—boys might find a more accessible path toward engagement with literacy. Thus, we were alert to the potential for both literacy-related problems and literacy-related progress. Further, given our experiences with and our readings of the literature on digital multimodality, we expected that children might find their sea legs where literacy is concerned through the mediation of multiple modes and computers, especially when they were allowed to draw upon popular culture and local knowledge. Thus, we were primed to take note of how the children made use of a variety of symbol systems, and whether and how communication, creation, and play via computers engaged them.

Finally, a theoretical concern in our previous work had centered on agency (Hull and Katz 2006). To what extent do individuals who face, even as children, a range of social and material constraints, nonetheless develop agentive senses of self when they are appropriately supported in that effort? We thus examined our data, including the children's digital stories, for indications that children were or were not constructing and enacting senses of self as able to impact their social worlds. In doing so, we found helpful the conceptualization of agency offered by Emirbayer and Mische as "a temporally embedded process of social engagement" (Emirbayer and Mische 1998, 963) that is shaped by understandings of relationships to the past, future, and present. We were cued, then, to examine how children represented past, present, and future selves. Finally, we examined what we call the "authorial agency" that we observed in the boys' digital stories. Drawing on our own past research (Hull and Katz 2006), as well as traditions from linguistic anthropology (e.g. Bauman and Briggs 1990, Dyson 2003), we noted instances of the powerful authorial moves of "decontextualization" and "retextualization," which can be glossed for our purposes as taking language, images, or ideas from one context and resituating them in another, making them serve one's own ends. As Bauman and Briggs explain: "To decontextualize and recontexualize a text is thus an act of control, and in regard to the differential exercise of such control the issue of social power arises" (Bauman and Briggs 1990, 76). This semiotic strategy may be an especially powerful one after-school, and it may be especially afforded by multiple modalities, as children are allowed and encouraged to draw upon local knowledge, popular culture, and multiple symbol systems as they create.

We used the above framework and methods to address the following research questions: What images of self were revealed in the boys' digital stories? What elements of popular and local culture did the boys appropriate for their stories and for what purposes? What were the constraints and affordances of digital multimodal composing and print-based composing for the boys? What features of their after-school space seemed most conducive to their participation and learning and to the construction of positive and possible "agentive" senses of self? To illustrate our findings, we turn next to a case study of one child, Taj.

The case of Taj: A vulnerable superhero

Nine-year-old Taj came to DUSTY's summer program with many, many questions. His first one, by way of introducing himself, was directed to his teacher, Miss Nora: "What kind of animation software do you have?" he inquired in his high-pitched voice, articulating his words precisely as was his style. When she answered that DUSTY used Adobe Premiere for its digital storytelling projects, Taj immediately queried her further about its 3-D functionality and animation components. This initial exchange hinted at what we were later to learn in much detail about Taj's talents, resources, and challenges. He was a boy who loved and was adept with computers, but he was in fact interested in, and he had questions about, a diversity of things. Here are excerpts from a long list of his multiplex interests provided by his mother, Sonja, as part of her e-mail efforts to find a compatible school for him the year after he participated in DUSTY. Taj, she explained, was interested in space, the 3rd and 5th dimensions, computerized games and computer animation of various kinds, drawing, cooking, the digeridoo and the cello, rugby and yoga, movies, building soundtracks for animations and stories, the beach, Greek mythology, Halloween and costuming, fantasy play with made-up characters, frilled lizards and komodo dragons, Alaska, Antartica, and the Aurora Borealis! What a magical list of diverse interests, a reminder of the rich panoply of topics, knowledge, modes, and activities that can captivate young minds.

Taj not only had many interests and a million questions to accompany each, he had very definite opinions about his dislikes. For example, he did not like noise in the classroom or at home. He noted on his "More about ….You!" DUSTY questionnaire, given to all children at the beginning of the program, that he did not like his neighborhood because "some people hang by the liquor sto[r]e talking loud all night." To sit still was a special torture for him, and he similarly thrived on digitally-afforded movement: quick transitions between pictures in an animation, lots of physical action in plotlines, fast-paced "techno" music, and the chance to flip back and forth among several open programs on a computer's desktop. He did not easily tolerate anything that he experienced as injustice or unfairness to himself, at DUSTY or at school, and he often demanded explanations from adults in situations when many children might simply be resigned. He took "why" questions to a new height and readily confessed, "I get on my teacher's nerves!" He had his own agendas for how he preferred to spend his time and the types of projects that he found engaging. For example, Taj came to DUSTY with one purpose and one purpose only, and that was to create an animated story, and it was hard to engage him in anything that he saw as straying from accomplishing his particular goal. All of this—his propensity to question, to complain, and to otherwise express himself, to move about, to be self-directed, and as we shall see in more detail below, to mediate his activities digitally and multimodally whenever possible—added up to a gigantic mismatch between Taj and his elementary school, on both an academic and a social level, and sometimes made him a bit of a lightning rod for negative attention from his peers, especially other boys.

In this case study we hope to reveal some of the social progress that Taj made at his DUSTY summer program, as he became more accepted by and accepting of his peers, and as he developed more trusting relationships with his summer teachers and tutors. This reorientation occurred partly, we will argue, through the social purchase that he acquired through his growing expertise with digital multimodality, and partly through his inventive use of popular cultural genre conventions and digital multimodal narration, which allowed Taj to reposition himself authorially. His reorientation had to do as well with the hybrid social space that was DUSTY, a space that joined some of the characteristics of school with some of the characteristics of play, and that provided access both to digital symbolic tools and to much social support in the form of teachers, assistant teachers, technology specialists, tutors, and children.

We will argue that Taj represents one important version of the child of the future, presuming that the future is a digital one, with his predilection for an assortment of the types of mediational tools that are available online or through software programs (Gee 2004). To be sure, some traditional literacy practices, such as writing by hand, were for Taj a tall hurdle. Yet of all the children we have known thus far at DUSTY, this young boy represented the tightest union of interests and talents with available digital tools and modes of expression. Thereby he taught us a great deal about the habits of mind and literate digital practices that may soon be commonplace for children growing up in this age (but likely will continue to elude many adults). "Dial up is old school," he once commented, and so it is to a child like Taj. However, at the same time that Taj was advanced technologically, he was an historically and socially situated young person, someone who struggled, as most of us must do, with finding a social niche, and also an ethnic and racial and gendered sense of self. We salute him as much for his engagement with his social becoming as we do for his ever-burgeoning technical and symbolic expertise.

"They think I'm Mexican"

Early on Miss Nora, the DUSTY instructor, and Taj's peers were introduced to his single-minded focus on things digital and technological as well as his intense need to have his own concerns attended to. The first week of the program one of the DUSTY volunteers, a university student, wrote a detailed set of field notes about the range of activities that occurred over a span of approximately 45 minutes. According to this tutor's notes, boys played action-oriented computer games, conferences with children were held, visitors came and went, and a rap song in which one of the DUSTY children had been featured as a back-up singer was shared with a small group of adult and child admirers. During all of these activities, Taj didn't leave his computer or engage with the visitors, tutors, or other children. Instead he focused with laser-like intensity on his self-determined task at hand, which was to locate the game "Crash Test Dummies" using the Google search engine. The undergraduate tutor noted that midway through the activities, "Taj was still searching for Crash Test Dummies, looking at prices on Ebay and getting pictures of the game from Google," an observation that served as a chorus throughout her notes.

Such focus and determination served Taj well in terms of his quickly accumulating technological expertise and very impressive knowledge base. Throughout our field notes and interviews with Taj and his mom, we noted again and again his impressive agility with software, Internet searches, what seemed to us very complicated users' guides, and a variety of software programs. In fact, when Taj came to DUSTY, according to our formal assessment of his technological skills as well as his own self-assessment, he had already mastered basic computer skills, such as organizing via folders and using email, and he knew as well how to use the Internet for searches. He did not know how to scan pictures or to use Adobe Photoshop to alter images or to use I-Movie or Adobe Premiere to create multimodal movies or narratives. But these technical skills he began to acquire with alacrity.

What was more difficult for Taj was learning to fit in socially. From the start he had difficulties even sitting next to his classmates, especially any one of four other boys: Angel, Loren, Brandon, and Jermaine. These four boys, two sets of brothers, comprised a group of longtime friends and neighbors. (Indeed, one volunteer noted in her field notes how many of the children at DUSTY seemed to be connected as family or friends.) All four of these boys participated actively on sports teams, and although he was the youngest of the four, Jermaine demonstrated many leadership qualities, traits according to his teacher that were acknowledged by his brother, his friends, and the rest of the class. Taj, on the other hand, was not athletic, being noticeably bow-legged and tending toward chubbiness, and he did not endear himself to most of the children. According to his teacher, he often loudly complained that the other boys were making too much noise, invading his "personal space," or not following rules, and he was not above "telling on" Angel, Loren, Brandon, and Jermaine, whenever an opportunity presented itself. Altercations were frequent, especially during outdoor play-time, when the more athletic and more popular boys proceeded with regularity to pelt Taj during the game of dodgeball. Yet Taj continually sought opportunities to play with them nonetheless. So salient for him were these events that they figured prominently, as we shall soon see, in the plot of his animated digital story.

The peer-related difficulties that Taj experienced are certainly not unusual, as most children vie for social status in peer networks that are of necessity influenced by adult cultures and societal values concerning the personal characteristics—skin color, physical build, personality, athleticism—that foster desire and carry cachet. Yet, Taj faced more challenges in this regard than most, for he stood out as different in a number of ways. In this largely African American neighborhood, most children and adults were easily identified as Black, and even children who were not Black were at least conversant with and often influenced by African American youth culture—enjoying, for example, rap music, and effortlessly absorbing Black speech forms—features of African American Vernacular English (AAVE)—into their language patterns. Taj was in fact African American on his mother's side with roots in Creole and Cajun culture, while his dad's heritage was East Indian by way of Trinidad. Taj was definitely aware of his rich mixed ancestry: "I'm actually Indian, Trinidadian, umm, Jewish, and Irish, and I can't think of the other one," he told Miss Nora. He also noted that when asked about his ethnicity, he usually chose not to respond "because it's a long list." But he did not seem to identify as African American, and unlike virtually all of his DUSTY classmates, Taj never code-switched from standard English to AAVE. When asked what ethnicity children associated him with, Taj replied, "They think I'm Mexican."

Indeed, Taj's DUSTY instructor believed that some of Taj's social difficulties arose because the other boys in the program "couldn't really figure out what to make of him" racially and ethnically. She subsequently discussed this possibility with Taj's mom and invited her to come to a DUSTY class, believing her identity as African American would take away some of the puzzle about Taj. On two occasions Sonja visited and interacted with the class, once leading a storybook reading and on the second occasion, using her expertise as a professional photographer, teaching the children basic photographic angles, such as a "bird's eye view." Miss Nora believed that these visits did have a positive effect on how children viewed Taj. However, being different seemed to be a central identity feature for Taj, one that persisted and that held both positive and negative consequences for him. On the one hand, he delighted in his own uniqueness and his status as an only and quite a special child. He wrote once on a DUSTY questionnaire that if he could live anywhere it would be "a private planet because it would be all mine;" and for another journaling exercise on being principal for a day, Taj chose to be the principal of a "science fiction school of weirdness." Yet, Taj worried about being picked on "because you're weird," and related a story about such a family member who'd been attacked and had later died. These are themes that bob to the top for Taj, not only in casual conversation and interactions, but as we shall see, in his digital story as well.

"I'm going to make movies and video games for a living"

One of the pedagogical practices in the DUSTY summer school was to address children with titles associated with the jobs or careers they expected to have when they grew up, thereby honoring and supporting the adult identities they were working toward. Thus, it was "Engineer Clinton" and "Dr. Cristina" and "Rapper Malcolm." Taj wanted to be an animator and movie-maker, as he would elaborate on to anyone who would listen, with or without their prompting. As he clicked on his movie icon on the desktop of a DUSTY computer in order to open it and show it a tutor, Taj noted:

> Taj: I'm going to make movies and video games for a living. My first one is going to be Zach the Opossum. It'll be done by 2007.
> Christine: How old are you now?
> T: Nine.
> C: And how old will you be when Zach the Opossum is done?
> T: Twelve.
> C: That's impressive.

Impressive indeed, as was the digital story that became the centerpiece of Taj's summer at DUSTY. Taj called his digital story "Delicate man: A one-eyed super hero." It consisted of 42 colorful images, each of which Taj painstakingly designed, drew, and illustrated using the software Adobe Photoshop, and then assembled using Adobe Premier. Taj had wanted to create a genuine animation with state-of-the-art software especially made for this work, but because DUSTY didn't have the particular software he needed, he made do with the tools at hand, juxtaposing his individually created images and linking them together to provide the illusion of movement. He narrated his images with his own voice recording, enacting the characters and the storyline. In the background he added fast-paced instrumental music that he had created himself at home, sampling and blending melodies he downloaded from the Internet.

Taj's story featured a fictional character, "Delicate Man," that he and his mom recalled he had originally created when he was six years old. The story begins with a boy at whom "a thousand people" threw dodgeballs (Figure 4-1). A scientist found the boy lying on the ground and transported him to his laboratory to examine him, where he accidentally dropped him into a mutating machine that turned him into Delicate Man. Delicate Man, a super hero whose only power was to break into pieces, had no arms but did have very long legs that allowed him to run quickly. "It was hard being Delicate Man," Taj explained in a draft of his story, because when someone bumped into him, he'd fall into pieces. However, falling into pieces did have its advantages, since Delicate Man could hurl his legs and use them as defensive weapons. This is indeed what happened in Taj's digital story: A robber (wearing a T-shirt proclaiming "Cops Stink") swung a dagger at Delicate Man, who pretended to be "sliced," but then ambushed the robber and put him in jail. Soon another bad guy appeared and likewise ambushed Delicate Man, threatening to blow him up and not put him back together. The story ends, in true episodic fashion, with a promise that it is "to be continued."

Figure 4-1. Screen shot from Taj's animation: Being Pelted with Dodge Balls

To view Taj's digital story is to be impressed with its inventiveness—his clever appropriation of the super hero genre, his expression of an aesthetics that is alert to color and shape and line, his sense for the dramatic and the enacted, and his sensitivity for braiding together, for orchestrating (Kress 2003, Mitchell 2004) different modes of expression for their best combined effect. Our first point, however, is that these multimodal talents and predilections did not map simply onto or follow linearly from print-based literacy. The curriculum for creating digital stories began with a variety of print-based activities: completing the boxes in a "Short Story Writer's Guide" that asked, for example, "What is your topic?" "Where will your story take place?" It proceeded toward a story map (with completion boxes for setting, characters, plot and events), multiple drafts of a written story, and then a "storyboard," which paired the text from the story with a description or drawing of the images that would be used to accompany the narration. Interestingly, in this technology-intensive program, much of the writing and drawing nevertheless was done with paper and pencil, and Taj in fact had great physical difficulty creating a legible text in this conventional way. After it became clear that he would not be able to compose or transcribe a story on paper, instructors wrote his words for him as he dictated. Multiple drafts emerged this way: a tutor's transcription in her handwriting of Taj's spoken story; several word-processed revisions of this text, done via Taj's directions; and finally, a word-processed version of his story that was divided into sections on the page—one that his helpers thought would facilitate Taj's oral reading of the story when he recorded his voice digitally.

Here, however, the most dramatic discontinuity emerged between the print-based practices that characterized much of the literacy-related work at DUSTY and Taj's own predilections for composing. When the time came for Taj to record his voice, reading from his prepared word-processed text divided neatly into segments, he instead performed his story, not even glancing at the paper version of it. Taj's performance followed the plotline, but dramatized it, as he took on the voices of his characters, and he transformed a third-person omniscient narration ("A scientist found him lying on the ground") to a first-person enactment ("Oooh, I found a boy on the ground!"). (See Table 2.) Remarkably, Taj performed the text from memory, having internalized the precise timing for each frame of his movie and its plot (Bennett 1991). Below is Taj's matter-of-fact account of what seemed to his instructor quite a creative architectural feat.[2]

> Miss Nora: When you wrote "Delicate Man" you wrote it down and it was really like you had everything word for word, but when you went into the voice capture with Ms. E you did kind of a different version right? You didn't just read off the paper.
> Taj: Uhhh no I just said it.
> N: So you already had it memorized in your head, right?
> T: Yeah, how long the movie was and how and what timing the voices would be and==
> N: ==Wow, so you remembered all that so when you were saying the voice capture==
> T: ==I just remembered how how minutes, what scenes in the movie took place.

N: Wow, and so you did the voice capture with each scene that you knew was coming up and you knew how long each scene was? Yeah?
T: Mmm hmm.
N: Wow, Taj that's amazing.

As a child at home in the digital age, and as a composer for whom the use of multiple modalities was normal rather than extraordinary, Taj's preferred process of representation seemed to privilege a seamless and transparent integration of visual, musical, linguistic, and technical elements. Indeed, his original creation of the character of Delicate Man was itself multimodal, drawing upon and combining a range of symbol systems, modes, and textual resources, as revealed in the following interview excerpt:

Miss Nora: So tell me about Delicate Man, how did, when did you think of Delicate Man?
Taj: Uhh, in the first grade.
N: And why did you pick the name "Delicate Man"?
T: Huh?
N: Why is his name "Delicate Man"?
T: I made it out of Tinker Toys==
N: ==OOOh
T: and I made it while I was near a piece of china.
N: Oh, so that's how you got the idea for the word "delicate"?
T: Yes.
N: What do you think "delicate" means, that word?
T: Easy to break.
N: Oh, so when you, when you made Delicate Man, was there, was there another, was there another super hero that he, that he reminds you of or is he totally different or==
T: ==Umm, No he actually looks like the guy in the *Odyssey*,
N: Which odyssey?
T: The story,
N: Oh the *Odyssey*?
T: Mmm Hmmm
N: Oh because he has one eye?
T: Yes.

What is very interesting to us here is that Taj reports that he originally created a stick figure of Delicate Man out of Tinker Toys—a resource that we later learned offered particular compositional constraints, such as long thin legs!—and that he later went on to translate this material stick figure into linguistic and digital multimodal form. We are also fascinated by the way that Taj willingly weaved for us a set of semantic influences that were the affordances for his creative process, influences that are textual, material, aesthetic, and generic and that thereby differ radically from the often more unimodal process of composing a linguistic text.

Original text episodes	Movie: Verbal
Delicate man is a boy and a thousand people threw dodge-balls at him. Each person had two dodge-balls.	Hey, why do you guys have dodge balls?
	We want to throw it at you
	Oh no!
	Uuuh!
A scientist found him lying on the ground.	Ooh, I found a boy on the ground
He picked him up and then he took him to the lab and examined him.	Maybe I should take him to my lab
He accidentally dropped him into a smoosher and mutating machine and that's how he turned into Delicate Man.	Oh no I […] made him fall into the mutating machine
The boy found out that he had no arms just legs His legs fell off.	Heeey I broke into pieces
The scientist put him back together. He's a super hero. His only power is that he breaks into pieces. He has big legs so he runs fast.	I'll put you back together
It was hard being Delicate Man. If somebody bumped into	

him they put him back together [until the scientist found him on the ground.]	
	Oops sorry
	Did I break you into pieces?
	Oh no You didn't
	Well I'm not putting you back together
	hah hah
	Hey!
	Let me put you back together
	long transition
Soon a bad guy walks down the street [and Delicate Man hits the bad guy with his big legs.]	Aahhh there's a robber

Table 4-2: Excerpts from Taj's written text and performed text

What we are arguing, then, is that in his out-of-school technology-intensive program, Taj was able to turn the available technological means toward the service of his own preferred creative predilections, and indeed, that the flexibility of an out-of-school, summer program fostered this kind of appropriation. We also want to argue that, by being able to make use of multimodal tools and to fashion an animation featuring his previously created character of "Delicate Man," Taj was able to create a representation of his social world that was agentive in helpful ways and that allowed him to give voice to possible identities and thereby to try on possible selves. It will not have escaped our readers' notice that Taj lifted his regrettable experiences of being pelted in the game of dodgeball and recontextualized them in his digital story (Bauman and Briggs 1990). But whereas the Taj of everyday life in DUSTY and at his school was routinely unable to turn the tables on the more athletic boys, witness the character of Delicate Man, who gained his magical powers by virtue of having been hit by not one but a thousand dodgeballs, then rescued by a scientist, accidentally mutated, and thereby changed into a super hero with special powers. It is an important authorial move, we would argue, to create a plot in which one becomes a super hero. Even more interesting to us is the nature of this super hero. We have witnessed many children adopt super hero characters from cartoons and comic books and recreate their exploits digitally.

It's more unusual, in our experience, for children to create their own super hero character, borrowing of course expertly from the genre—offering, for example, a creation story. Taj knew exactly what features of Delicate Man were unique. "He's one of a kind," commented Taj's DUSTY instructor, expressing her admiration of Taj's creation of Delicate Man. "'Cept for him getting mutated. That's not original," replied the honest author Taj. It is especially unusual to craft a super hero who goes against the masculine grain. There is some precedent, to be sure, to create less than traditionally masculine characters, to wit, mild-mannered Clark Kent of Superman fame. But in all of the cases with which we are acquainted, once the mild-mannered characters are transformed into super heroes, their powers become formidable—Superman's ability to leap tall buildings with a single bound, for example. Yet, Taj created a "vulnerable" super hero, one with the less than spectacular power of falling apart. This, we believe, was in keeping with his sensitivity to himself and certain other friends and relatives as different, as not-so-athletic, and as sometimes picked-upon. "Mostly everybody's out to get him," Taj noted about Delicate Man, "'cause he's weird." Taj's mom mentioned to us in an e-mail that sometimes Taj gets labeled as "weird" too, particularly by same-age friends and cousins who "are striving to be African-American hip-hop cool…athletic" and who consequently don't know what to make of Taj, with his mixed-race heritage and his unconventional version of a masculine self that is vulnerable rather than tough.

A good day at school: "Nobody getting beat up and teachers wouldn't get so mad"

The beginning of Taj's summer at DUSTY was filled with altercations. During one especially bad incident, Taj and the two brothers, Brandon and Jermaine, sat around a table and kicked each other, accidentally and otherwise. This horseplay eventually degenerated into boasts and threats. "I'm gonna come by and shoot up your house," Brandon told Taj, apparently in an attempt to one-up Taj's somewhat milder previous promise that he'd have his friends pay Brandon and Jermaine a visit, friends who "have very bad tempers." Over the course of the summer, however, we saw evidence that Taj was learning to be more social and less self-focused, even on the dodgeball court. Late in the summer one tutor noted:

> On the dodge-ball court, everyone, even Ms. Nora… is playing. The girls are just as active as the boys, although among the boys Taj and Miguel seem less dominant…. Clinton gets smacked by one of the balls and sits off on the side and complains to the teacher. Taj looks frustrated at getting hit a few times, but unlike before, makes little of it and plays along.

We also observed that Taj had started to gain in social stature with the other children, a transformation that we attribute in part to the growing respect he was garnering for his digital work. His DUSTY instructors and tutors praised his story with genuine enthusiasm at every turn and took obvious pride in what he had accomplished. And digital expertise was something that the students, such as the popular athletic boys Angel, Loren, Brandon, and Jermaine, valued too, as we shall see in subsequent sections of this paper. They were each, after all, willing participants in a summer digital storytelling program, where cool kids could also be computer experts, and computer nerds could also be cool kids. It was likely also the case that Taj's mastery of the super hero genre, popular especially among the boys, brought him a bit of cachet. By the end of the summer, Taj had even gained entry into the previously closed social group of popular African American boys. Most noticeably, Jermaine had relented in his previously staunchly oppositional stance toward Taj. After a culminating summer activity, a daylong fieldtrip to the university, Taj's DUSTY instructor noted with some surprise that "Jermaine and Taj were like best friends," and that Taj had even bought a soda for Jermaine at the end of the day (a gesture, however, that Taj later professed not to remember.)

When Taj returned to school and the fourth grade the summer after DUSTY, he had a difficult year, not getting along with his teacher, feeling oppressed in her classroom, and generally experiencing a grave mismatch between his love of computers and his need for movement, and a school environment where "we rarely do computers" and where a premium was placed on order and staying in one's seat. A good day a school, Taj said, would be one in which no one gets beat up and teachers don't get so mad. Although resource specialists at Taj's school had conducted numerous tests to determine the cause for his disruptive classroom behavior and his difficulties with fine motor movement, his mother became exasperated by evidence that the school was not complying with the IEP, or Individualized Education Program, that had been agreed to, and she began to search for other schools and considered home-schooling for a time. She was clear that many children, including Taj, "have different needs, postures, attitudes, ways of processing information and ways of learning than do the children for whom this present educational system was designed," and she worried about schooling's effects on "our African American children and other children of color—particularly the boys." She was determined that her son would not be a casualty. Outside of school Taj continued to flourish in his technologically-mediated world, gaining more and more expertise at animation and thriving on the acquisition of insider knowledge about software and hardware and an amazing array of other topics. He showed his "Delicate Man" movie at a local film festival, accepting kudos and questions from the audience with panache.

Of the focal children in our larger project, Taj was the most proficient technologically and among the least proficient socially. In addition, he was among the most unhappy children at school, as well as among those children who presented the greatest dilemmas for many of their school-day teachers. He defied racial and gender stereotypes, not identifying in obvious ways with African American youth culture or hegemonic forms of masculinity. Despite his great facility with and interest in technology, he was at-risk of school failure, and the new multimodal literacies that gave him social purchase and allowed him agentive expression out-of-school, did not always have noticeable value during the school day. We appreciated the chance to write about Taj precisely because he complicated many of the expectations about kids at risk, especially boys, that are prevalent in the literature. Further, analyzing his creative work and his participation at DUSTY gave us a roadmap for thinking about the other boys in our study. It would be a grave analytic mistake, we would argue, to dismiss Taj as merely different, as just an interesting outlier in terms of his great digitally-mediated potential and the equally large lack of fit between his habits of mind and body and the participant structures and instructional modes of traditional schooling. Rather, we see him as different in degree, not in kind, and in his extremity able to call our attention in very helpful ways to the dilemmas and challenges and resources of other young children coming of age in a digital era.

Conclusion

While we do not expect all children to take up the available technological means with as much eagerness and ease as Taj, we are primed by his example to examine exactly how their multimodal composing interface with their expressive intentions, desires, and resources, including knowledge about print-based composing and knowledge about local and popular culture. We are interested as well in the representations of self that children construct through multimodal means. While we do not anticipate that all children will draw so transparently upon their day-to-day lives to fashion themselves as super heroes, the case of Taj reminds us to be alert to the multiplex possibilities for self-fashioning embedded within narration and storytelling. Finally, we illustrated above how Taj achieved greater social acceptance and increased sociability through his growing technological achievements in a particular kind of social space.

At a time when after-school programs are under pressure to be extensions of the school day, we want to argue, not for an isolated autonomy, but for recognition of and support for the special functions they currently can serve as alternative spaces for learning and identity formation, spaces that can offer different participant structures, literacies, relationships, and ideologies. Such features are often unavailable, for a whole variety of reasons—administrative, pedagogical, epistemological, economic—during the school day. Especially during periods of intense standardization, back-to-basics, testing and accountability, not to mention competition for resources, after-school programs can be islands in the storm for children and their families who are most in need. They do so, for example, by providing culturally-alert and critically-attuned creative activities, relationships with caring adults, and pathways toward positive social futures and imagined selves. Although marginal in power when juxtaposed to institutions such as school, church, and government, after-school programs have the advantage of working outside the usual institutional constraints and habits of mind, bringing together diverse talents and identities, a range of resources both social and material, and a commitment to and knowledge of local communities. We hope that our analyses of children's participation in one after-school program, the DUSTY project, are suggestive of these rich possibilities.

Most research on after-school programs is evaluative in nature, seeking to provide project funders and designers with evidence that programs have made a difference in learning outcomes. We took and recommend, in addition, a different approach: the study not only of outcomes but of identity formation and learning processes and practices. If after-school programs can act, as we believe they can and should, as alternative learning spaces, then there will be much to discover about how children grow and learn from their participation in these contexts that will not be apparent elsewhere. In our research we focused particularly on how boys' identity enactments were afforded both by characteristics of their after-school social space, such as its particular types of participant structures, and the symbolic means and subject matters privileged therein, principally digital multi-modal narratives and popular culture. We documented how successful all of these children were at digital multi-modal composing, provided they were given appropriate social support and a range of entry points to the process (rather than, for example, being required to begin by writing). We discovered anew the importance of popular culture for these young authors—the appropriation of themes, images, and sounds from television and cartoons, music and movies—in particular, the ways the boys re-purposed this material in their own stories. To those educators who worry that children, and especially boys, are too immersed in mediatized worlds, we would point out that their active use of such symbolic material in their stories often serves important, often invisible ends—for example, the reworking of one's social world in agentive ways.

Notes

[1] The authors gratefully acknowledge the following for their contributions to the research reported in this article: Ananda Esteva, Ali Foresman-Schneider, Pauline Pearson Hathorne, Stacy Marple, Sonja Melton-Ramsar, Laura Nicodemus, Mark Nelson, Jeeva Roche-Smith, Jennifer Tilson, and Jean Wing. We also thank the University of California, Berkeley undergraduate tutors and the DUSTY staff. A special thank you to the children who have participated in after-school and allowed us to share what we have learned about their creativity and learning, especially Taj, whose work is highlighted in this chapter. Finally, we thank the Robert Bowne Foundation, which funded the research on which this chapter is based. The chapter is based on a monograph published by the Bowne Foundation (Hull, Kenney, Marple, Forsman-Schneider 2006), and we gratefully acknowledge their willingness to reprint portions of that monograph here.

[2] In this and subsequent transcriptions, we use the symbol == to indicate moments in which two utterances follow each other without any perceptible pause or even over-lap each other, as one person begins to speak before the other person has stopped. "Latching" and overlapping of conversational turns can indicate interlocutors' comfort and familiarity with each other, but they can also suggest a person's eagerness to take the floor or willingness to interrupt. In the case of Taj and Miss Nora, these features suggest to us both the child and his teacher's ease with each other, but also Taj's propensity to interject himself at will into most

conversations. For a detailed explanation of transcripts and their analysis and interpretation, see Duranti (1997).

References

Bauman, R., and C. L. Briggs. 1990. Poetics and performance as critical perspectives on language and social life. *Annual Review of Anthropology* 19: 59-88.

Bhabha, H. K. 1994. *The location of culture*. London: Routledge.

Bennett, A. 1991. Discourses of power, the dialectics of understanding, the power of literacy. In *Rewriting literacy: Culture and the discourse of the other,* ed. C. Mitchell and K. Weiler, 1-13. New York: Bergin and Garvey.

Brown, J. A. 1999. Comic book masculinity and the new black superhero. *African American Review* 33(1): 25-42.

Bruner, J. 1994. The "remembered" self. In *The remembering self: Construction and accuracy in the self-narrative*, ed. U. Neisser and R. Fivush. Cambridge: Cambridge University Press.

Collins, A., D. Joseph, and K. Bielaczyc. 2004. Design research: Theoretical and methodological issues. *Journal of the Learning Sciences* 13(1): 5-42.

Curtis-Tweed, P. 2003. Experiences of African American empowerment: A Jamesian perspective on agency. *Journal of Moral Education* 32(4): 397-409.

De Certeau, M. 1984. *The practice of everyday life*. Berkeley, CA: University of California Press.

Duranti, A. 1997. *Linguistic anthropology*. Cambridge: Cambridge University Press.

Dyson, A. H. 1997. *Writing superheroes: Contemporary childhood, popular culture, and classroom literacy*. New York: Teachers College Press.

—. 2003. *The brothers and the sisters learn to write: Popular literacies in childhood and school culture*. New York: Teachers College Press.

Dyson, A. H., and C. Genishi. 2005. *On the case: Approaches to language and literacy research*. New York: Teachers College Press and the National Conference on Research in Language and Literacy.

Emirbayer, M., and A. Mische. 1998. What is agency? *American Journal of Sociology* 103(4): 962-1023.

Fairclough, N. 1989. *Language and power*. London: Longman.

Freedman, S. W., and D. Abazovic. 2006. Growing up during the Balkan wars of the 1990s. In *International perspectives on youth conflict and development,* ed. C. Daiute, L. Nucci, C. Higson-Smith, Z. Beykont, 57-72. Oxford: Oxford University Press.

Gee, J. P. 2004. Millennials and bobos, *Blue's Clues* and *Sesame Street*: A story for our times. In *Adolescents and literacies in a digital world,* ed. D. E. Alvermann, 51-67. New York: Peter Lang.

Greene, J. P. 2002. *High school graduation rates in the United States.* New York: The Manhattan Institute for Policy Research, http://www.manhattan-institute.org/html/cr_baeo.htm (retrieved January 13, 2008).

Hall, S. 1996. Introduction: Who needs identity? In *Questions of cultural identity,* ed. S. Hall and P. du Gay, 1-17. London: Sage.

Halpern, R. 2003. *Making play work: The promise of after-school programs for low-income children.* New York: Teachers College Press.

Holland, D., W. Lachicotte, Jr., D. Skinner, and C. Cain. 1998. *Identity and agency in cultural worlds.* Cambridge, MA: Harvard University Press.

Howard, S., ed. 1998. *Wired-up: Young people and the electronic media.* London: Routledge.

Hudak, G. M. 1999. The "sound" identity: Music-making and schooling. In *Sound identities: Popular music and the cultural politics of education,* ed. C. McCarthy, G. Hudak, S. Miklaucic, and P. Saukko, 447-474. New York: Peter Lang.

Hull, G. 2008. Foreword: After-school talks back. In *Afterschool matters: Creative programs that connect youth development and student achievement,* ed. S. Hill, 447-474. New York: Peter Lang.

—. 2003. Youth culture and digital media: New literacies for new times. *Research in the Teaching of English* 38(2): 229-33.

Hull, G., and M. James. 2007. Geographies of hope: A study of urban landscapes, digital media, and children's representations of place. In *Blurring boundaries: Developing writers, researchers, and teachers. A tribute to William L. Smith,* ed. Peggy O'Neill, 250-89. Cresskill, NJ: Hampton Press.

Hull, G., and M.-L. Katz. 2006. Crafting an agentive self: Case studies on digital storytelling. *Research in the Teaching of English* 41(1): 43-81.

Hull, G., N. Kenney, S. Marple, and A. Forsman-Schneider. 2006. *Many versions of masculine: Explorations of boys' identity formation through multimodal composing in an after-school program.* The Robert Bowne Foundation's Occasional Papers Series. New York: Robert Bowne Foundation.

Hull, G., and M. Nelson. 2005. Locating the semiotic power of multimodality. *Written Communication* 22(2): 224-61.

Kelley, R. D. G. 1997. *Yo' mama's disfunktional! Fighting the culture wars in urban America*. Boston: Beacon Press.

Kellner, D. 1995. *Media culture: Cultural studies, identity and politics between the modern and the postmodern*. London: Routledge.

Kirsch, I., H. Braun, K. Yamamoto, and A. Sum. 2007. *America's perfect storm: Three forces changing our nation's future*. Princeton, NJ: Educational Testing Service.

Kress, G. 2003. *Literacy in the new media age*. New York: Routledge.

Lundby, K. 2005. Digital storytelling on life and faith: Options and limitations for youth in the church of Norway. Paper presented at the Conference on Childhoods 2005, in Oslo, Norway.

McDonald, K. 1999. *Struggles for subjectivity: Identity, action, and youth experience*. London: Cambridge University Press.

Miles, M. 1994. *Qualitative data analysis: An expanded sourcebook*. Thousand Oaks: Sage.

Miller, P. 1994. Narrative practices: Their role in socialization and self-construction. In *The remembering self: Construction and agency in self narrative,* ed. Neisser and Fivush, 158-179. Cambridge: Cambridge University Press.

Mitchell, W. J. T. 2004. Sounding the idols. Keynote address, Conference on Visual Culture, University of California, Berkeley.

Noam, G. G., ed. 2004. *After-school worlds: Creating a new social space for development and learning*. New Directions for Youth Development Series. San Francisco: Jossey-Bass.

Ochs, E., and L. Capps. 1996. Narrating the self. *Annual Review of Anthropology,* Vol. 25, pp. 19-43.

Ochs, E., and L. Capps. 2001. *Living narrative: Creating lives in everyday storytelling.* Cambridge, MA: Harvard University Press.

Scott, J. 1985. *Weapons of the weak: Everyday forms of peasant resistance*. New Haven, CN: Yale University Press.

Sefton-Green, J., ed. 1999. *Young people, creativity and new technologies: The challenge of digital arts*. London: Routledge.

Soep, E., and V. Chavez. 2005. Youth radio and the pedagogy of collegiality. *Harvard Educational Review* 75(4): 409-34.

Walker, S. W., and J. R. Snarey. 2004. Race matters in moral formation. In *Race-ing moral formation: African American perspectives on care and justice,* ed. V.S. Walker and J. R. Snarey, 1-14. New York: Teachers College Press.

Wardrip-Fruin, N., and P. Harrigan, ed. 2004. *First person: New media as story, performance, and game*. Cambridge: MIT Press.

Wasserman, S. 1991. Cafes, clubs, corners, and candy stores: Youth leisure-culture in New York City's Lower East Side during the 1930s. *Journal of American Culture* 14(4): 43-48.

Wenger, E. 1998. *Communities of Practice: Learning, meaning and identity*. Cambridge: Cambridge University Press.

Wolf, M. J. P., and B. Perron, ed. 2003. *The video game theory reader*. New York Routledge.

CHAPTER FIVE

FROM MULTIMEDIA TO MULTIPLE VOICES: CONFLICTS IN COLLABORATIVE LEARNING CULTURES [1]

SARITA YARDI

Over 87 per cent of youth in America between the ages of 12 and 17 use the Internet and usage spikes from 60 per cent in the sixth grade to 82 per cent by seventh grade (Lenhart and Madden 2005). Teens are actively creating blogs and webpages, posting original artwork, photography, stories or videos online and most teens have accounts on MySpace, Facebook, or Xanga. Teens also keep in touch through a vast array of communication tools, such as instant messaging, email, message boards, or chat rooms. This activity, in combination with the increasingly globalized socially networked information economy, indicates a need for researchers, teachers, parents, and policy makers to better understand the influence of these media and activities on the changing dynamics of classroom collaborative culture. In particular, we need a better understanding of the ways in which youths' use of technology in their informal learning environments influences their use in the classroom.

Many of today's new media technologies are highly social in nature. Similarly, youths' uses of these digital media in their informal environments are highly collaborative and communicative as suggested by the popularity of these environments, such as GarageBand, Flickr, MySpace and YouTube. Despite their enthusiasm using computers and the Internet, they express a strong lack of interest in pursuing careers and academic disciplines using computers, technology, and digital media. Youths' perceptions of these tools in formal educational environments are that they are often boring, anti-social, and lacking real world implications (Margolis 2002). Their lack of interest poses a problem in today's expanding, Internet-based, global economy. Opportunities at companies like Yahoo!, Google, or Electronic Arts reveal that there is a demand for youth to become experts in their use of digital media. The skills required in today's economy include practices related to media remixing, reuse, and appropriation. However, these practices often exist in contrast to the individual nature of much of today's standards-based school curricula. What is considered sharing or appropriating in an informal environment becomes cheating or stealing in a formal environment. In my prior work, I describe the role of collaboration in kids' informal activities (Yardi and Perkel 2007). In this chapter, I expand on this discussion, focusing more specifically on the challenges faced in informal digital media environments versus formal computing classes. The role of computers, technology, and the Internet in our everyday lives is rapidly expanding in unexpected and unforeseen ways. At the same time, educators are encouraging the use of computers and new media in the classroom. As technical proficiency becomes a fundamental skill within a reading and writing curriculum, the nature of how youth should interact in these environments becomes more complex. In this chapter, I explore these conflicting collaborative computing cultures. I frame my argument in Mikhael Bakhtin's theory of dialogism to suggest ways of understanding these emerging mediums and how to design collaborative learning cultures.

Collaborative storytelling: A case study

We conducted a digital media storytelling after school program twice a week for two months (Yardi and Perkel 2007). Our goal was to determine requirements for an online, collaborative storytelling environment to help youth learn principles of non-linear, narrative construction using multiple digital and physical expressive mediums. The story creation process involves developing ideas and constructing knowledge through personally meaningful forms of self-expression. Recent projects have looked to design interactive storytelling environments to support the creation, production, consumption, and sharing of stories. For example, The POGO environment describes the use of active tools and the performance of the stories to the group (Decoritis and Rizzo 2002). Similarly, the design of KidPad and Klump centered on the notion of "shoulder-to-shoulder collaboration," as two or more children share an interface in the process of creating a story (Benford, et al., 2003, Hourcade, 2002). StoryMat examines collaboration in storytelling and addresses the importance of the "collective sharing" that allows story producers to "change point of view and acquire a different perspective" (Cassell and Ryokai 2001). In StoryBuilder, kids can either add a new page to an existing story that has been created by other kids or they can create pages and use an "email to a friend function" to create a shared story with a known group of friends (Antle 2003). The collaborative process between the kids, as authors, happens during the creation of the story, but the latter method requires direction communication through an existing relationship. Collaboration between kids, as both author and audience, shapes the meaning of the story to both.

In our program, we designed our curriculum to teach fundamental storytelling concepts, with each session focused on a particular theme, such as non-linear narration or character development. We chose storytelling as a valuable and engaging medium through which we could explore the ways kids used digital media to describe the world around them. We conducted hour and a half long sessions, twice a week, at the school's computer lab (see Fig. 5-1). The study involved eight fifth-grade students, five boys and three girls, and a team of five researchers. Our lead researcher ran each session, with support from the other researchers, who played the interchangeable roles of participant observer, note-taker, videographer, and teaching assistant. We videotaped all the sessions and conducted pre, mid, and post-interviews with the participants. We also conducted formal interviews with each of the participants. Four of the interviews were with individual participants and two of them were in paired groups.

Fig. 5-1. After school program.

Our program was based on Backyard Transformations, a project that was conducted at Apple Computer's Vivarium Research Lab from 1989 to 1990 (Strickland and Wright 1991). Backyard Transformations combined story construction with collaborative play in a form that encouraged children to be imaginative and creative. The system combined two components: the first consisted of 174 video clips that provided evocative and unusual scenes of characters played out in one of the creator's backyard. The other component was a set of improvisational storytelling games designed to help children learn principles of narrative construction. Children played these games in groups that included a teacher or coach. They used physical "cards" that depicted key frames from the video clips and then used the cards to construct specific activities for developing ideas, sharing, and creating story sequences.

Sharing ideas: Collaboration or cheating?

Storytelling is often perceived as an individual process in which stories are attributed to a single author. However, there are usually many influences that may have contributed to the creation of the story. Walter Ong (2002) described the weaving of stories by ancient rhapsodes who pieced together memorized sections for the benefit of their audience. Explicit references to remixing emerged in the 1970s in context of multi-track music recordings and developed through the 1980s in context of video remixing, such as synthesizing, sampling, and looping (Manovich 2001). The storytelling process in our program involved remixing, revising, and appropriation of others' ideas. Many new media environments have looked for innovative means to create collaborative storytelling cultures through this type of remixing. For example, Penguin Books created an online remix contest in which they provided thirty classic novels that could be downloaded and creatively recomposed into novel compositions.[2] Our activities fostered a culture that strongly encouraged media reuse and sharing. However, we did not attempt to establish any norms or rules for sharing, attributing ownership, or claiming ideas, artefacts, and stories as one's own. We thus observed that the participants struggled with a sense of uncertainty throughout their evolving storytelling processes. Their acts of sharing and appropriation revealed the tensions between collaboration, copying, and cheating in their uses of various forms of digital media. In our storytelling environment, who owned the components within their story sequences?

During one session in our project, Toby selected a card from the deck and created Count Whistleboy, an imaginary character based on the image on the card, but with its own unique fantastical and distinct features, which Andrew then used in his own story. Did that act carry the same implications as when Iris used the disposable camera to take a picture of her family cat and uploaded the digitized version to the lab computer, which Dionne then used in her story? When was borrowing a peer's idea collaborating and when was it stealing? We found that our participants preferred to collaborate during the idea generation process, often struggling to produce ideas on their own. For example:

> Researcher: What do you like about working with other kids?
> Andrew[3]: I think it would go faster if I worked by myself but Miguel has some good ideas.... Miguel watches a lot of TV and gets good ideas from TV. There's a lot of good ideas on TV.
> Iris: Giving me some ideas. Ideas are basically like all you need.
> Miguel: I like working with other people better 'cause usually I don't have all the ideas and other people can help.
> Researcher: Would you rather work with [other kids] or by yourself?
> Iris: I think it would go faster if I worked by myself but Miguel has some good ideas.
> Researcher: What kind of ideas?
> Iris: He said let's put the policeman in the fight but then we tried to do that but it showed the policeman over the robot so you couldn't see the robot. And then we decided to put him after the fight ... Miguel watches a lot of TV and gets good ideas from TV. There's a lot of good ideas on TV...

However, while they sought out their peers and other external resources for ideas, they also expressed a desire to be given credit for ideas that were used by others. We frequently heard comments such as "Hey, you stole my idea!" or "That was my idea![5] In the following episode, Toby presented his story in iMovie to the group:

> Toby: This is Madame Peacock.
> Jason: He stole the idea. He stole the idea!
> Toby: She's crawling because she has no feet. How do I know? I can't see her feet. She is 13 years old. She is small as a squirrel. It lives in a wooden house. Its favorite thing to do is hunt the Invisible Woman.... Their greatest hope is to destroy the Invisible Woman.
> Jason: [under his breath] Oh come on. [reaches across the table and points at the screen] He stole that. [points finger in Toby's face] You stole that!

In another similar episode, Toby described a character he had created called Count Whistleboy:

> Toby: This is a human. His name is Count Whistleboy. He is ten years old. He is ten inches tall... and um it dislikes the ... the dark... the moon the most because it goes "raar" and becomes a vampire. And um... and um... his friends are his whistles.
> Jason: Wait, did you do Count Whistleboy or did you? [*pointing first to Toby and then to Andrew*]
> Toby: I did Count Whistleboy.

Andrew: So did I.

While tensions dissolved as soon as the owner of an idea was given public acknowledgement for his or her idea, character, or artifact, at the same time, their interactions brought to light the potential sources of complexity and confusion regarding the proper uses of shared artefacts and artistic creations. The kids looked to one another as sources of creative inspiration, yet they wanted to simultaneously maintain a sense of individual authorship. While it is important to acknowledge that productive creative activities can occur in isolation, design research studies suggest that "the role of interaction and collaboration with other individuals is critical to creativity" (Fischer 2005). The romantic notion of the individual author as creative genius was criticized as too centered on the individual (Barthes 1978) and has more recently given way to notions of authorship as an interwoven system of creative collaborations. Creativity is fostered through the interactions of multiple ideas and thoughts and the social and cultural contexts in which they are shared. In this discussion of the modern informal remix culture, creative collaborations thus directly rely on the participation of multiple individuals engaged in one or more interactions. These creative environments are valuable because they allow a variety of new and different cultural forms to be created - one artist can comment on another's creativity in ways that the original creator did not anticipate or foresee. This expands the cultural enjoyment because it gives the audience more to experience and enjoy, and it can also inspire new creativity in the original artist. Enabling a culture in which people can comment on and reinterpret the works of others is a powerful form of self-expression.

Our participants expressed a number of ways through which they sought out creative opportunities and outlets: "I don't like that you have limits of characters. I wish you could, like, build characters from your own imagination so you don't have to keep on using the same people." We encouraged this collaborative idea generation by working with them to develop their stories, as well as by encouraging participants to provide feedback on one another's stories. In one case, a researcher prompted Dionne with series of interactive questions about her character, Ms. Laugh A Lot, such as: "How old is she? Does she laugh in her sleep? What is her typical day like? Does she know that she annoys the teachers and other students?" As Dionne developed the character on the whiteboard, the researcher further probed:

Researcher: Why is her body so small? Other than the fact that it's goofy…

> Dionne: Because she laughs a lot. And as she laughs a lot her body gets smaller… and smaller. And her head gets bigger… and bigger…
> Researcher: How does her head get bigger?
> Dionne: Because she laughs and her mouth gets bigger and stretches out her head.

In the following subsequent exchange, Tia then played the role of researcher with Dionne to offer Dionne ideas for her story:

> Tia: Well the two things that I don't like is that I think she could encounter more problems in her life. Not just that the only bad thing that happens to her is that her head gets bigger. And… is there anything else about her? Because all you said was that she had a big head, a lot of hair, and a small body.
> Tia: And two good things are, I think your character is funny, and I like how her head gets bigger when she laughs. I think that's a good idea.
> Dionne: [*off camera*] Thank you.

We later witnessed Dionne incorporate Tia's feedback into her revised character depiction, writing down Tia's feedback on the whiteboard then drawing variations that implemented some of Tia's suggestions. She then approached Tia and asked if the revised drawings were what she had in mind or if she had other suggestions. In this activity, participants had a common understanding that feedback provided by them to their peers gave right to the author or artist to appropriate and incorporate the suggested ideas into their work.

How should these practices, which are simultaneously individual and collaborative, be understood when the rules behind the sharing of ideas and artefacts are subtle or unclear? More specifically, what is the role of collaboration in increasingly technology rich classrooms where a culture of remixing and reusing is pervasive? Computer science and technology classes in particular, are becoming core courses in many formal educational curricula, taking their place within the more traditional reading, writing, and arithmetic classes. I suggest that Bakhtin's theory of dialogism provides a useful framework through which to understand the culture of collaboration within these learning environments. In the following sections, I first describe Bakhtin's dialogic theory. I then frame formal computing curricula in the context of dialogism. Finally, I suggest ways of understanding collaboration in formal educational environments and how to promote a culture of collaboration in formal learning environments.

Framing classroom culture in a theory of dialogism

The perceived dialogic nature of a medium and how it is used in the classroom correlates to whether students will be inclined to use it collaboratively or individually. I use a definition of dialogue as consisting of one or more speakers, listeners, and the relationships among them (Bakhtin 1981). Bakhtin used the term "utterances" to describe the situated act of dialogic discourse as a unit of analysis (Bakhtin 1986). I thus characterize dialogue as the inscriptions, implications, and intersections that are embedded within words, texts, gestures, intonations, voices, responses, and other communication utterances. While others have described the nature of dialogue as it occurs between man and machine (Meadow 1970), I focus on dialogue as it takes place between man and man, where the machine is the mediating agent among two or more humans. It is useful to ground this discussion of these varied learning environments by describing them in terms of categories of genres. Bakhtin described speech genres as characteristic patterns of speech within the realms of dialogue and text (Bakhtin 1986). He distinguished between primary genres, which legislate words, phrases, and expressions that are acceptable in everyday life, and secondary genres, which are characterized by various types of text. Examples of genres vary from simple forms such as greetings, farewells, congratulations, or information about health, to more complex forms such as novels, dramas, or scientific research (Bakhtin 1986). In our project, genres emerged through the different ways that the kids used the media that we provided for them. Some were simple forms, such as talking, laughing, shouting, and playing. Others were more complex, such as visual art, software-based, acting, and written stories. Bakhtin would characterize these forms as types of literary discourse, or individual literary "texts", as an intersection of multiple textual surfaces rather than as a fixed point or meaning.

Multivocality is defined by Bakhtin as the ways in which multiple voices can be discerned in a text (Bakhtin 1981). The role of multivocality in collaborative learning spaces is less clearly understood in these emerging new mediums. What happens when there are multiple voices, listeners, and possible interpretations in a given utterance? A speaker's utterance, as a type of message, has historical roots in oral storytelling. However, what implications does the speaker's original ownership have as the utterance evolves through multiple dynamic and untraceable states? According to Bakhtin, "language is not a neutral medium that passes freely and easily into the private property of the speaker's intentions; it is populated–overpopulated–with the intentions of others" (Bakhtin 1981). One of the challenges we faced was that, in contrast to text and language, which offer a more binary distinction between speaker and listener (although they are not always explicitly delineated), the boundaries are less obvious when the utterance continues to be used and reused beyond the speaker's original intention, as was the case in our multimedia environments. Multiple layers of meaning are added and interwoven as the utterance is appropriated throughout its lifecycle. Perhaps the sender's original message remains embedded somewhere in the medium but it will become convoluted and masked over time. The ability for messages to be mediated through both the students and the medium can influence the ways in which its dialogism evolves. What are the roles of the sender and receiver within these mediums?

In our study, for example, Miguel discovered an obscure built-in sound pattern in iMovie and proudly maximized the volume to broadcast his find to the computer lab. Toby crossed the room to see the sound source and promptly incorporated it into his own story (see Fig. 5-2). Miguel's re-broadcast of his iMovie tune throughout the lab is a type of indirect speech, which Wertsch and Toma (1995) describe as instances in which speakers incorporated text from prior talk. In this example, Miguel was actively interpreting these utterances and the boundary between speaker and listener - and unanticipated future listeners - was not clearly demarcated.

Bakhtin describes the process of appropriation as taking something that belongs to others and making it one's own. "The word in language is half someone else's. It becomes 'one's own' only when the speaker populates it with his intention, with his own accent, when he appropriates the word, adapting it to his own semantic and expressive intention" (Bakhtin 1986).

Fig. 5-3. Types of broadcasting in Backyard Transformation activities.

Appropriation begins to pose a problem when students are encouraged to dissect, transform, or remix artefacts and ideas as part of their individual and collaborative learning processes. What rules define the boundaries between copying an idea versus copying an expressive form? The question of the differences between transformation of a work versus derivation of a work, in terms of copyright, is an important but separate discussion. Bereiter (1994) stated that "classroom discussions may be thought of as part of the larger ongoing discourse, not as preparation for it or as after-the-fact examination of the results of the larger discourse... The important thing is that the local discourses be progressive in the sense that understandings are being generated that are new to the local participants and that the participants recognize as superior to their previous understandings." As prior scholars of Bakhtin have done (e.g. Kozulin, 1996), I extend and generalize Bakhtin's theory of dialogism in text and language to apply it to multiple modes of communication that are used in the classroom, such as audio, video, verbal, spatial, and gestural. While dialogic theory can be applied across a range of formal and informal learning environments, I focus here on its intersections within computer science and emerging new media. Dialogism provides a framework for understanding computer science and programming environments as a form of collaborative storytelling, in which bits of code are used and reused to fit the goals of the person who is writing the program. In formal educational environments, the dialogic nature of digital media, and how they are used in the classroom, is fluid and can be manipulated by the teacher to encourage collaborative learning environments.

Computing culture: Collaborative or individual?

Researchers in computer science education have long questioned the role of collaboration in assignments, looking to understand at what point collaboration ends and plagiarism or cheating begins (Stewart-Gardiner et al., 2001, Sheard 2002, Harris 1994, Roberts 2002). When should teachers encourage students to collaborate? Should the students discuss the ownership of that code? If ownership is not properly acknowledged or attributed, are they cheating? Where does the line fall between collaboration and cheating? Rick and Guzdial (2006) found that faculty attitudes and models of collaboration presented a cultural barrier to collaboration: "If the culture of the context is not compatible, the medium will not succeed." One civil engineering faculty member who assigned only individual work stated "But engineering students should have only single-answer problems!" further declaring that he didn't believe that collaboration was important. Such faculty attitudes were commonly expressed among professors in science, engineering, and math related fields, explaining why some students in these classes were fearful that group discussions would be equated with cheating: "What was I supposed to do… Those who answered questions were severely criticized by [the teacher]" (Rick and Guzdial 2006). Related studies in collaborative learning indicate that the perception of single-answer assignments hinders collaboration, instead suggesting that open-ended, ill-structured problems tend to encourage productive group learning. If the students perceive that there is only one answer, they do not see a need for working collaboratively (Cohen 1994). Because they were accustomed to computer science syllabi that were based on individual coding assignments, computer science students actively resisted collaborating, even though they were encouraged to do so.

In contrast, students in an architecture design class, who frequently engaged in formal and informal dialogues during their group activities, actively adopted the collaborative opportunities that they were offered. Courses where the collaboration was the most successful were focused on dialogue rather than rote learning. "It was more just the ideas bouncing off each other. I don't think this class would have been as much fun if I wasn't able to collaborate." Similarly, "It's not just about the class… People talk about anything, it's a little bit more friendly than just 'here's your assignment'" (Rick and Guzdial, 2006). The technical affordances offered in their online medium were successfully interwoven with the social and interactive learning environments within that disciplinary culture. The framework of dialogism helps to guide the importance of considering *how* the medium is implemented based on its constraints and affordances. The physical properties of the medium influenced the extent to which students perceive it to encourage creativity and collaboration. The dialogism of the medium is not embedded in the medium itself but instead emerges through the specific ways in which the medium is implemented and used within the learning environment. I found that the technical affordances of the medium deeply influenced the ways in which the students felt they could become more creatively engaged with the tool. They were particularly excited when they could transfer ideas between multiple media, especially when their creative inspirations were transferred from physical expressions to digital formats (see Fig. 5-3).

Fig. 5-3. Exploring creative media.

Many new software environments have been designed to foster collaborative learning of computer science principles. These tools have carefully constructed technical affordances for constructing arguments using drag and drop style tangible interfaces. Traditional computing processes, such as that of a software development life cycle, clearly define the goals, roles, and individual contributions within the collaborative product development process. Tools like CVS[4] are designed to support these processes by identifying each person's individual contribution in terms of code written, time of contribution, and implicitly, the value to the final outcome of the product. In today's culture of remixing, reusing, and sharing online, the traditional notions of computing are being redefined. New models are emerging that no longer delineate individual roles and contributions in the collaborative development process. In MySpace, for example, youth can customize their pages by copying selected sections of HTML from existing MySpace accounts and appropriating them for their own use. There are few rules – either explicit or implicit – for restricting the copy and reuse of another's MySpace page.

A more formal example is Scratch[6] (see Fig. 5-4), a programming language that makes it easy to create stories, animations, games, music, and art while learning about the process of design and computational thinking. Studies show that kids made connections to computer science using Scratch (Peppler and Kafai 2006).

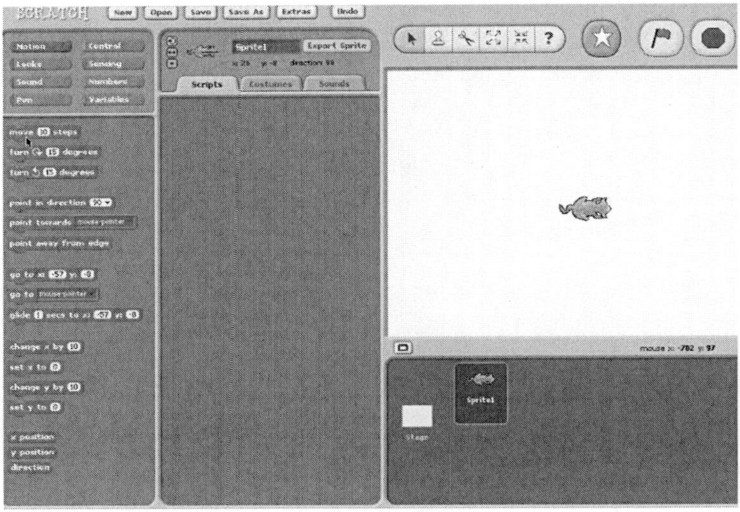

Fig. 5-4. Scratch drag and drop programming interface.[7]

Scratch is different from many traditional programming environments because it explicitly encourages reuse and remixing of media. "[Students] were able to repurpose code in a meaningful way and accomplish artistic design goals for the piece by taking pieces of code and creatively recombining them for new characters" (Peppler and Kafai 2006). Scratch is inspired by the hip hop remixing culture where multiple sounds are generated on a vinyl record player. Using Scratch, kids can mix different types of media, such as graphics, photos, and music, to create new digital stories. Mitchell Resnick states that "we want people to start from existing materials - grabbing an image, grabbing some sound, maybe even bits of someone else's program and then extending them and mixing them to make them their own." A student can visit the Scratch gallery and download specific projects they like and reuse characters, images, or ideas in their own story. Furthermore, Scratch users can then share their creations in a public user gallery, similar to YouTube or Flickr. They can also embed their creations in other social networking sites, such as

MySpace or Facebook. Thus, the model for sharing, reusing, and copying becomes explicitly encouraged. The social nature of the medium suggests that collaboration is not only accepted, but is encouraged. Users who upload their projects to the Scratch gallery are choosing to make their projects publicly available and culture of reuse is therefore built into the nature of the medium. The technical affordances of the site convey to the user that their projects will be used by others. A specific "Share" link communicates to the user that the project is being made public to the world and a "Download this project screen" indicates that anyone can download a project that is publicly available (see Fig. 5-5).

Fig. 5-5. Scratch sharing features.

In these environments, authorship becomes a dialogue between multiple voices, in which specific utterances may manifest themselves as text, images, graphics, sounds, and ideas. Collaboration – even when users are not physically co-located becomes built into the system itself.

From Individual authorship to multivocality

I propose that through the lens of dialogism, educators can construct collaborative learning experiences both in formal and informal environments by designing around these factors. Kids and teenagers are passionately engaged in their computing cultures and express an interest in learning more about these environments. Our participants expressed an inclination for taking existing media and repurposing it for their own uses. For example, Iris said "I think it's easier because you already have clips. So it makes it more fun because you already have some clips you can watch. And then put another thing together with it. If you had a picture of a birthday party with a war scene then it's kind of cool because you can put them together in different ways. As you think of it." In one session, Iris drew from her existing knowledge of online environments but used paper and pen during her initial idea generation process to flesh out her "mini iMac" commercial. Her plot evolved from ideas about a girl bringing a pocket-sized computer to a birthday party, to the girl being sucked into her computer, and finally discovering something about it:

> Iris: Here's what I have so far: [*holding up paper with first drawings*] She's sitting at home bored when suddenly she sees her mom, OH! [*puts down the paper and begins drawing*].
> Iris: We need some kind of adventure, maybe she gets sucked into the computer? When she's in the computer, she goes to… [*writes: Ida is amazed she can go anywhere she wants*].
> Iris: She goes to…Google! [draws Google and a search box] What should she type in? … OH! [writes "mini iMac" in the search box and then draws a search button.

In this sense, the dialogue is carried on as a continuous dialogue between other artefacts, authors, and audiences. The dialogue does not merely extend other works, but is iteratively informing and being informed by these works. The dialogue moves bi-directionally, shaping and evolving over time. In follow-up interviews with junior high and high school aged teenagers I found that they were creative, passionate, and enthusiastically engaged in their online digital media environments. They are actively creating blogs and web pages, posting stories and videos online, and remixing art, images, and digital media. When I asked them "If you could learn something new on the computer, what would it be?" they responded "probably like Garage-Band. I think it's cool how you can make music" and "editing videos and stuff" and "iTunes and Photobooth are really cool." Our results suggest that there is an opportunity to establish guidelines for collaborative uses of technology among teenagers by bridging the gap between their perceptions of individual and group roles in their uses of new media. Furthermore, the number of tools and software environments that support collaborative remixing on the web is growing rapidly (Wong and Hong 2007). These environments are becoming easier to use and are more widely accessible to youth, regardless of their technical abilities. Although early web tools, such as mashups and APIs, required programming expertise in areas such as web crawling, text parsing, pattern matching, and databases (Wong and Hong 2007), the recent release of intuitive, drag-and-drop tools like Scratch, Yahoo! Pipes[8], or Microsoft Popfly[9] have eased web development into the realm of non-programmers. The decreasing need for technical skills in these environments offers a wide range of entry points for youth to merge their activities in their formal and informal environments.

Designing the collaborative classroom

Although the contexts of use of the environments I have discussed, from storytelling to computer science programming software, differ significantly, there are common threads across them as dialogic mediums. In a software coding environment that is consistently perceived to be a dialogic genre, the technical affordances that are core properties of that genre can convey to the student how it should be used. Embedded features such as "publish my code to the class" or "download module from group" can help the students to perceive their actions using these features as collaborative, rather than cheating. Similarly, in multimedia environments, features such as "share this picture with the class" or "download character from group repository" can help the students to perceive their actions as encouraged creative reuse. The genre might provide the option for students to associate their name to a section of code–their "utterance"–in order to maintain a sense of individual ownership within the group's final artefact. If the authorship option is disabled, students will be made aware that their code contribution will be incorporated into a group-owned artefact that may not acknowledge individual ownership. In each of these examples, if the teacher can control these types of features by enabling or disabling options during certain phases of students' projects, the students will be more clearly cued into the extent of the dialogic, and accordingly, the collaborative, nature of their activities.

My goal in this chapter is to suggest the potential for designing collaborative classrooms through the lens of this dialogic framework while also exploring open questions about its applications in emerging learning environments. I propose that through the lens of dialogism, educators can construct collaborative learning environments by designing around these factors. In order to facilitate similar perceptions in the classroom, teachers thus need to explicitly specify rules and clarify expectations to avoid potential misunderstandings. Many incidents of cheating in computer science courses have been due to the differences in awareness and expectations between students and teachers. If students perceive a clearly defined culture of dialogism, they will be better prepared to determine when collaboration is or is not encouraged. The communicative, many-to-many properties of new media suggest that instances of multivocality in the classroom may become more ubiquitous, playing themselves out in novel and unpredictable ways. As researchers and educators, we need to support students in developing literacy skills and critical thinking skills to reflect on the emerging role that technology plays in their formal and informal everyday lives.

Notes

[1] I thank the Digital Youth research group at UC Berkeley's School of Information and Dan Perkel, in particular, who ran the storytelling project and without whom the project would not have taken place. I thank the rest of the research team, Rachel Strickland, Carrie Burgener, and Nick Reid as well as the MacArthur Foundation for their time and resources. Finally, I thank the eight fifth grade students for their enthusiasm and participation in our project.
[2] Penguin Launch Remix Project. http://www.djmag.com/newsfeat118.php.
[3] Pseudonyms are used to protect the identity of the participants. All media is reproduced with the consent of the participants and their parent(s).
[4] See Yardi and Perkel (2007) for more details.
[5] See http://www.nongnu.org/cvs/
[6] See http://scratch.mit.edu/
[7] See http://scratch.mit.edu/
[8] See http://pipes.yahoo.com/pipes/
[9] See http://www.popfly.ms/

References

Antle, A. 2003. *Case study: The design of CBC4Kids' StoryBuilder.* In Proceedings of the 2003 Conference on Interaction Design for Children, in Preston, England.

Bakhtin, M. 1981. Discourse in the novel, trans. M. Holquist and C. Emerson. In *The dialogic imagination*, ed. M. Holquist, 259-422. Austin: University of Texas Press.

—. 1986. The problem of speech genres, trans. V. McGee. In *Speech genres and other late essays*, ed. C. Emerson and M. Holquist, 60-102. Austin: University of Texas Press.

Barthes, R. 1978. *Image, music, text: The death of the author*. New York: Hill and Wang.

Bereiter, C. 1994. Implications of postmodernism for science, or, science as progressive discourse. *Educational Psychologist* 29(1): 3-12.

Cassell, J., and K. Ryokai. 2001. Making space for voice: Technologies to support children's fantasy and storytelling. *Personal Ubiquitous Computing* 5(3): 169-190.

Cohen, E. 1994. *Designing group work: Strategies for the heterogeneous classroom* (2nd ed.). New York: Teachers College Press.

Fischer, G. 2005. Distances and diversity: Sources for social creativity. Proceedings of Creativity and Cognition, London, April.

Harris, J. 1994. Plagiarism in computer science courses. In Proceedings of the Conference on Ethics in the Computer Science Age.

Hourcade, J.P., B. Bederson, A. Druin, and G. Taxen. 2002. KidPad: Collaborative storytelling for children. In Proceedings of CHI 2002. ACM.

Kozulin, A. 1996. A literary model for psychology. In *Discourse, Learning, and Schooling,* ed. D. Hicks, 145-164, New York: Cambridge University Press.

Lenhart, A., and M. Madden. 2005. Teen content creators and consumers. Washington, DC: Pew Internet and American Life Project.

Manovich, L. 2001. *The language of new media*. Cambridge MA: MIT Press.

Margolis, J. and A. Fisher. 2002. *Unlocking the clubhouse: Women in computing*. Cambridge, MA: MIT Press.

Meadow, C.T. 1970. *Man-machine communication*. New York: Wiley.

Ong, W. 2002. *Orality and literacy: The technologizing of the word.* London: Routledge.

Peppler, K., and Y. Kafai. 2006. Creative codings: Personal, epistemological, and cultural connections to digital art production. In Proceedings of the International Conference of the Learning Sciences, Bloomington, IN.

Rick, J., and M. Guzdial. 2006. Situating CoWeb: A scholarship of application. *International Journal of Computer-Supported Collaborative Learning* 1(1).

Sheard, J., M. Dick, S. Markham, I. Macdonald, and M. Walsh. 2002. Cheating and plagiarism: Perceptions and practices of first year IT students. ACM SIGCSE Bulletin. In Proceedings of the 7th annual conference on Innovation and Technology in Computer Science Education (ITiCSE 2002) 34(3): 183-187.

Stewart-Gardiner, C., D. G. Kay, J. C. Little, J. D. Chase, J. Fendrich, L. A. Williams, and U. Wolz. 2001. Collaboration vs plagiarism in computer science programming courses. In Proceedings of the Thirty-Second SIGCSE Technical Symposium on Computer Science Education. New York: ACM Press.

Strickland, R., and J. Wright. 1991. Backyard transformation: An interim project report. Research report at Apple Computer's Vivarium Research Program.

Wertsch, J., and C. Toma. 1995. Discourse and learning in the classroom: A sociocultural approach. In *Constructivism in education*, ed. L. Steffe and J. Gale, 159-174. Mahwah, NJ: LEA.

Wong, J., and J. I. Hong. 2007. Making mashups with marmite: towards end-user programming for the web. In Proceedings of the SIGCHI conference on human factors in somputing systems: 1435–1444.

Yardi, S., and D. Perkel. 2007. Understanding classroom culture through a theory of dialogism: What happens when cheating and collaboration collide? Paper accepted to the Computer Supported Collaborative Learning Conference, July 16-21, at Rutgers University, NJ.

CHAPTER SIX

(STUDENT) LIFE'S A GAME: PERSONAL DEVELOPMENT PLANNING AS AN INTERACTIVE SIMULATION

GRAEME KIRKPATRICK, GUY LANCASTER AND JOHN W. G. WILSON

In recent years the British government has made personal development planning (PDP) a compulsory part of course delivery for all educators, from primary schools through to higher education (HE). In 2007, PDP will even be mandatory for post-graduate students. The impetus for introducing it at university level came from the 1997 Dearing Review, which made a number of specific recommendations for universities, including the suggestion that "progress files" should be introduced as part of a "structured and supported process undertaken by an individual to reflect upon their own learning, performance and/or achievement and to plan for their personal, educational and career development" (National Committee 1997, Recommendation 20). In May 2000, this idea was made mandatory for all universities by the Quality Assurance Agency.

As its name suggests, PDP is concerned with the non-academic aspects of an individual's progress through a course of study. Enlarging one's knowledge of a discipline is invariably at the same time related to processes of personal growth. Understanding the relationship between intellectual and other aspects of personal development is gained by reflection on the part of the student. Educators are now obliged to support this process by creating space and time for reflection in curriculum planning and by providing students with appropriate resources to help. It is now incumbent upon educators to provide time and resources for their students to engage in critical self-reflection aimed at enabling students to turn themselves into better, more efficient learners who make strategic choices in other areas of their lives in order to enhance their academic performance.

The underlying belief that motivates PDP in HE is that reflection on one's skills and periodic reassessment of their domain of application is essential to personal fulfilment, as well as professional success. To foster this reflective process, the government initially introduced PDP in schools, usually in the form of a diary-like "progress file" or other paper based medium. Students are supposed to use these to record their achievements, keep records of their marks and to reflect on what they have done and how they might improve their performance in the future. The best paper progress files made use of questionnaires, with which students could assess their own performance and reflect on weaknesses and strengths. Scores derived from these exercises might be used to direct students towards appropriate resources for them within the institution.

Paper progress files were quickly followed by on-line PDPs developed by many university departments in the first few years of this century. In the on-line PDP, reflection is instilled through different modalities of action and interaction within a technologically supported environment. Typically, the following facilities have been made available from Intranet sites:

- Interactive questionnaires that give instant feedback, including personality assessments and situation diagnostics.
- Discussion, or bulletin boards, with topics given over to reviewing the results of reflection, including tutor input.
- An evolving store of links and documents aimed at supporting student reflection and planning.
- Guidance tutor drop in sessions, often delivered using the "chat" facility, especially where an integrated web platform has been used such as "Blackboard" (see Kirkpatrick 2005).
- Opportunities for student initiated critique, review and improvements to the PDF facility itself.

These kinds of facilities have been developed by most university departments, probably in part motivated by the desire to find cost-effective ways of implementing PDP.

The theoretical potential of computer games for PDP

Self-reflection of the kind envisaged by PDP has a surprisingly similar structure to play with a computer game: each requires us to make decisions, act upon them and live with the consequences. In both cases, reflection centres on the success or failure of previous decisions followed by experimentation with alternative approaches in future. Sid Meyer, designer of the game "Civilization", has famously said that "a game is a series of interesting choices". We might add that successful players pursue varied strategies until they hit upon the right one for the attainment of their objective. This is often the situation students face too as they attempt to become better, more fulfilled learners.

The process of critical self-reflection that is the goal of PDP is produced in a computer game by encouraging the game's player to reflect upon, or "play with" her identity in the manner theorised by James Paul Gee (Gee 2003). Gee asserts that "video games recruit identities and encourage identity work and reflection on identities in clear and powerful ways" (Gee 2003, 51). According to Gee's theory, the relationship of a real person to a virtual character results in three separate identities: a *virtual* identity (the player's identity as a virtual character in the game world), a *real-world identity* (the player's own identity as a really existing individual), and, importantly, a *projective identity* (produced by the interface, or interactions, between the real-world person and the virtual character).

The projective identity is crucial for understanding the learning potential of this game (and, Gee argues, of computer games in general). This identity plays on two senses of the word "project": 1) "to project one's values and desires on to the virtual character" and 2) "seeing the virtual character as one's own project in the making, a creature whom I imbue with a certain trajectory through time defined by my aspirations for what I want that character to be and become (within the limitations of her capacities, of course)" (Gee 2003, 55). The projective identity is therefore aspirational: it is the sort of character the player *wants* her virtual identity to become, and reflects the player's values, meaning that in the course of play the player has to think critically and reflect upon those values.

The measure of success in establishing the projective identity is therefore the consistency between the values the player wishes to impose upon the game character, or virtual identity, and the actions the game character is made to perform in the game: "The projective identity… as a project… in the making can fail because I… have caused… the virtual me to do something in the game that the character I want… to be would not or should not do" (Gee 2003, 57). Failure of consistency in establishing a projective identity does not entail making a mistake at playing the game, or breaking the game's rules, but attributing feelings and motives to a game's character and then performing actions in the game world that would be inconsistent with the actions and motives of someone who truly had those feelings and motives.

It is important to note that the feelings and motives attributed to the projective identity need not coincide with those of the game's player, or "real-world identity". For example, many PC role-playing games offer the opportunity for the player to play as either a good or an evil character (a good example here would be LucasArts' *Star Wars: Knights of the Old Republic* series of games). A player may well choose to play as an evil character, but may at some point in the course of play do something "good", an action inconsistent with the evil persona she has decided to assume in the game world, either out of curiosity or expediency or for some other reason. Of course, were the player somehow actually transported, as it were, into the game world, she might wish to behave in a totally different way from that she has chosen to assign to her (in this case, evil) projective identity. The point is that the player *recognises* her projective identity as an identity with a *separate* set of values and desires from her own, and measures how successful she has been in establishing this projective identity by comparing it to her virtual identity, produced by the actual (as opposed to aspirational) results of her playing of the game, and it is this act of measuring which results in the critical self-reflection which the PDP game is specifically designed to encourage. Gee sums this process up in what he calls the "identity principle" of learning:

> Learning involves taking on and playing with identities in such a way that the learner has real choices (in developing the virtual identity) and ample opportunity to meditate on the relationship between new identities and old ones. There is a tripartite play of identities as learners relate, and reflect on, their multiple real-world identities, a virtual identity, and a projective identity (Gee 2003, 67).

In an illustration of this point, Norbert Braun at the University of Trier has developed an interactive game that teaches students about Medieval German history, essentially by simulating dialogues with characters from the past and allowing them to enter the historical narrative as spectators and participants (Braun 2002). This method of participation in the period of history being taught allows the type of projective identity construction described by Gee and which is much more difficult to produce in a traditional classroom setting.

PDP game design

Despite these important examples, so far as we have been able to tell no one has previously modelled the actual process of personal self-reflection, central to becoming a more effective and active learner, through the medium of the interactive computer game. The idea pursued here was to develop a game that encouraged the player to reflect on her role as a player in the game and, by implication, in her life as a student. The game simulates student life and offer players a series of scenarios in which they have to make choices that will determine their success or failure as students. In line with PDP's emphasis on reflection as a process that has implications for all areas of life, the kinds of choices made in the game will impact upon the player's standing on three levels: socially, financially, and academically. Success in the game, as in life, depends first upon managing the interplay of these dimensions of experience and learning. Winning the game consists in finding the optimal balance between them.

Although the game models critical self-reflection, it was never intended to be unduly serious. This would conflict with the nature of play as a freely chosen and inconsequential activity. We anticipate that many students, particularly on multiple playthroughs when differing projective identities are developed, will choose simply to explore the consequences in the game world without directly aiming to "win" the game. We managed the tension between game and reality, however, by ensuring that the rewards for success in the game world were consistent with its character as a game. This includes the possibility of winning the "departmental prize," if a player completes the game with a high score for academic performance. Game messages that relate play successes to the realities of student life will do so with a certain degree of irony, perhaps promoting the idea that a strategic assessment of the relevance of play actions and successes might itself be something worth reflecting upon. The game does not promise to provide a recipe for success; rather it will be presented as a way of highlighting the centrality of reflection to becoming a more effective learner. In this way the PDP game is intended to allow students to "play" at being students by giving them the core aspect of a game – a series of interesting choices – in a simulation of student life.

A number of initial considerations determined the basic structure of the game. Firstly, the game obviously had to be playable by someone with no experience of playing computer games, which meant that it needed to be extremely simple in terms of both graphical representation and control method (for example, a sophisticated 3-D graphical representation would necessarily entail a potentially complicated – to those unfamiliar with 3-D graphical representations of virtual spaces – control system). Arguably, then the PDP game is not quite a computer game in the regular, or commercial, understanding of the term, in which the control method and game interface form a substantial part of the game's aesthetic appeal (Kirkpatrick and Wilson 2005).

Secondly, the game needed to be short, to encourage multiple playthroughs, and consequently the development of new projective identities in each playthrough. In commercial massively-multiplayer online role-playing games (MMORPGs), players invest a great deal of time (and money) in a single avatar, but this would not be appropriate for the PDP game, not only because of the time it would take for players to develop a sufficiently complex character to make the game worthwhile, but principally because the game is designed to simulate *playfully* a real experience, that of being a student, for someone who is actually undergoing (or about to undergo) that experience in reality. This actually makes the game quite unusual. Simulation programmes are usually designed to be played either as a substitute for the real experience (e.g. driving games) or as part of a course of professional training (e.g. professional flight simulators). Even computer sports games are designed to allow their players to play at a level that they would not be able to in reality (e.g. a player of a football game like the *Pro Evolution Soccer* series of games might very well play real games of football, but she would not compete at an international level!). However, the PDP game is intended to represent being a student in a virtual world to a player who is a student in the real world, and this has important consequences for the game's design.

It is crucial to emphasize that the PDP game is not designed to directly train or instruct, as it were, its player on *how to be* a student in the way that a professional flight simulator programme trains its user on how to fly a plane. It is doubtful that a PDP game that sought to train its player in this direct way could be successful or even feasible. For these reasons, it was decided not to develop a game that required a long-term process of development of a single virtual avatar or identity, partly because of practical reasons (students might not complete the game) but mainly because the critical process of reflection then becomes solidified around a single virtual identity which gradually loses correspondence between the real and virtual worlds as the simulation becomes more detailed. By keeping the virtual world as generalised as possible, it was hoped, perhaps ironically, to keep it more convincing.

The basic design of the PDP game was then to be a short game based on a relatively low number (between twenty and thirty) of choices. These choices would affect a series of digital values intended to approximate the experience of being a student. Three different, fairly self-explanatory values were chosen: academic, social and financial. These values were chosen because the beginning of an undergraduate degree course is usually the first time in their lives that first-year students in the U.K. have a significant measure of independent self-control in each of these three areas of life; going to university is usually the first experience that British 18-19-year-old students will have of going into debt, and it is also often the first time students will be living away from the family home and the social supervision of their parents or guardian. These three values are also fairly independent: a student's bank manager is not usually concerned with her academic record; a student's academic supervisor does not usually concern herself with how rich her student is, and a student's friends do not know everything about her academic scores or her bank balance.

It is possible to argue that the delineation of student life into these three categories is already prevalent in the organisation of many British universities; it is equally arguable that such delineation represents a gross simplification of the complexities of student life. However, such simplification actually functions in the PDP game as a major initial factor prompting the type of critical self-reflection produced by the player's construction of a projective identity, as the player realises: "This is how the game is organised, but it's not quite like this in real life, because real life is much more complicated…" This conclusion – that real student life is a great deal more complex than a crude simulation could hope to model, in other words a critical reflection on the properties of student life and the challenges that the student player will face – is precisely the sort of reaction that we hope the game will produce.

The language and the accompanying illustrations with which each choice is presented is, as stated above, deliberately informal and ironic, reminding the player that the game (to be more precise, the *experience* of *playing* the game) is ludic and unserious, and to distinguish the game from other PDP material with which the player might be involved (such as personal journals or message boards). The humorous tone of the game is designed to encourage repeat plays and not immediately to discourage (what the game would define as) failure. Although it is expected that on an initial playthrough, players would make choices similar to those they would make in real life, the brevity of the game encourages repeat playthroughs in which the player might attempt to construct a projective identity which would be very different from how they regard themselves. For example, a player who would think of herself as very level-headed and financially parsimonious would probably initially play the game in such a way as to maintain a high financial score, but on a second play session decide that she will play the game as a profligate social butterfly, just to see how quickly she can go bankrupt. (As noted above, if, during such a playthrough, the player decides not to go bankrupt but modify her virtual behaviour, so she can continue the game a little longer, such a decision represents a modification of her projective identity.)

By encouraging the player to construct, and moderate, numerous projective identities through repeated play sessions, the potential of the PDP game to promote self-aware critical reflection that is the goal of the PDP programme, is maximised. Although the playthrough time of the game is relatively short, we anticipate that critical reflection does not primarily occur *as the game is being played*. Rather, it is *after* each play session that the player-student is encouraged to ask herself questions such as: "Are the consequences of each of my decisions that the game calculates really like the consequences that would obtain in the real world?", "Are the situations the game presents ones which I am really likely to encounter during my time at university?", and, perhaps fundamentally, "Which of my projective or virtual identities am I most like in reality?". Even if the player decides that the game does not properly describe what her experience of university is really like, nevertheless the fact that she has undergone the process of critical self-reflection that is required to actually formulate an answer (even though it is a negative one), means in our view that the PDP game has been successful in achieving its goals.

PDP game play

Good game play is normally characterised by intense concentration and focus on game objectives. There is widespread consensus among game designers that this pleasurable state, in which the learner-player is constantly receiving and acting on information from their senses is caused by "flow" (Csikszentmihalyi 2002). Flow is a function of "skill" and "challenge", where skill denotes game playing ability and challenge the nature of the obstacles put in our path by the game. Flow can be represented in the following way:

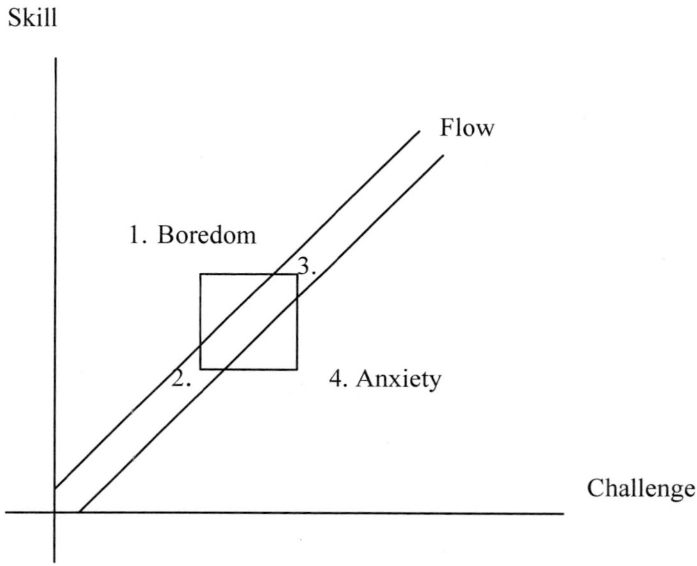

Figure 6-1. Flow (Source: Salen and Zimmerman 2004)

Maintaining flow is achieved by keeping players in the central channel, where they feel that their skills are sufficiently challenged to ward off boredom but not overwhelmed by the difficulty of the game, causing anxiety. In the diagram, positions 2 and 3 represent "flow", while positions 3 and 4 will precipitate player disengagement (Salen and Zimmerman 2004).

In the PDP game, skill is defined in terms of player understanding of the impact of their decisions and choices on game outcomes. A skilful player will master the art of recognising which choices are likely to result in the outcome she seeks, from the specific scenarios favoured by the game. Challenge will be defined in terms of the scenarios. A challenging scenario will involve a set of complex variables drawn from student life and their interplay in a dramatic context. Skilful play will involve maintaining high values attached to the following game variables, each reflecting a crucial dimension of the student experience:

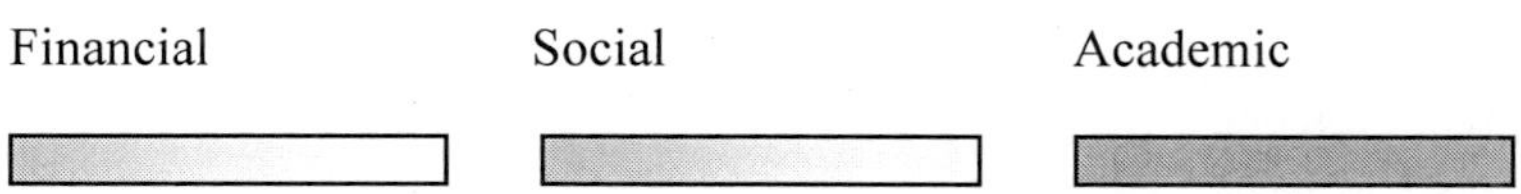

Figure 6-2. Status bars in the PDP game

Each will be represented, as here, by a bar showing the player's current status. As well as offering players "flow", a successful game also requires clear goals – players need to know what they are trying to achieve at any given point. In the PDP game, the primary goal is survive a series of "attacks" from circumstance, without allowing the value of any of the variables shown above to fall below zero. For example, stage four describes a scenario where the player must decide between going to a friend's birthday party, and completing an essay due for the following day. This early stage presents a fairly obvious conflict between social and academic game values and an open choice between them.

The obviousness with which decisions impact upon values will become more opaque as the player progresses through the game and successful variable management will require more reflection by the player on her previous choices. The more complex stage ten describes a scenario in which the player's grandmother becomes ill and the player must choose between visiting her at home, sending her a get well card and phoning home constantly to check on her condition, while "trying not to let her grandmother's condition distract her from her work". Each choice the scenario offers results in a negative value to a game variable: the lesson here is that the player-student will, inevitably, be faced during her studies with situations where there is no obvious "good" outcome and she will be forced to choose between the lesser of two (or, in this case, three) evils.

Stage ten is a good example of how, in the words of game theorist Jesper Juul, "fiction *matters* in games and it is important to remember the duality of the formal and the experiential perspectives on fiction in games" (Juul 2005, 199). The player's grandmother's illness in stage ten is entirely fictional, and the correct choice for the player in terms of the abstract game mechanics would be to select whichever game option is appropriate in terms of her current score in each of the game's three values. However, by playing, as it were, on the player's strong emotional attachments to her real family (emotional attachments which will very often be powerfully strengthened by the homesickness felt by many new students, especially those living far away from the family home) the fiction of the game overpowers the abstract rules in a way which effectively promotes the kind of critical self-reflection that is the ultimate goal of the game.

As the game progresses, the level of ironic humour in the game scenarios also increases; consistent with the idea that students learn best when they are enjoying themselves (Ramsden 1998). This can be seen in stage 20, in which the player can choose to lie in bed when the fire alarm in her accommodation goes off, but if she does so, she "dies" and the game is immediately over. The obvious lesson here is that, although in reality choosing to lie in bed when the fire alarm goes off will not *inevitably* result in one's death in a blazing inferno, it is nevertheless *always* a good idea to get out of bed when one hears the fire alarm; it is in fact the ironic inflexibility of the game's rules that allows the player to draw this conclusion.

The formal goal, once players have learned to survive, will be to reach the end of the game with a high enough score attached to each variable to qualify for "excellence", or game success, represented in the game as the successful awarding of the student's degree.

According to Roger Caillois (1958), at the heart of any game play we usually find some combination of four elements: competition; gambling or risk taking; mimicry (assuming a role, or play-acting), and a kind of reverie associated with respite from the demands of reality. The PDP game offers experiences of all four kinds. Players compete with the program to try and survive and ultimately to attain excellence. The game involves an element of risk because; although strategy will be informed by reflection on past experience each game scenario will require some experimentation and, inevitably, the experience of defeat. The player who is running low on finances, for instance, might just scrape through choosing a night out with their friends – the pay-offs for which will be high in the other two dimensions – but they might not. Weak decisions may not always be what they seem and occasionally, as in life, players might get away with making them. This adds to the excitement essential to any good game. The game involves role-playing, as discussed above and there are "rewards" and "punishments" for success and failure, ranging from winning the departmental prize to finding oneself ejected from university for failing to pass exams.

From the perspective of the player, the core mechanic of the game centres on:

- Balancing values against each other – over-achievement in one will have negative consequences for the others, with excessive socialising leading to a reduction in one's "study" score, for example.
- Maintaining high values in all three bars, without reaching the "tipping" point – some scenarios will have unexpectedly high scores for specific variables, unexpectedly impacting negatively on the others.
- Achieving the goal of survival and then of survival with high "study" value, the (initially concealed) key to achieving "excellence".

If successful, these principles would be implemented in a game that is both fun for students to play and a tool that promotes critical self-reflection.

Computer game play as a repertoire of learning

As stated above, the majority of PDP activity in British universities now occurs in a digital, on-line environment. Consequently the digital context against which the PDP game is to be played is, on the whole, pedagogic and therefore serious: because of the finite amount of IT equipment available to most British universities, frivolous or playful use of university-owned computers is generally discouraged or frowned upon by the institutional authorities, in order that IT resources might be concentrated upon purely productive tasks. This has the adverse effect of leading students to regard the PC in an institutional context as limited to those specific uses sanctioned by the university authorities, which in turn discourages free or creative use of PCs by students, especially those who do not have access to the technology outside of the university: such use of university owned PCs is regarded as transgressive of university protocol.

However, if students are to engage meaningfully with PCs and other digital technologies, they must feel able to learn from them informally, in a play context, as well as in formally planned and/or supervised interactions. After all, it was in an informal play context (students playing around with university owned computers) that the very first computer game, *Spacewar!*, was created, eventually giving rise to today's computer game industry. The PDP game is thus intended to allow its student players to feel able to engage creatively and playfully with the digital technology (not just the computers themselves, but also the digital PDP materials) that their university offers them without committing themselves to doing "work" that will reflect on their permanent academic record, or transgressing their university's codes of conduct. The PDP game is intended to offer a virtual space for digital play, to complement the virtual space for digital work that has become an integral part of the curriculum of British universities.

Technical implementation

1. Requirements

The specification of the game required a system that would allow many students to play the game concurrently (with the potential for different groups of students to play different versions of the game at the same time). Student details would need to be entered manually or downloaded from a university central student database. Individual students should be able to make life choices, taking them from an initial state (the start of their course) to subsequent states (with updated academic, social and financial scores), until they reached a terminal state.

It was required that the content developer of the game be different from the programmer of the game. This was done with a game management system that would allow a non-technical manager to add and change new scenes (as opposed to a system needing new programming for new scenes).

2. Technology solution

A web-based user interface was chosen for reasons of familiarity and easy off-site access.

A database was needed to allow storage of student details and analysis of played games. Server-side (as opposed to client-side) technology was used to free the game from specific client hardware or browser platforms. This also removed the need for testing every possible hardware platform, operating system and browser combination. LAMP (Linux/Apache/Mysql/Php) server technology was chosen, being free and widely used in academia. The relational database consisted of normalised (efficiently designed) data tables, with data tables for:

- students/managers
- games
- game pages
- game page options
- rules
- student play log

Login data was passed from screen to screen using cookies. The state of the game for each student at any given time was stored in the student database table. Information entered by students was passed from screen to screen as part of the URL (web page address).

3. Game management system

The game management system is entered via a logon page. This allows managers to access screens for:

- display of game(s)
- display of student activity (from the log file)
- student data, e.g. name, student id, password
- game manager data, e.g. name, staff id, password

- initialisation of all students' playing states
- update game – allowing the manager to add, delete or change a game
- copy game - allowing different versions of the game to be developed (e.g. for speculative modified versions to be tested, as well as different department/institution versions to be run)
- logout

Games contain:

- a description
- initial academic, social and financial scores
- pages, organised into stages

The Pages of Games contain:

- text (the scenario)
- a picture (with an alternative text description – required for SENDA accessibility compliance)
- student selectable Page options.

The Options of Game Pages (usually three) contain:

- text (the description of the possible student choice)
- an optional message to be displayed on selection of that option
- fixed and recurrent changes to the financial, social and academic scores
- the page to be displayed on selection of the option.

Additional to this functionality are rules, which may be linked to particular pages or active throughout the game. These rules specify that if social, financial or academic scores lie within certain values, then a message may be displayed and/or a jump may be made to a specific page. These rules take precedence over the next page calculation described in the previous paragraph. One use of the rules function is to terminate students having an unacceptable financial, social or academic score.

4. Student playing system

The student playing system starts with a login page. It requires that the students enter their public id and a password.

The screen below (Figure 6-3) is the initial playing page, but has a similar format to all subsequent pages except the terminating page. It displays the student's name, game name, scores, and messages from previous screens (if any), scenario and options.

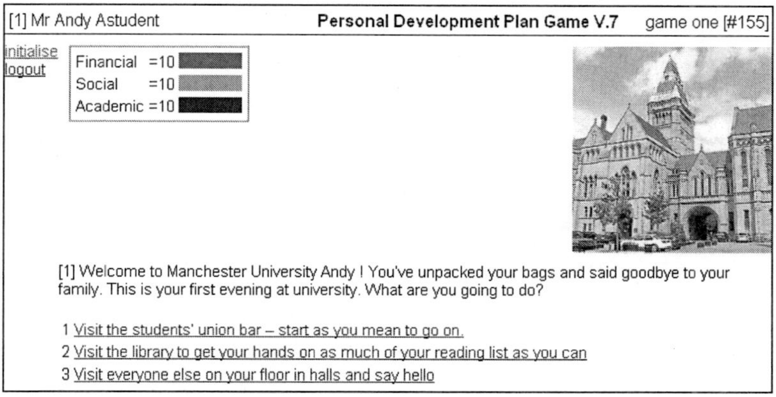

Figure 6-3. Initial playing page of the PDP game

Once a selection is made, then the new financial, social and academic scores are calculated. This is done from:

- existing fixed financial, social and academic scores
- existing recurrent financial, social and academic score changes
- fixed scores changes from the selection just made
- recurrent score changes from the selection just made.

An example of fixed score change is *going to the library*, which might increase the student's academic score. An example of a recurrent score change is *choosing to use busses without buying a bus pass*, which results in a negative recurrent financial score.

The selection that the student makes decides which next page is displayed. The next page may however be overridden by game or page rules, which inspect the scores, and if they lie within particular ranges, then a new page will be selected. Examples of this include:

- If the Financial score is low but positive, then a bank manager's letter will be displayed
- If Financial score is negative, then financial collapse causes a termination page to be displayed

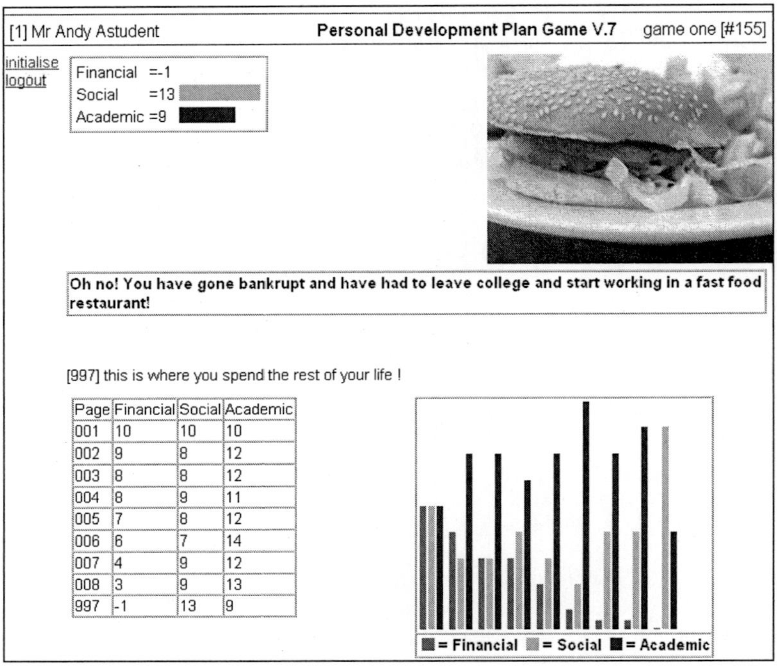

Page	Financial	Social	Academic
001	10	10	10
002	9	8	12
003	8	8	12
004	8	9	11
005	7	8	12
006	6	7	14
007	4	9	12
008	3	9	13
997	-1	13	9

Figure 6-4. Terminating page of the PDP game

The terminating page (Figure 6-4) provides graphical data not represented on previous screens which show the students how their scores have lead to their demise or success.

Possible future game implementations and suggestions

The game prototype has currently been programmed with around twenty-five questions or stages designed to reflect a general conception of student life. The game engine is fully reprogrammable to allow either new questions (e.g. those specific to certain institutions, courses or student groups) or modification of existing questions in response to player feedback, which can be taken into account when any modifications are made.

When introducing students to the game for the first time, we recommend emphasising the ludic quality of the PDP game, and clearly stating that players will *not* be assessed or judged on the basis of how they play the game, so that they are free to play through the game as and how they choose to. This is the best way of promoting the critical reflection that the game is designed to produce. Unlike other PDP materials, the PDP game is intended to work best when players are entirely free to govern their own interactions with the programme, and if players feel that anything depends on how well they play the PDP game, or whether they win or lose, the game will not be as useful.

References

Braun, N. 2002. Narrative semiotics for computer games. Paper presented to The Challenge of Computer Games conference, 25th-27th October, University of Łodz, Poland.

Caillois, R. 1958. *Man, play and games*. Illinois: University of Illinois Press.

Csikszentmihalyi, M. 2002. *Flow: The classic work on how to achieve happiness*. New York: Rider and Co.

Dewey, J. 2004. *Democracy and education*. New York: R.A. Kessinger.

Gee, J. P. 2003. *What video games have to teach us about learning and literacy*. Basingstoke: Palgrave Macmillan.

Griffiths, M. D., and M. N. O. Davies. 2002. Excessive online gaming: Implications for education. *Journal of Computer Assisted Learning* 18: 379-380.

Juul, J. 2005. *Half-Real: Video games between real rules and fictional worlds*. Cambridge, MA: MIT Press.

Kirkpatrick, G. 2005. On-line chat rooms as pedagogic tools. *Active Learning in Higher Education* 6(1): 145-159.

Kirkpatrick, G., and J. W. G. Wilson. 2005. Plastic homunculus: Controllers, hands and ludo-eyes'. Paper presented to the Playful Subjects conference, 13th-14th May, University of the West of England, Bristol.

National Committee of Enquiry into Higher Education. 1997. Chair Ron Dearing, http://www.leeds.ac.uk/educol/ncihe/ (retrieved February, 2006).

Ramsden, P. 1998. *Teaching and learning in higher education*. London: Routledge.

Salen, K. and E. Zimmerman. 2004. *Rules of play: Game design fundamentals*. London: MIT Press.

CHAPTER SEVEN

WHEN ALL ELSE FAILS: THE INTERNET AND ADOLESCENT-IMMIGRANTS' INFORMAL LEARNING [1]

NELLY ELIAS AND DAFNA LEMISH

Every year, thousands of people, many of them children and adolescents, cross the borders of various countries in search of an improved standard of living, family unification, or political asylum. Accordingly, many immigrants experience what is considered to be one of the most difficult, complex processes in a person's life - one that requires long-term social learning and adaptation to new and unfamiliar surroundings.

Extensive academic research has examined the various roles the mass media, and especially television in the host and native languages, fulfill in the process of immigrants' social and cultural learning (e.g. Chaffee, Naas and Yang 1990, Stilling 1997). Though the media in the immigrants' native language have generally been perceived as a main tool for cultural preservation, and on occasion seen as counter influence to the acculturation effect of host-language media (Lee and Tse 1994, Stilling 1997), more recent studies (e.g. Elias forthcoming, Hwang and He 1999) have found that media in the host country produced especially for immigrants in their native language was a more effective means of social learning due to cultural proximity and ability to overcome the language barrier.

Yet, very little is known about the socializing roles that mass media, in general, and the Internet, in particular, have in the lives of immigrant children and adolescents who are faced with unique personal and social challenges, above and beyond those of the adult immigrants. In addition to the turbulent period of adolescence, characterized, among other things, with a disassociation from family and old role models and the search for a mature identity, young immigrants also find themselves confronted with the difficulties involved with migration to a new, and often quite hostile, society. Both existential processes - adolescence and migration in one junction in life - require on-going, active adjustments. The weakening of "old" socialization agents - be they friends, teachers, or parents - that occurs during adolescence (Buhrmester 1996, Kroger 1996, Steinberg 1990) is even more dramatic for immigrant teenagers who have been uprooted from their native land.

Moreover, in the relocation process, the clearly defined hierarchy between children and parents is significantly challenged, since immigrant parents are often dependent on their children as their guides into the new surroundings due to the latters' advanced linguistic capabilities. Immigrant parents can suffer from a dramatic decline in their professional and employment status, and find themselves at a severe social disadvantage as they struggle to adjust to the new society. Hence, alongside a "natural" decline in parental authority typical to coming of age, immigrant teenagers may be even more critical of their "incompetent" parents (Sluzki 1979).

At the same time, immigrant teenagers often experience disappointment in the new teachers they encounter in their host country, as their different teaching methods are frequently interpreted as a lack of professional skills (Horowitz 1999). Their approach to the new educational system is characterized by distrust and disrespect as they nostalgically glorify the familiar educational system from which they were abruptly uprooted. Additionally, young immigrants often have difficulty finding a new referent group among local peers due to the language and cultural barriers and, as a result, they can develop a strong sense of alienation (Gottesfeld and Mirsky 1992, Mirsky 2001). With the weakening of the traditional socializing agents, on one hand, and distrust of the local socializing agents, on the other hand, the mass media become central agents of socialization, providing young immigrants with important sets of knowledge about their new society, its mores, norms, and behavioral patterns.

In an illustrative example, Zohoori (1988) found that television appears to be an important source of education and information about their new society for children who immigrated to the United States. Likewise, our on-going research on immigrant children from the Former Soviet Union (FSU) to Israel and Germany (Elias and Lemish 2006, 2008) suggests the growing importance of the mass media during the initial stage of settling down and adjustment to the new society. We found that media play a central role both in the immigrant children's orientation "inward" to their home-culture and family consolidation (e.g. instilling linguistic skills, transmitting cultural heritage, and spending family leisure time together) as well as in "outward" integration into the host culture and local peer group (e.g. instilling linguistic skills of host-language, adoption of local youth culture, and spending time with peers).

Alongside the importance of "traditional" media in the lives of immigrant children and adolescents, we learn from the extant literature on non-migrant children that the Internet, too, might play a central role in the process of social learning and adjustment, as it can simultaneously serve as a source of information, a cultural resource, and the only "safe" area for trying on new social roles and identities (e.g. gender, ethnicity, age) without fear, typical to immigrant adolescents, of being punished due to "inappropriate" behavior or unaccepted appearance (Suler 2002, Turkle 1996, Valkenburg, Schouten, and Peter 2005).

Indeed, the current discussion of the Internet as an alternative model of learning suggests that this medium moves us away from a linear transmission model of learning to an active, "learning by doing" model that breaks down knowledge hierarchies and emphasizes learning how to find information instead of presenting the information. Such theorizing suggests that the Internet reverses the modern model of structural-institutional learning and brings learning back into the home and to the leisure environment (Livingstone 2002).

In order to pursue this line of thought, the present study sought to investigate the roles of the Internet as an emerging agent of informal learning and socialization for immigrant teenagers from the FSU to Israel. In doing so, we focused on the roles and meanings these adolescents assign to the Internet use in the entangled transitions they are making into both adolescence and to a new society, at one and the same time.

Methodology

In order to investigate this question we conducted in-depth interviews in 2005 with 70 immigrant youth aged 12-18 who had been living in Israel between six months and five years. The sample consisted of 27 boys and 43 girls, and was solicited using the "snow-ball" non-random sampling method (Deacon, Pickering, Golding, and Murdock 1998). While the sample is not representative, a special effort was made to recruit youth representing different profiles of the immigrant population from the FSU. The sample was equally divided between the urban center of Israel and the periphery, in this case smaller towns in the southern part of the country, and between the more veteran immigrants who have been living in Israel three to five years and newcomers who have been living between six months and three years. The interviewees' age and the time lived in Israel are indicated in parenthesis as (16, 1½).

The interviews took place in the youths' bedroom and lasted on an average one hour. The interviews focused on the main patterns of media usage, while distinguishing between different print and electronic media in the Russian, Hebrew and English languages; the gratifications sought and acquired from these media; and the roles of different media in the interviewees' social and family lives. In addition, a series of open-ended questions were asked about various aspects of the interviewees' social and cultural integration, such as the use of Russian and host languages in everyday life; friendships with Israeli-born children; and the sense of belonging to the host society and to the original homeland.

Even though the interviews did not focus intentionally on the Internet, this medium emerged as a central theme. As a result, a significant part of the interview was directed to questions regarding the interviewees' access to the Internet; how much time they spent surfing the Internet; favorite websites, their main characteristics and the reasons for surfing these sites; other Internet-related activities; and patterns of Internet surfing before the immigration.

The interviewees agreed to participate in the research willingly, and we encountered only a few refusals. At the end of each interview, the interviewee received a small payment (equivalent to 12 $) as a token of appreciation for her/his time and attention. Two trained research assistants of Russian origin conducted all interviews in Russian. The interviews were tape-recorded, transcribed per verbatim, and submitted to a grounded analysis from which emerged the main themes discussed by the full complement of interviewees.

Findings

The many roles that the media play in the lives of immigrant families that emerged from this study are discussed elsewhere (Elias and Lemish 2006, 2008). Here we focus on the central roles that the medium of the Internet was playing in these young immigrants' lives. What we learned was that many of the uses of the Internet were involved in an intensive learning process about the new society. This use stands in stark contrast to the findings from studies of the Internet usage of non-migrant teenagers, who devoted most of their Internet time to school work, personal communication, and to gaming (see for example, Livingstone and Bober 2005). The following findings reveal the various learning related roles of Internet in the lives of immigrant teenagers, as they take their first steps to settling down into their new home.

First, most of the interviewees started using the Internet only after the immigration to Israel. Before immigration, only 15 of the 70 interviewees had any access to the Internet, whereas in Israel 62 interviewees used Internet regularly, at least once a week. The average time of surfing was two hours per day. 52 interviewees had an Internet connection at home, and 38 had one in their bedroom. Having a computer in their bedroom usually meant that the interviewee had exclusive access to the Internet, though sometimes they had to share it with their father or with younger brothers and sisters. Ten interviewees, who stated that they surf regularly but do not have a computer at home, usually had access at school and more rarely at their friends' house.

Analysis of the interview-transcripts revealed that Internet surfing served a number of functions for the immigrants: Their socialization was advanced since the Internet was used as the main tool for learning about their new social and cultural surroundings; it helped them gain recognition and respect because it was used to engage in informal instruction of their Israeli peers about their homeland; and as an information-source that facilitated learning in the areas of personal interest to reinforce their self-confidence and positive image in the eyes of their local mates. We turn now to a discussion of these three complementary aspects of informal learning from the Internet by immigrant adolescents.

Learning about the host society

The most urgent task involved with the relocation of immigrant youth into the new society is the need for adjustment of the former lifestyle to the new cultural demands, meeting the challenges posed by the need to learn the host language, norms of behavior, customs, and the like. Our findings suggest that Russian-speaking adolescents find the Internet to be a very accessible and useful tool for such conscious efforts. By accessing Russian-language websites that offer information about Israeli society, the Internet enables them to overcome language barriers, so central to cultural integration. At the same time it provides the young immigrants with a non-threatening environment within which to explore their budding Hebrew skills, without being a target of ridicule or misunderstandings.

The information sought on the Internet extends along a continuum: from the macro issues of understanding Judaism and Jewish life in Israel, learning about Israeli politics and the local youth culture to the micro level of practical information related to everyday life in school, behavioral patterns expected in the local discotheques, courting behaviors, youth-fashion, and the like. The illustrations below suggest how many of these themes are entangled with one another in the interviewees' spontaneous responses. Moreover, it was evident in many interviews that immigrant teenagers were aware of their parents' incompetence regarding various aspects of life in Israel; hence, instead of consulting with them they surfed the Internet for both practical information and prospects for a better future. For example, Jenia (16, 1), uses a Russian-language Internet website to learn about her reality in Israel, including information about other Israeli cities, in search of a better place to live in the future:

> There is this site that translates things from Russian to Hebrew. That's important. It helps me survive. There are news sites, about the political and economic situation in Israel. They explain the world we live today. And besides this, there is this *mail.ru*. I use it more for chats. I enter a chat, choose a topic and correspond. I can ask all kinds of questions and receive all kinds of answers; for example, about life in a different city. Let's say, Herzelia [a prestigious town in the center of Israel]. Is it good or bad there? What's interesting there, how is the weather? We don't plan to live in Beer-Sheva [a peripheral city in the south] forever. Later we will decide where we wish to live.

It could be seen from Jenia's quote that the Internet also facilitates inter-personal communication within the Russian-speaking immigrant community through the chats. In this way, the more experienced immigrants serve as additional agents of socialization for the newcomers and transmit to them valuable knowledge about the host society. For immigrant teenagers, in particular, it is also the easiest way to conduct an exchange with other adults who might have more knowledge about the new surroundings than do their own parents.

Likewise, Niya (15, 1½) is also very goal-oriented in her Internet usage. She explained:

> I search for everything on the Internet. A vacation in Eilat [a resort town on the Red Sea], for example. I look at pictures […] about Haifa [a port city in the north of Israel] or the Mediterranean Sea. And I registered on a portal that has all kinds of important and interesting things – jokes, stories, techniques, trips, and vacations. In techniques I am interested in information about cars, trips – where is there a good place to travel.

In contrast to interviewees like Niya and Jenia, who were searching for practical information about material aspects of life in Israel (e.g. most popular cars, prestigious towns, or trendy trips abroad, thus adjusting their aspirations and goals to those of the local Israelis), other interviewees were looking for more "spiritual" information, such as insights into Israeli cultural traditions and Judaism. Since most of the interviewees were recent immigrants who still had difficulty reading Hebrew, Russian-language websites originating in Israel became a most useful resource for such information. Thus, Misha (13, 1.5) said:

> I use the Internet a lot. You can learn on the Internet about customs, holidays, kosher laws and [Jewish] tradition. I have an address of such sites in Russian. I have seen Internet sites that explain about Israeli customs.

In the interview, Misha related how the information he finds on the net is often in contradiction to what his history teacher claims. Hence, the Internet provides him an oppositional reading of the non-Jewish identity ascribed by the teacher to new immigrants from the FSU.

Likewise, Masha (12, 1.5) turns to the Russian-language Internet sites to explore Judaism, its practices and meanings:

> Lately it is more important for me to know what's happening here. It is not strange that I read news about Israel in Russian on the Internet. I want to be sure that I understand things accurately... Sometimes I enter *istoki.ru* – it's a Russian-language website about Judaism. I like to surf it and read about the Jewish family, about the roles of the woman in the family, about [Jewish] lifestyle. It attracts me. […] But once I also ran into an interview with a very important religious person from Israel. He said that those who came from Russia – are not real Jews; that we should not be accepted [as Jews and therefore as Israelis]. I try not to pay attention. But why does he get to determine who is a real Jew and who is not?[...] I don't understand this.

Notice, that Masha also used Russian-language Internet sites to learn about Israel, thus overcoming the language limitations she still has as a relatively newcomer to Israel. As is evident in Masha's recollection of her Internet experience, she does not just absorb Internet information uncritically, but challenges and negotiates it. This pattern repeated itself in many of the interviews, but almost exclusively in regard to the treatment of "Russians" by the native-born Israelis. This reinforces the argument that the more familiar one is with the subject matter appearing in the media and the more one has invested interest in it, the more capable one is of being critical and argumentative with the mediated version (Lemish 2007).

Moreover, both Misha and Masha express a deep sense of estrangement from and mistrust in native-born Israelis, be they a teacher of history or a religious authority. In both cases interviewees complained of the lack of acceptance facing Russian-speaking immigrants by their local counterparts, a lack that, in their view, stemmed from their being labeled as non-Jews by the religious authorities, among other reasons. Hence, in order to learn more about Judaism, both interviewees turned to the Internet as the best of all choices. In this way the Internet could also serve as an important tool for these teenagers personal empowerment, since it provided them with information about the issues that were perceived as "closed" to them due to their questionable Jewishness.

Another type of informal learning through the Internet related to incorporation into their new society was found in several interviews where immigrant teenagers tried to correspond with their local counterparts in order to improve their language skills. Many interviewees complained of a lack of personal contacts with their local peers or of painful consequences of unsuccessful attempts to establish such connections. On the other hand, contacts established through the Internet provided them with a relatively safe environment where they could initiate contacts with the local teenagers without fear of being mistreated or ridiculed. Thus, Elina (15, 1.5) recalled:

> Once I surfed to a chat room in Hebrew and started corresponding with some Israeli guy. […] It was very difficult for me to write in Hebrew, so I wrote Hebrew words with Latin letters. […] I would like to continue to correspond with him in order to improve my knowledge of the language through such writing.

In addition to direct questions on Internet uses for learning purposes, the interviewees were also asked more specifically to describe what they would do with media if they had a friend from their homeland visiting them. This question was based on our assumption that the interviewees would mention those media that helped them learn about the new society. And, indeed, this is what happened in most of the interviews. Many mentioned the Internet as a means of introducing Israel to newcomers. For example, Andrei (16, 5) responded:

> I am used to entering news-sites in Israel. Is there a [teacher] strike? Are there any news about Beer-Sheva [his hometown]? If a friend from Russia will come visit me, I'll show him pictures from my trips. And of course – there is the Internet! I can show him what I like on the Internet – the Golan Heights, the desert, the blossom in the Galilee. All kinds of pictures you can find on the Internet.

We can conclude that of all media available to new FSU immigrant youth, including various media in their mother tongue, such as television channels, radio stations and newspapers, the Internet was the one more often cited and elaborated upon as the major source of much valued information and learning in their on-going process of cultural integration and socialization into the new society.

Teaching about the homeland

In order to investigate the potential of the Internet in learning about the former homeland and its culture, we asked the interviewees how they would use the Internet to teach their local mates about Russia. This theme was often brought up more as a "wishful" function, rather then an actual one, something one "could do" or "wish to do" rather than something one actually does on a regular basis. For example, Olga (17, 5) responded directly to a question about how to break social barriers with Israeli youth and to familiarize them with the immigrants' Russian origins:

> If I had to tell Israelis about Russia, I would use the Internet first of all. Pictures of Moscow, St. Petersburg. And it is very important to tell them about the Russian village. I can download from the Internet pictures of villages. Here children do not know what a Russian village is. They are familiar with a kibbutz, but they don't know what it's like to guard the cows, run after the ducks… that's what they don't have here. That's what I miss, too.

Similarly, Kiril (16, 3) explained:

> I search on the Internet for all the information I need. Through Google I can find pictures of Minsk [the city he came from]. I have entered many times in order to look at pictures of Minsk… it's the homeland. I download these pictures so that later I can show them to my Israeli friends: "See where I lived! It is not Beer-Sheva" [the Israeli city were he currently lives in, is, according to him: "a small town, dirty and crowded – in comparison to Minsk].

The nostalgic feelings and sense of pride involved in the potential use of the Internet for re-connecting to the homeland and for introducing it to Israelis is very evident in the following example. Jenia (16, 1) expressed her feelings and gratitude for the Internet as follows:

> It is outstanding that we have the Internet. Thanks to whoever created it. Thanks to the Internet, I can feel the homeland closer to me, as if part of it exists on the Web. I wish I could show Russia to Israelis. On the Internet I can find information about the big theaters, famous statues, big factories,

> about St. Petersburg. You can download pictures. There is this site of the iron-plant in Magnitogorsk [a big industrial city in Siberia where she was born]; it's in our city. How they established it, how it is developing – here in Israel there aren't things like that.

However, the Internet is perceived as a double-edge sword: It is a medium where both negative stereotypes and put-downs against Russians thrive, just as it is a reliable and legitimate resource, a cultural "witness," for discrediting these common attitudes. The frustration and pain over social stigmas expressed in the following quote is very evident. Rita (13, 5) shared the emotional pain she is experiencing and the relief she feels from being able to access the Internet:

> Russians are treated badly, not only by Israelis, but also by Americans on the Internet. I surf many USA and Israeli forums. Everybody makes fun of Russians. They think that we are primitive. For example, they think that when in all the other countries people were studying and developing new ideas, in Russia people just drank vodka. They said that the Russians are primitive and live like animals. That's how our [Israeli] teacher taught us. But I know this is not true. You can surf the Russian Internet and see that this is not true! There is abundance of information about Russian history, scientists, inventors, about culture and art… It is a fact that people lie about the Russians, but that's how it is customary to think around the world. It's a fact. I wish I was without a nationality, just like that, a citizen of the world.

Here, too, as in the case of learning about Israeli society through the Internet, some of the young users are actively engaging with the medium, if not in real interactive manner, then in a form of mental dialogue. Such an example is provided by Andrei (16, 5) who related his desire to react to social stigmas on the Internet:

> In the Internet there are many negative responses about Russians. In the news sites [in Hebrew] there are news and then comments. Everyone can comment. So first I read the news – and then the comments. When I read an unjustified critic of Russians, I feel like writing something… very long… for example, when they write that all the Russians are drunk, I feel like responding – but I am not! This topic, the attitude towards the Russians, really bothers me a lot. Those stigmas that Russians are drunk, that they don't want to learn Hebrew […] I love my neighborhood, but I still can't say that I feel really at home. I feel like a guest.

The desire to use the Internet as a source of "evidence", a "show and tell" of how things "should be" following the homeland model is evident even in personal matters, such as codes of dress and the definition of "attractiveness." Anastasia (13, 2) confessed the following:

> I don't like Israeli boys. They walk around in dirty and torn clothes. In our place in the Ukraine everybody was clean, dressed nicely. When I am sad, I surf the Internet. I can find pictures there, interesting stories about Russia, even to remind myself what a man should look like. I wish I could show this to my classmates at school. So they would see how everything there is so handsome… I do very much want Israelis to understand how they should dress. This is very important if we are to raise the Russian immigrants' status […] Israelis don't like the Russian immigrants. They like other Israelis. […] They hate the Russians; they just hate.

The Internet, so it seems, serves as a central arena for learning about societal stereotypes associated with one's ethnic identity and at the same time it is a resource for countering them and reinforcing pride in one's origins and cultural background. This is immediately related to our third theme, which deals with the personal implications of this duality for young immigrants' personal self-confidence and self-esteem.

Learning from the internet and self-confidence

One of the central themes that emerged in the analysis was the role the Internet plays in the construction of identities of these immigrant youth (see Elias, Lemish, and Khvorostianov 2008). More specifically related to this chapter, informal learning from the Internet was often immediately relevant to these adolescents' formation of self-confidence and construction of a positive self-image. For example, Ania A. (12, 1.5) explained how the Internet helped her reduce some of her anxieties and insecurities:

> First of all I enter Google and read the news in Hebrew. Through the news I discovered that in Israel there are sports, concerts. I discovered that Israel is not a completely different world. It gave me a sense of security that I am not in a totally foreign world. When we came to Israel, we thought that Israel is a completely new country, and that we will need to learn everything anew, but it turned out that the difference is only in the language.

Several of the interviewees related how they use knowledge gained through the Internet to improve their social status. Masha (13, 3) shared the following:

> My favorite site is one that a girl from my class built about our school: about teachers and students, what happens during the day, who fought with whom, who made friends with whom. I don't like so much to stick my nose in things that are not my business, so at school I am not involved. So I enter the Internet site to find out what's happening in school. I don't like to hang around and ask about things, and this way I just read one opinion, just to be in. I mean that if someone asks me about something, at least I can respond. When I come to school I know what's going on. It is quite understandable, since in school I am not at the center of things. I tried to improve my status, but it's not working out.

Ania B. (12, 5) tells us that she is very persistent in recruiting the Internet as a means of providing her with a relative advantage over her Israeli classmates. She explained:

> I like Google. It's a search engine. I search everything for homework. All kinds of interesting things. I like to search for new information, new knowledge [...] Sometimes I feel worthless. As if Russians are not as good as Israelis. And I try to be better than them. In schoolwork, in general knowledge, in those things that Russians are better at. I am proud of the fact that I am a good student, that I know lots of things. But knowledge – it's only the amount of information you collected, it is not really wisdom. And I try to cope with it. Thanks to the Internet I always have something to say.

However, the Internet is used not only to reduce anxieties and improve one's status within the peer group, it is also applied to challenge the new, formal socializing agents - like teachers in the Israeli educational system. For example, Misha (13, 1.5) related the following incident:

> In my opinion our teacher doesn't even know what is Tu-Beshvat [Jewish holiday celebrating the spring renewal of trees and nature]. Once she told us something, and I remembered it very well, because my grandma explained it to me almost the opposite way. So I checked on an Internet site called 'Rabbis' and my grandma was right. I didn't argue with the teacher. There is no point. I just know that I am right.

The Internet, in this case, served to confirm information provided by a source that Misha deemed credible (his grandmother), in opposition to the less credible new sources of information available to him - his teacher, and thus he acts as a "neutral" judge resolving a conflict between the "old" and the "new" socializers.

Like Misha, Marat (15, 1.5) explained that he does not trust his Israeli karate instructor (his favorite hobby), so he checks the Internet for better explanations of the new moves. This helps him to raise his self-confidence and makes him feel better prepared for a fight:

> I visit websites of famous athletes. Read about them, look at their pictures. I am an athlete myself. […] I study karate. In Russia I didn't have access to the Internet, so I learned in class, it was enough. Here, in Israel, the karate instructors are not good. That's why I am looking for the websites dedicated to karate. For example, in class we learn some new moves, and then I look for explanations on the Web. For more nuances how to perform it right. In karate it is even important where you look while doing a certain move. In the Internet you can find everything.

The view that it is possible to find on the Internet any kind of information in order to satisfy personal interests emerged, too, in an interview with Nina (15, 4):

> There are several things that interest you and you'd like to know more about them, but at home we don't have books, whereas on television it is not deep enough. Therefore, if you're very interested in some topic, you'd rather surf the Internet. There you can find detailed information and other people's opinions on this subject, which is also very interesting. For example, I visited a website 'Cats' portal' [in Russian] and there I found a list of literature about cats […]. So I started looking for these books and read them and it was very interesting. Otherwise, without the Internet, I would never hear about such books. Another example, I was looking for information to what species my cat belongs. It was important for me to know. So I visited several sites on cats' species and looked at the pictures of different cats.

It can be seen from this quote that Nina (as well as other immigrant teenagers) suffers from a lack of books at home that could satisfy her curiosity. She defined the Internet as the richest and most available source of information, also in comparison with television, whose potential to fulfill her intellectual interests and distinguish her as a unique individual is far more limited.

Discussion and conclusions

The evidence presented in this chapter suggests that adolescents who have immigrated from the Former Soviet Union to Israel perceive the Internet to be a central - as well as most credible - source of information that provides a wide range of possibilities for informal learning about their new society, about their former homeland, as well as, for maintaining their high self-esteem and personal hobbies and interests. Some of the expressions they use - such as "It is outstanding that we have the Internet. Thanks to who ever created it. It helps me survive" - highlight the empowering potential they assign to this medium and their heavy dependency on it for easing their way into a new and sometimes hostile environment. In particular, we found that the Internet provides the young immigrants with an extremely accessible and effective tool for informal learning under severe shortage of material and informational resources and the weakening of social resources typical to immigration. This was found to be particularly true for those youths who have spent less than two years in Israel, suggesting that the initial, most difficult stage of adjustment, requires the recruitment of all possible resources they can put at their disposal.

It is interesting to note that the Internet also helps to ease the most important cultural barrier of all - the linguistic one, as it frees immigrant youth from their linguistic disadvantages. Many reported accessing Russian-language websites on a regular basis to retrieve information about Israel and Judaism. At the same time, the opposite was also found to be true, when those immigrants who had no access to Internet at home often surfed the Hebrew-language websites at school for information about their homeland. This seeming contradiction suggests that the linguistic diversity offered by the Internet releases the pressure associated with acquisition of the host language, and the social negative sanctions applied by peer groups for using the Russian language that marks one as an "outsider." On the Internet, one is free to live in one's chosen linguistic virtual world and to access information in the language of one's choice.

Beyond the language diversity, the Internet provided the most easily accessed and widely applicable source of information for immigrant youth who need to study almost everything from scratch - from names of streets to fashion codes, from Jewish traditions to places to go on vacation. The Internet offered the adolescent immigrants access to all of this in a private and efficient manner. Furthermore, in contrast to other media, the Internet requires an active learner who directs the search for information, not a passive viewer, reader, or listener who is at the mercy of mass media offerings.

Finally, it is important to emphasize that the Internet offers immigrant adolescents not only the "formal" and unidirectional information provided by electronic newspapers or websites belonging to organizations, but also information created by other surfers, be they immigrants like themselves or local residents. This facilitates a transfer of valuable knowledge from more experienced to more recent immigrants. In other words, through the different forms of interpersonal communication based on Internet technology, such as chats and forums, immigrant adolescents easily establish contacts with other users, and in this way they gain access to information regarding any aspect of the host society or their personal interests. This finding is especially important due to the fact that host residents usually fail in the role of socialization agents due to mutual mistrust and prejudices as well as their having only occasional, superficial contacts with the new immigrants (Al-Haj 1998, Leshem 1998, Pfetsch 1999). It seems that the Internet helps to break this barrier, as it provides the new immigrants with less stressful opportunities to address their local counterparts, without fear of being rejected or misunderstood. We can therefore conclude that when all others fail - parents, teachers, local peers, and even other immigrants - it is the Internet that serves as the most important teacher of all.

These conclusions can have significant implications for formal learning, as well. As noted, we have found that there is a gap between informal and formal use of the Internet. Young immigrants are much more motivated to use the Internet informally in their process of learning about the host culture and are quite suspicious of formal socializing agents. The formal education system, for its part, has yet to recognize the potential advantages of the Internet as a major resource for immigrant adolescents' education and socialization. Such an initiative, for example, might be development of a formal program that can assist young immigrants to select and to access appropriate educational and informational websites that provide them with much needed, accurate, diverse, and rich information, crucial for their integration (e.g. websites dealing with the state of Israel, cultural life in the country, Judaism, the Middle East conflict, etc). Taking advantage of their special interest in and dependency on the Internet could be accompanied by efforts to promote Internet literacy among immigrant students in order to assist them to maximize the benefits of the medium.

Notes

[1] The authors would like to thank the Israel Foundations Trustees for their generous support of this study.

References

Al-Haj, M. 1998. Soviet Immigration as viewed by Jews and Arabs: Divided attitudes in a divided country. In *Immigration to Israel*, ed. E.

Leshem and J. Shuval, 211-228. New Brunswick and London: Transaction.

Buhrmester, D. 1996. Need fulfillment, interpersonal competence, and the developmental contexts of early adolescent friendship. In *The company they keep: Friendship in childhood and adolescence*, ed. W. M. Bukowski, A. F. Newcomb, and W. W. Hartup, 158-185. New York: Cambridge University Press.

Chaffee, S. H., C. I. Naas, and S. M. Yang. 1990. The bridging role of television in immigrant political socialization. *Human Communication Research* 17(2): 266-288.

Deacon, D., M. Pickering, P. Golding, and G. Murdock. 1999. *Researching communications: A practical guide to methods in media and cultural analysis*. London: Arnold.

Elias, N. (forthcoming). *Coming home: Media and returning diaspora in Israel and Germany*. New York: SUNY Press.

Elias, N., and D. Lemish. 2006. Between three cultures: Media in the lives of immigrant children in Israel and Germany. Paper presented at the Annual Conference of the International Communication Association, June 19-22, in Dresden, Germany.

Elias, N., and D. Lemish. 2008. Media uses in immigrant families: Between "inward" and "outward" paths of integration. *International Communication Gazette* 70(1): 23-42.

Elias, N., D. Lemish, and N. Khvorostianov. 2008. Re-inventing homeland identities: The Russian internet in the lives of immigrant adolescents from the FSU in Israel. In *New media and innovative technologies*, ed. T. Samuel-Azran and D. Caspi, 188-210. Beer-Sheva: Ben-Gurion University Press.

Gottesfeld, J., and J. Mirsky. 1992. To stay or to return: Rapprochement processes in the migration of adolescents and young adults. *Journal of Contemporary Psychotherapy* 21(4): 272-284.

Horowitz, T. 1999. *Children of perestroika in Israel*. Lanham: UPA.

Hwang, B., and Z. He. 1999. Media uses and acculturation among Chinese immigrants in the USA. *Gazette* 61(1): 5-22.

Kroger, J. 1996. *Identity in adolescence: The balance between self and other*. London: Routledge.

Lee, W., and D. Tse. 1994. Changing media consumption in a new home: Acculturation patterns among Hong Kong immigrants to Canada. *Journal of Advertising* 23(1): 57-70.

Lemish, D. 2007. *Children and television: A global perspective*. Oxford: Blackwell.

Leshem, E. 1998. The Israeli public's attitudes toward the new immigrants of the 1990s. In *Immigration to Israel*, ed. E. Leshem and J. Shuval, 307-332. New Brunswick, NJ: Transaction.

Livingstone, S. 2002. *Young people and new media*. London: Sage.

Livingstone, S., and M. Bober. 2005. *UK children go online: Final report*. London: London School of Economics.

Mirsky, J. 2001. Psychological independence among immigrant adolescents from the former Soviet Union in Israel. *Transcultural Psychiatry* 38(3): 363-373.

Pfetsch, B. 1999. In Russia we were Germans, and now we are Russians: Dilemmas of identity formation and communication among German-Russian Aussiedler. Paper presented at the Annual Conference of the International Communication Association, May 27-June 1, 1999 in San Francisco.

Sluzki, C. 1979. Migration and family conflict. *Family Process* 18: 379-390.

Steinberg, L. D. 1990. Interdependence in the family: Autonomy, conflict and harmony in the parent-adolescent relationship. In *At the threshold: The developing adolescent*, ed. S. S. Feldman and G. R. Elliott, 255-276. Cambridge, MA: Harvard University Press.

Stilling E. A. 1997. The electronic melting pot hypothesis: The cultivation of acculturation among Hispanic through television viewing. *Howard Journal of Communication* 8(1): 77-100.

Suler, J. 2002. Identity management in cyberspace. *Journal of Applied Psychoanalytic Studies* 4: 455-460.

Turkle, S. 1996. Parallel lives: Working on identity in virtual space. In *Constructing the self in a mediated world: Inquiries in social construction*, ed. D. Grodin and T. R. Lindlof, 156-175. Mahwah, CA: Sage.

Valkenburg, P. M., A. P. Schouten, and J. Peter. 2005. Adolescents' identity experiments on the internet. *New Media and Society* 7(3): 383-402.

PART III:

PERSPECTIVES FOR EDUCATION

CHAPTER EIGHT

LEARNING THEORY, VIDEO GAMES, AND POPULAR CULTURE

JAMES PAUL GEE

Today, children's popular culture is more complex than ever before (Johnson 2005). A game like Yu-Gi-Oh—a card game played by children as young as 7, either face-to-face or on a GameBoy handheld game machine—involves the sorts of complex language, vocabulary, and thinking skills we associate with the advanced grades in school (Gee 2004). Children today "multi-task" across multiple modalities, playing a video game like Age of Mythology, reading and writing about mythology, researching it on the Internet, and, maybe, even contributing to web sites devoted to the game and wider topics in mythology (Jenkins 2006).

Concentrating on good modern video games, I will argue that children today often engage in cutting-edge learning in their popular cultural practices, learning of a sort that fits well with what the Learning Sciences have discovered about optimal human learning, but not necessarily well with how current schools operate (Bransford, Brown, and Cocking 2000; Gee 2003, 2004, 2005). At the same time, good video games — like contemporary research in the Learning Sciences — challenge us to truly integrate cognition, language, literacy, affect, and social interaction in our ideas about learning and the organization of learning inside and outside schools (Gee 1996, 2004; Damasio 1994).

Much of what I have here to say about video games is equally true when comparable games are played face-to-face with no digital technology involved, whether this be Yu-Gi-Oh or Dungeon and Dragons. However, digital technology does add certain features to the learning, features that are, we will see, reminiscent of how scientists use simulations to learn and to produce new knowledge.

But we need to discuss two points before starting our discussion of games and learning: content and technological determinism. First, content. Media discussions of video games often focus on the content of video games, especially if that content is violent (though many games are not violent, including the best-selling game of all time, The Sims). More generally, non-gamers tend to view video games in the same way in which they view films and novels: content is what determines the nature and value of the work. However, in video games — unlike in novels and films — content has to be separated from game play. The two are connected, but, to gamers, game play is the primary feature of video games; it is what makes them good or bad games (Koster 2004, Juul 2005, Salin and Zimmerman 2003).

The content in a game like Grand Theft Auto: San Andreas involves poverty, an African-Americans community, and crime. However, the game play involves solving problems strategically, problems like how to ride a bike through city streets so as to evade pursuing cars and follow a map to end up safely where you need to go. In games like this, elements of content could be changed without changing the game play—for example, in some cases, taking pictures of people instead of shooting them or secretly planting a message rather than a bomb in their car would leave the problem solving and its difficulty pretty much the same. Critics of games need to realize that players, especially strategic and mature players, are often focusing on game play more than they are on content per se.

Content in a game sets up, but does not fully determine, game play. It also determines the basic themes, metaphors, and emotional valences of the game, beyond the emotions of challenge, frustration, competition, and accomplishment that are determined by game play. However, the two inter-relate in complex ways, for example, in a role-playing game one's pride in accomplishment or regret for poor decisions can easily be projected onto the character the player is playing in the game. Equivalently, the power, problems, or fascinating features and accomplishments of a character in a game can be transferred as emotions to the player (e.g. feeling "cool" while being Solid Snake in Metal Gear Solid or empathy with the main character in Grand Theft Auto: San Andreas).

Then, too, video games, like most popular culture media, reflect back to us, in part, the basic themes and even prejudices of our own society. The Grand Theft Auto series is made in Scotland, but it clearly recycles U.S. media images from television and film. In this respect, games are no different than popular films and television. Some people think they are more powerful than these other media, because the player acts in games. But the fact is that while humans react emotionally to images (television, film, games, even pictures) in much the way they do to real life (Reeves and Nass 1999), this does not mean they are tempted to act on these emotions in real life—people do, after all, have higher thought processes in terms of which they make decisions and decide what is and is not real.

We also need to realize that video games involve content in a quite broad sense. Video gaming has turned out — despite early predictions to the contrary — to be a deeply social enterprise (Steinkuehler 2006, Taylor 2006). Even single-player gaming often involves young people in joint play, collaboration, competition, sharing, and a myriad of websites, chat rooms, and game guides, many of them produced by players themselves. But the social nature of gaming goes much further. Multiplayer gaming — games where small teams play against each other — is very popular among many young people. And massively-multiplayer games — games where thousands or millions of people play the same game — have recently (thanks, in part, to the tremendous success of World of WarCraft) become mainstream forms of social interaction across the globe. Such games are introducing new "states" (six million people world wide for World of WarCraft) or "communities" into the world. In such games, people are learning new identities, new forms of social interaction, and even new values, a broad form of "content," indeed (Steinkuehler 2006, Taylor 2006).

There is, indeed, much space for critique and critical theory in regard to video games, though that is not my topic here. My remarks about content are meant to suggest some of the issues particularly germane to video games as a media that need to be considered for such critique not to mistake games for books or films. But there is another issue relevant to anyone who wants to engage in critical theory in regard to games: technological determinism.

The media often discuss video games as if they are inherently good for people or bad for them. This is a form of technological determinism. Technologies—including television, computers, and books, as well as games—are neither good nor bad and have no effects all by themselves, though, like all tools, they have certain affordances (Greenfield 1984, Sternheimer 2003). Rather, they have different effects, some good, some bad, some neutral, depending on how they are used and the contexts in which they are used (Hawisher and Selfe 2007). One important aspect of use is, as I have already mentioned, the ways in which the player engages with the game's game play as opposed to its content or graphics ("eye candy"). Players can be more or less reflective, strategic, and focused on game play rather than content or graphics. Critics of games need to consider how games are "consumed" by different people in different contexts. Blanket general claims—either for the good or the bad effects of games—are close to useless.

Finally, let me say that my discussion below—about the powerful ways in which video games can recruit learning as a form of pleasure—is as much about the potential of games as we spread them to new contexts and design new types of games as it is about the present of games. Video games are a relatively new form of popular culture and no one should mistake their present state—for example, deeply influenced as it is by a Hollywood blockbuster mentality that often drives out innovation—for their future potential in the context of a diverse array of new technologies, designers, players, and learning and playing situations.

Video games are good for learning, but not just because they are games

Video games are good for learning (Shaffer, Squire, Halverson, and Gee, in press; Gee 2003, 2005). What I mean by this is that good commercial video games build in good learning principles, learning devices that are supported by recent research in the Learning Sciences (Gee 2003, Sawyer 2006), though, of course, how these learning principles are picked up will vary across users and contexts, as I pointed out above. This claim does not just mean we should use video games for learning in and out of schools. It also means that we should use the learning principles built into good video games in and out of schools even if we are not using games. These learning principles can be built into many different curricula.

What makes video games good for learning is not, by any means, just the fact that they are games. Furthermore, the video games that are most interesting for learning are not just any video games. Different types of games can have different effects. Puzzle games like Tetris and Bejeweled may very well exercise pattern recognition capacities; Trivial Pursuit games may well make learning facts fun. But these are not, in my view, the sorts of video games which are most interesting in regard to learning.

Before I say what makes video games good for learning, let me be clear about just what type of video game I am interested in in this article. First, consider simulations in science, say a digital simulation of an electro-magnetic field, a solar system, or an ecological system. Sometimes scientists use such simulations to test hypotheses. But very often they use them to examine systems that are so complex that it is hard to make specific predictions about outcomes ahead of time (take weather for example). In this case, they design these simulations ("virtual worlds"), "run them" (i.e. let many variables interact across time), and see what happens. Then they seek explanations for the outcomes, build new theories about the complex system being simulated, run the simulation again and again in order to improve the theory, and, maybe, eventually, get better at making actual predictions.

These scientific digital simulations are not video games. However, the video games in which we are interested here—for example, in the case of commercial games, games like Deus Ex, Half-Life, The Sims, Rise of Nations, SWAT IV, Civilization, The Elder Scrolls III: Morrowind—are, indeed, simulations. They are worlds in which variables interact through time. What makes them interestingly different from scientific simulations is that the player is not outside, but, rather, inside the simulation (the virtual world). There are also cases like flight simulators and games like Full Spectrum Warrior which are used, in one form, as professional training devices and, in another form, as games for the commercial market.

The player has a surrogate in the simulation (game), namely the virtual character or characters he or she controls in the virtual world (e.g. Solid Snake in Metal Gear Solid, a Sim family in The Sims, or citizens, soldiers, and buildings in Rise of Nations). Through this character or characters the player acts and interacts within and on the simulation. The player discovers or forms goals within the simulation, goals that the player attributes to his or her surrogate in the world. In order to reach these goals, the player must recognize problems and solve them from within the inside of the simulated world. This essentially means that the player must figure out the rule system (patterns) that constitutes the simulation (the rules that the simulation follows thanks to how it is designed). The player must discover what is possible and impossible (and in what ways) within the simulation in order to solve problems and carry out goals. Achieving these goals constitutes the win state for the player.

So the video games in which I am interested, the ones that I think are most interesting for learning, are digital simulations of worlds that are "played" in the sense that a player has a surrogate or surrogates through which the player can act within and on the simulation and that have "win states" (reachable goals that the player has discovered or formed through his or her surrogate). By the way, in augmented reality games, a person can be playing a virtual role (e.g., urban planner, toxic spill specialist, detective) in a rule system that is designed to play out partly in a virtual world and partly in the real world (Klopfer and Squire, in press).

Take Thief: Deadly Shadows as an example. Thief is a simulated world that is built around light and dark spaces, places good for hiding (dark) and places where one is exposed to detection (light). The world is medieval, filled with police and guards, as well as citizens, some of them well armed. Players must move through this world to accomplish specific goals, but they have little physical power and no powerful weapons for melee combat. Face-to-face confrontations are possible, but difficult and can quickly lead to defeat. The player plays the master thief Garrett — Garrett is the player's surrogate in the virtual world. Using Garrett's body (which comes equipped with the ability to meld into the shadows), players must move carefully and hide often, engaging in stealth. All the while they are trying to figure out how best to get where they need to be and how best to accomplish their goals, for example, infiltrating a museum and stealing a well-protected precious object. Using and understanding this world (spaces, light conditions, virtual people and objects) and understanding the rule system it incorporates—a system that facilitates some actions, defacilitates others, and makes some others downright impossible—to successfully accomplish various smaller and bigger goals is the win state for the player.

So why would a learning theorist be interested in video games like these? For all sorts of reasons. A good number of these reasons have nothing to do with the fact that video games are game. I will first discuss a few such reasons that have little to do with the fact that video games are games and then turn to some reasons directly connected to the fact that video games are games.

Embodied empathy for a complex system

Let's go back to those scientific simulations—simulations of things like weather systems, atoms, cells, or the rise and fall of civilizations. Scientists are not inside these simulations in the way in which players are inside the simulated worlds of games like Thief: Deadly Shadows. The scientist doesn't "play" an ant in his or her simulation of an eco-system. The scientist doesn't discover and form goals from the perspective of the ant in the way I do from the perspective of Garrett in Thief.

However, it turns out that, at the cutting edge of science, scientists often talk and think as if they were inside not only the simulations they build, but even the graphs they draw. They try to think from within local regions of the system being simulated, while still keeping in mind the system as a whole. They do this in order to gain a deeper feel for how variables are interacting in the system, for the range of possibilities and impossibilities in the system. Just as a player becomes Garrett, a scientist can talk and think as if he or she were actually an electron in a certain state or an ant in a colony. For example, consider the following talk from a physicist talking to other physicists while looking and pointing to a graph on a blackboard:

> But as you go below the first order transition you're (leans upper body to right) still in the domain structure and you're still trying to get (sweeps right arm to left) out of it. Well you also said (moves to board, points to diagram) the same thing must happen here (points to the right side of the diagram). When (moves finger to left) I come down (moves finger to right) I'm in (moves finger to left) the domain state (Ochs, Gonzales, and Jacoby 1996, 330-331).

Notice the "you's" and "I's". The scientist talks and acts as if he and his colleagues are moving their bodies not only inside the graph, but inside the complex system it represents, as well. In reality he is talking about atomic particles and the states they can be in. So, though video games and scientific simulations are not the same thing, video game can, under the right circumstances, encourage and actually enact a similar "attitude" or "stance". This stance involves a sort of "embodied empathy for a complex system" where a person seeks to participate in and within a system, all the while seeing and thinking of it as a system and not just local or random events. Squire's (2005, Squire and Jenkins 2004) work on Civilization III and other games has shown that even young learners can enter a game as a complex system and learn deep conceptual principles about history and the social sciences. Halverson (2005) is designing a video game in which adult educational leaders can use the game to understand modern principles of school leadership within a framework that sees schools as complex systems interacting with a variety of other complex systems.

Action-and-goal-directed preparations for, and simulations of, embodied experience

Video games don't just carry the potential to replicate a sophisticated scientific way of thinking. They actually externalize the way in which the human mind works and thinks in a better fashion than any other technology we have.

In history, scholars have tended to view the human mind through the lens of a technology they thought worked like the mind. Locke and Hume argued that the mind was like a blank slate on which experience wrote ideas, taking the technology of literacy as their guide. Much later, modern cognitive scientists argued that the mind worked like a digital computer, calculating generalizations and deductions via a logic-like rule system (Newell and Simon 1972). More recently, some cognitive scientists, inspired by distributed parallel-processing computers and complex adaptive networks, have argued that the mind works by storing records of actual experiences and constructing intricate patterns of connections among them (Clark 1989, Gee 1992). So we get different pictures of the mind: mind as a slate waiting to be written on, mind as software, mind as a network of connections.

Human societies get better through history at building technologies that more closely capture some of what the human mind can do and getting these technologies to do mental work publicly. Writing, digital computers, and networks each allow us to externalize some functions of the mind. Though they are not commonly thought of in these terms, video games are a new technology in this same line. They are a new tool with which to think about the mind and through which we can externalize some of its functions. Video games of the sort I am concerned with are what I would call "action-and-goal-directed preparations for, and simulations of, embodied experience". A mouthful, indeed, but an important one—and one connected intimately to the nature of human thinking — so, let's see what it means.

Let me first briefly summarize some recent research in cognitive science, the science that studies how the mind works (Bransford, Brown, and Cocking 2000). Consider, for instance, the remarks below [in the quotes below, the word "comprehension" means "understanding words, actions, events, or things"]:

> … comprehension is grounded in perceptual simulations that prepare agents for situated action (Barsalou 1999a, 77)

> … to a particular person, the meaning of an object, event, or sentence is what that person can do with the object, event, or sentence (Glenberg 1997, 3)

What these remarks mean is this: human understanding is not primarily a matter of storing general concepts in the head or applying abstract rules to experience. Rather, humans think and understand best when they can imagine (simulate) an experience in such a way that the simulation prepares them for actions they need and want to take in order to accomplish their goals (Barsalou 1999b, Clark 1997, Glenberg and Robertson 1999).

Let's take weddings as an example, though we could just as well have taken war, love, inertia, democracy, or anything. You don't understand the word or the idea of weddings by meditating on some general definition of weddings. Rather, you have had experiences of weddings, in real life and through texts and media. On the basis of these experiences, you can simulate different wedding scenarios in your mind. You construct these simulations differently for different occasions, based on what actions you need to take to accomplish specific goals in specific situations. You can move around as a character in the mental simulation as yourself, imaging your role in the wedding, or you can "play" other characters at the wedding (e.g. the minister), imaging what it is like to be that person.

You build your simulations to understand and make sense of things, but also to help you prepare for action in the world. You can act in the simulation and test out what consequences follow, before you act in the real world. You can role-play another person in the simulation and try to see what motivates their actions or might follow from them before you respond in the real world. So I am arguing that the mind is a simulator, but one that builds simulations to prepare purposely for specific actions and to achieve specific goals (i.e. they are built around win states).

Video games turn out to be the perfect metaphor for what this view of the mind amounts to, just as slates and computers were good metaphors for earlier views of the mind. Video games usually involve a visual and auditory world in which the player manipulates a virtual character (or characters). They often come with editors or other sorts of software with which the player can make changes to the game world or even build a new game world (much as the mind can edit its previous experiences to form simulations of things not directly experienced). The player can make a new landscape, a new set of buildings, or new characters. The player can set up the world so that certain sorts of actions are allowed or disallowed. The player is building a new world, but is doing so by using and modifying the original visual images (really the code for them) that came with the game. One simple example of this is the way in which players can build new skateboard parks in a game like Tony Hawk Pro Skater. The player must place ramps, trees, grass, poles, and other things in space in such a way that players can manipulate their virtual characters to skate the park in a fun and challenging way.

Even when players are not modifying games, they play them with goals in mind, the achievement of which counts as their "win state". Players must carefully consider the design of the world and consider how it will or will not facilitate specific actions they want to take to accomplish their goals. One technical way that psychologists have talked about this sort of situation is through the notion of "affordances" (Gibson 1979). An "affordance" is a feature of the world (real or virtual) that will allow for a certain action to be taken, but only if it is matched by an ability in an actor who has the wherewithal to carry out such an action. For example, in the massive multiplayer game World of WarCraft stags can be killed and skinned (for making leather), but only by characters that have learned the skinning skill. So a stag is an affordance for skinning for such a player, but not for one who has no such skill. The large spiders in the game are not an affordance for skinning for any players, since they cannot be skinned at all. Affordances are relationships between the world and actors.

Playing World of WarCraft, or any other video game, is all about such affordances. The player must learn to see the game world—designed by the developers, but set in motion by the players, and, thus, co-designed by them—in terms of such affordances (Gee 2005). Broadly speaking, players must think in terms of "what are the features of this world that can enable the actions I am capable of carrying out and that I want to carry out in order to achieve my goals?"

The view of the mind I have sketched argues, as far as I am concerned, that the mind works rather like a video game. For humans, effective thinking is more like running a simulation in our heads within which we have a surrogate actor than it is about forming abstract generalizations cut off from experiential realities. Effective thinking is about perceiving the world such that the human actor sees how the world, at a specific time and place (as it is given, but also modifiable), can afford the opportunity for actions that will lead to a successful accomplishment of the actor's goals. Generalizations are formed, when they are, bottom up from experience and imagination of experience. Video games externalize the search for affordances, for a match between character (actor) and world, but this is just the heart and soul of effective human thinking and learning in any situation. They are, thus, a natural tool for teaching and learning.

As a game player you learn to see the world of each different game you play in a quite different way. But in each case you see the world in terms of how it will afford the sorts of embodied actions you (and your virtual character, your surrogate body in the game) need to take to accomplish your goals (to win in the short and long run). For example, you see the world in Full Spectrum Warrior as routes (for your squad) between cover (e.g. corner to corner, house to house), because this prepares you for the actions you need to take, namely attacking without yourself being vulnerable to attack. You see the world of Thief: Deadly Shadows in terms of light and dark, illumination and shadows, because this prepares you for the different actions you need to take in this world, namely hiding, disappearing into the shadows, sneaking, and otherwise moving unseen to your goal.

While commercial video games often stress a match between worlds and characters like soldiers or thieves, there is no reason why other types of games could not let players experience such a match between the world and the way a particular type of scientist, for instance, sees and acts on the world (Gee 2004). Such games would involve facing the sorts of problems and challenges that type of scientist does face and living and playing by the rules that type of scientist uses. Wining would mean just what it does to a scientist: feeling a sense of accomplishment through the production of knowledge to solve deep problems.

I have argued for the importance of video games as "action-and-goal-directed preparations for, and simulations of, embodied experience." They are the new technological arena—just as were literacy and computers earlier—around which we can study the mind and externalize some of its most important features to improve human thinking and learning.

Distributed intelligence via the creation of smart tools

Consider how good games distribute intelligence (Brown, Collins, and Duguid 1989). In Full Spectrum Warrior, the player uses the buttons on the controller to give orders to two squads of soldiers (the game SWAT 4 is also a great equivalent example here). The instruction manual that comes with the game makes it clear from the outset that players, in order to play the game successfully, must take on the values, identities, and ways of thinking of a professional soldier: "Everything about your squad," the manual explains, "is the result of careful planning and years of experience on the battlefield. Respect that experience, soldier, since it's what will keep your soldiers alive" (THQ nd, p. 6). In the game, that experience — the skills and knowledge of professional military expertise — is distributed between the virtual soldiers and the real-world player. The soldiers in the player's squads have been trained in movement formations; the role of the player is to select the best position for them on the field. The virtual characters (the soldiers) know part of the task (various movement formations) and the player must come to know another part (when and where to engage in such formations). This kind of distribution holds for every aspect of military knowledge in the game.

By distributing knowledge and skills this way—between the virtual characters (smart tools) and the real-world player—the player is guided and supported by the knowledge built into the virtual soldiers. This offloads some of the cognitive burden from the learner, placing it in smart tools that can do more than the learner is currently capable of doing by him or herself. It allows the player to begin to act, with some degree of effectiveness, before being really competent—"performance before competence." The player thereby eventually comes to gain competence through trial, error, and feedback, not by wading through a lot of text before being able to engage in activity.

Such distribution also allows players to internalize not only the knowledge and skills of a professional (a professional soldier in this case), but also the concomitant values ("doctrine" as the military says) that shape and explain how and why that knowledge is developed and applied in the world. There is no reason why other professions—scientists, doctors, government officials, urban planners (Shaffer 2004)—could not be modeled and distributed in this fashion as a deep form of value-laden learning (and, in turn, learners could compare and contrast different value systems as they play different games). Shaffer's (2004, 2005) "epistemic games" take this principle much further and demonstrate how even young learners, through video games embedded inside a well-organized curriculum, can be inducted into professional practices as a form of value-laden deep learning that transfers to school-based skills and conceptual understandings.

Cross-functional affiliation

Consider a small group partying (hunting and questing) together in a massive multiplayer game like World of WarCraft. The group might well be composed of a Hunter, Warrior, Druid, Mage, and Priest. Each of these types of characters has quite different skills and plays the game in a different way. Each group member (player) must learn to be good at his or her special skills and also learn to integrate these skills as a team member within the group as a whole. Each team member must also share some common knowledge about the game and game play with all the other members of the group — including some understanding of the specialist skills of other player types — in order to achieve a successful integration. So each member of the group must have specialist knowledge (intensive knowledge) and general common knowledge (extensive knowledge), including knowledge of the other member's functions.

Players — who are interacting with each other in the game and via a chat system—orient to each other not in terms of their real-world race, class, culture, or gender (these may very well be unknown or if communicated made up as fictions). They must orient to each other, first and foremost, through their identities as game players and players of World of WarCraft in particular. They can, in turn, use their real-world race, class, culture, and gender as strategic resources if and when they please, and the group can draw on the differential real-world resources of each player, but in ways that do not force anyone into pre-set racial, gender, cultural, or class categories.

This form of affiliation—what I will call cross-functional affiliation—has been argued to be crucial for the workplace teams in modern "new capitalist" workplaces, as well as in contemporary forms of social activism (Beck 1999, Gee 2004, Gee, Hull, and Lankshear 1996). People specialize, but integrate and share, organized around a primary affiliation to their common goals and using their cultural and social differences as strategic resources, not as barriers.

Let me say here, too, that what is really important about today's massive multiplayer games, like World of WarCraft, Lineage, EverQuest, City of Heroes, and Guild Wars, is the ways in which, sometimes for better and sometimes for worse, people are creating new ways to build and share knowledge. They are also forming new forms of learning communities. We have much to learn from these games about new ways to socially organize learning in tomorrow's classrooms, libraries, workplaces, and communities (Steinkuehler 2005, in press).

Situated meaning

Words do not have just general dictionary-like meanings. They have different and specific meanings in different situations in which they are used and in different specialist domains that recruit them (Gee 2004). This is true of the most mundane cases. For instance, notice the change in meaning in the word "coffee" in the following sentences which refer to different situations: "The coffee spilled, go get the mop" (coffee as liquid), "The coffee spilled, go get a broom" (coffee as grains), "The coffee spilled, stack it again" (coffee in cans). Or notice the quite different meanings of the word "work" in everyday life and in physics (e.g., I can say, in everyday life, that I worked hard to push the car, but if my efforts didn't move the car, I did no "work" in the physics sense of the word).

A good deal of school success is based on being able to understand complex academic language (Gee 2004)—like the text printed below from a high-school science textbook. Such a text can be understood in one of two different ways: either verbally or in a situated fashion. When students understand such language only verbally, they can trade words for words, that is, they can replace words with their definitions. They may be able to pass paper and pencil tests, but they often can't use the complex language of the text to facilitate real problem solving, because they don't actually understand how the language applies to the world in specific cases for solving such problems. If they do understand how the words apply to specific situations and for specific problem solutions, they understand the words in a situated fashion. We have known for years now that a great many school students can get good grades on paper and pencil tests in science, but can't use their knowledge to solve actual problems (Gardner 1991).

People acquire situated meanings for words—that is, meanings that they can apply in actual contexts of use for action and problem solving—only when they have heard these words in international dialogue with people more expert than themselves (Tomasello 1999) and when they have experienced the images and actions to which the words apply (Gee 2004). Dialogue, experience, and action are crucial if people are to have more than just words for words, if they are to be able to cash out words for experiences, actions, functions, and problem solving. They must be able to build simulations in their minds of how the words are used in talk and action in different specific contexts. As they can do this for more and more contexts of use, they generalize the meanings of the word more and more, but the words never lose their moorings in talk, embodied experience, action, and problem solving.

Since video games are "action-and-goal-directed preparations for, and simulations of, embodied experience" they allow language to be put into the context of dialogue, experience, images, and actions. They allow language to be situated. Furthermore, good video games give verbal information "just in time"—near the time it can actually be used—or "on demand"—when the player feels a need for it and is ready for it (Gee 2003). They don't give players lots and lots of words out of context before they can be used and experienced or before they are needed or useful. This is an ideal situation for language acquisition, for acquiring new words and new forms of language for new types of activity, whether this be being a member of a SWAT team or a scientist of a certain sort.

Open-endedness: Goals and projects that meld the personal and the social

We need to say more about goals, since this leads to yet another good reason why video games are good for learning. In a video game, the player "plays" a character or set of them. The player must discover what goals this character has within the game world and carry them out, using whatever abilities the character has (remember affordances and smart tools). In Thief: Deadly Shadows, the player comes to realize that Garrett has specific goals that require stealth, for which Garret is well suited, to carry out. These are the "in game" goals the player must discover and carry out.

But in good open-ended games, games like The Elder Scrolls III: Morrowind, Arcanum, The Sims, Deus Ex 2, Mercenaries, Grand Theft Auto, and many more, players also make up their own goals, based on their own desires, styles, and backgrounds. The player must then attribute these personal goals to the virtual character and must consider the affordances in the virtual world (psych out the rule system) so as to get these personal goals realized along with the virtual character's more purely "in game" goals.

For example, in The Elder Scrolls III: Morrowind, a player may decide to eschew heavy armor and lots of fighting in favor of persuasive skills, stealth, and magic, or the player can engage in lots of face-to-face combat in heavy armor. The player can carry out a linear sequence of quests set by the game's designers or can make up his or her own quests, becoming so powerful that the designer's quests become easy and only a background feature of the game. In Grand Theft Auto III , the player can be evil or not (e.g. the player can jump in ambulances and do good deeds), can do quests in different orders, and can play or not play large pieces of the game, for example, he or she can trigger gang wars or avoid them altogether. Even in less open-ended games, players, even quite young ones, set their own standards of accomplishment, replaying parts of the game so that their hero pulls things off in the heroic fashion and style the player deems appropriate.

This marriage of personal goals and "in game" goals is a highly motivating state. When a person is learning or doing science, they must discover and realize goals that are set up by the scientific enterprise as a domain and as a social community. These are equivalent to "in game" goals. But they also, when effective, marry these goals to their own personal goals, based on their own desires, styles, and backgrounds. They try to be scientists of a certain type. When they do this, there is no great divide between their scientific identity and their "life world", their personal and community-based identities and values. Good video games readily allow such a marriage, good science instruction should too.

This issue of marrying personal and "in game" goals, leads to the issue of identity. Video games are all about identity The player "plays" some character; the player takes on, carries out, and identifies with some special identity in a virtual world. When I have married my personal goals and values to the virtual character's "in game" goals, I see the game as both a project that the game designers have given to me and, simultaneously, I project my own goals, desires, values, and identity into the game world, melded with the "in game" identity and goals of the virtual character. The "project" now becomes "mine" and not just something imposed on me, because I have "projected" myself into it.

Good science instruction should involve, as well, a marriage of "science's" goals and mine. I should see the project given to me by the classroom or the current state of science as something into which I can also project my own goals, values, desires, and identities. Good science instruction should, then, be "open-ended" in the way in which some good video games are.

Learning features connected to games as games

In addition to the learning features we have discussed thus far—features that are not directly connected to the fact that video games are games—there are a bevy of learning features (features that make video games good examples of good learning) that are more directly connected to the fact that video games are games. I will briefly discuss some of these features here.

First, good learning requires that learners feel like active agents (producers) not just passive recipients (consumers). In a video game, players make things happen. Players don't just consume what the "author" (game designer) has placed before them. Video games are interactive. The player does something and the game does something back that encourages the player to act again. In good games, players feel that their actions and decisions—and not just the designers' actions and decisions—are co-creating the world they are in and the experiences they are having. What the player does matters and each player, based on his or her own decisions and actions, takes a different trajectory through the game world.

The Elder Scrolls: Morrowind is an extreme example of a game where each decision the player makes changes the game in ways that ensure that each player's game is, in the end, different from any other player's. But at some level this is true of most games. Players take different routes through Castlevania: Symphony of the Night and do different things in different ways in Tony Hawk's Underground.

Second, people cannot be agents of their own learning if they cannot make decisions about how their learning will work. At the same time, they should be able (and encouraged) to try new styles. Good games achieve this goal in one (or both) of two ways. In some games, players are able to customize the game play to fit their learning and playing styles. In others, the game is designed to allow different styles of learning and playing to work. For example, Rise of Nations allows players to customize myriad aspects of the game play to their own styles, interests, and desires. Deus Ex and its sequel Deus Ex: Invisible War both allow quite different styles of play and, thus, learning, too, to succeed.

Third, deep learning requires an extended commitment and such a commitment is powerfully recruited when people take on a new identity they value and in which they become heavily invested (diSessa 2000)—whether this be a child "being a scientist doing science" in a classroom or an adult taking on a new role at work. Good games offer players identities that trigger a deep investment on the part of the player. They achieve this goal in one of two ways. Some games offer a character so intriguing that players want to inhabit the character and can readily project their own fantasies, desires, and pleasures onto the character. Other games offer a relatively empty character whose traits the player must determine, but in such a way that the player can create a deep and consequential life history in the game world for the character.

For example, Metal Solid Gear offers a character (Solid Snake) that is so well developed that he is, though largely formed by the game's designers, a magnet for player projections. Animal Crossing and The Elder Scrolls: Morrowind offer, in different ways, blank-slate characters for which the player can build a deeply involving life and history.

Fourth, given human creativity, if learners face problems early on that are too free-form or too complex, they often form creative hypotheses about how to solve these problems, but hypotheses that don't work well for later problems, even for simpler ones, let alone harder ones (Gee 2004). They have been sent down a "garden path". The problems learners face early on are crucial and should be well-designed to lead them to hypotheses that work well, not just on these problems, but as aspects of the solutions of later, harder problems, as well. Problems in good games are well ordered. In particular, early problems are designed to lead players to form good guesses about how to proceed when they face harder problems later on in the game. In this sense, earlier parts of a good game are always looking forward to later parts.

Fifth, learning works best when new challenges are pleasantly frustrating in the sense of being felt by learners to be at the outer edge of, but within, their "regime of competence" (diSessa 2000). That is, these challenges feel hard, but doable. Furthermore, learners feel—and get evidence—that their effort is paying off in the sense that they can see, even when they fail, how and if they are making progress. Good games adjust challenges and give feedback in such a way that different players feel the game is challenging but doable and that their effort is paying off. Players get feedback that indicates whether they are on the right road for success later on and at the end of the game. When players lose to a boss, perhaps multiple times, they get feedback about the sort of progress they are making so that at least they know if and how they are moving in the right direction towards success.

Sixth, expertise is formed in any area by repeated cycles of learners practicing skills until they are nearly automatic, then having those skills fail in ways that cause the learners to have to think again and learn anew (Bereiter and Scardamalia 1993). Then they practice this new skill set to an automatic level of mastery only to see it, too, eventually be challenged. In fact, this is the whole point of levels and bosses. Each level exposes the players to new challenges and allows them to get good at solving them. They are then confronted with a boss that makes them use these skills together with new ones they have to learn, and integrate with the old ones, to beat the boss. Then they move on to a new level and the process starts again. Good games create and support the cycle of expertise, with cycles of extended practice, tests of mastery of that practice, then a new challenge, and then new extended practice. This is, in fact, part of what constitutes good pacing in a game.

Seventh, failure works very differently in good video games from the way it does in school, for example. In a good video game, players are encouraged to take risks, explore, and try new things, because the price of failure is not terribly high. If the player fails, he or she can start back at the last game save or checkpoint. Furthermore, failure in games is seen by players as crucial to learning. No player expects or even wants to beat a boss on the first try. Rather, the player expects to learn from failing to kill the boss initially what patterns to look for and how to do better on the next chance.

Conclusion: Beyond commercial games

None of this is to say that video games do these good things all by themselves. It all depends on how they are used and what sorts of wider learning systems (activities and relationships) they are made a part of. None of these reasons why video games are good for learning stems primarily from a game's great 3-D graphics and many of them do not stem from the fact that a video game is a game in the general sense of "game". The cutting edge of games and learning is not in video game technology—although great graphics are wonderful and technical improvements are important. The cutting edge is realizing the potential of games for learning by building good games into good learning systems in and out of classrooms and by building the good learning principles in good games into learning in and out of school whether or not a video game is present.

Our discussion has centered around commercial games. However, thanks to the fact that commercial industry is part of the lager global media entertainment complex, such games stress content that is, for the most part, not academic or socially activist (though there are exceptions like Civilization). So called "serious games" devoted to such content are beginning to appear, games like A Force More Powerful (devoted to the spread of democracy), Re-Mission (a game to help and inform young cancer patients), or Dimenxian (a shooter recruiting algebra learning). One key question for some educators has been whether the learning principles in commercial games can be moved effectively into games teaching more school-based content, though not in ways traditionally associated with formal schooling.

One of many current examples of such games, and the research associated with them, is an "epistemic game" designed by David Shaffer called Madison 2020. In this project, Shaffer and Kelly Beckett at the University of Wisconsin have developed, implemented, and assessed a game and accompanying learning system that simulates some of the activities of professional urban planners (Beckett and Shaffer 2005, Shaffer 2007, see also Shaffer, Squire, Halverson, and Gee 2004).

Shaffer and Beckett call their approach "augmented by reality", since a virtual reality i.e. the game is augmented or supplemented by real-world activities, in this case further activities of the sort in which urban planners engage. As in the commercial game SimCity, in Shaffer and Beckett's game, students make land use decisions and consider the complex results of their decisions. However, unlike SimCity, they use real-world data and authentic planning practices to inform those decisions.

Shaffer and Beckett argue that the environmental dependencies in urban areas have the potential to become a fruitful context for innovative learning in ecological education. Cities are comprised of simple components, but the interactions among those components are complex. Altering one variable affects all the others, reflecting the interdependent, ecological relationships present in any modern city. For example, consider the relationships among industrial sites, air pollution, and land property values: increasing industrial sites can lead to pollution that, in turn, lowers property values, changing the dynamics of the city's neighborhoods in the process.

Shaffer and Beckett's Madison 2020 project situated student experience at a micro level by focusing on a single street in their own city (Madison, Wisconsin):

> Instead of the fast-paced action required to plan and maintain virtual urban environments such as SimCity, this project focused only on an initial planning stage, which involved the development of a land use plan for this one street. And instead of using only a technological simulation [i.e., the game, JPG], the learning environment here was orchestrated by authentic urban planning practices. These professional practices situated the planning tool in a realistic context and provided a framework within which students constructed solutions to the problem (Beckett and Schaffer 2005, 11-12).

Professional urban planners must formulate plans that meet the social, economic, and physical needs of their communities. To align with this practice, students received an informational packet addressed to them as city planners. The packet contained a project directive from the mayor, a city budget plan, and letters from concerned citizens providing input about how they wished to see the city redesigned. The directive asked the student city planners to develop a plan that, in the end, would have to be presented to a representative from the planning department at the end of the workshop.

Students then watched a video about State Street, featuring interviews with people who expressed concerns about the street's redevelopment aligned with the issues in the informational packet (e.g. affordable housing). During the planning phase, students walked to State Street and conducted a site assessment. Following the walk, they worked in teams to develop a land use plan using a custom-designed interactive geographic information system (GIS) called MadMod built into a SimCity like game.

MadMod allows students to see a virtual representation of State Street. It has two components, a decision space and a constraint table. The decision space displays address and zoning information about State Street using official two- or three-letter zoning codes to designate changes in land use for property parcels on the street. As students made decisions about changes they wished to make, they received immediate feedback about the consequences of changes in the constraint table. The constraint table showed the effects of changes on six planning issues raised in the original information packet and the video: crime, revenue, jobs, waste, car trips, and housing. Following the professional practices of urban planners, in the final phase of the workshop, students presented their plans to a representative from the city planning office.

In Madison 2020 students are gaming at two levels, within a virtual SimCity like world and via role-playing in the real world. Of course, Madison 2020 in some respects stretches the notion of a game. In my view, video games are simulations that have "win states" in terms of goals players have set for themselves. In this case, the students have certain goals and the game lets them see how close or far they are from attaining those goals. At the same time, the game is embedded in a learning system that ensures that those goals and the procedures used to reach them are instantiations of the professional practices and ways of knowing or urban planners.

Shaffer and Beckett show, through a pre-interview/post-interview design, that students learning through the game were able to provide more extensive and explicit definitions of the term "ecology" after their learning experience than before it. The students' explanations of ecological issues in the post-interview were more specific about how ecological issues are interdependent or interconnected than in the pre-interview. Concept maps the students drew showed an increased awareness of the complexities present in an urban ecosystem. Thus, students appear to have developed a richer understanding of urban ecology through their work in the project.

100 per cent of the students said the workshop changed the way they thought about cities and most said the experience changed the things they paid attention to when walking down a city street in their neighborhood. Better yet, perhaps, Shaffer and Beckett were able to show transfer: Students' responses to novel, hypothetical urban planning problems showed increased awareness of the interconnections among urban ecological issues. All these effects suggest, as Shaffer and Beckett argue, "that students were able to mobilize understanding developed in the context of the redesign of one local street to think more deeply about novel urban ecological issues" (Beckett and Schaffer 2005, 21).

We seem now far from a commercial game like Thief, though not so far from SimCity, but, in reality, all these games cause players to look at and live in a world in a distinctive way, to find patterns, and to solve problems. And these games give players the tools with which to accomplish these goals. Madison 2020 simply builds a more comprehensive learning system around the game and more integrally relates the game to the real world. In the end, however, it is an open research question as to how far we can go in moving the learning principles in good commercial games outside the entertainment sphere those games inhabit and the distinctive pleasures they offer.

References

Barsalou, L.W. 1999a. Language comprehension: Archival memory or preparation for situated action. *Discourse Processes* 28(1): 61-80.

—. 1999b. Perceptual symbol systems. *Behavioral and Brain Sciences* 22(4): 577-660.

Beck, U. 1999. *World risk society*. Oxford: Blackwell.

Beckett, K. L., and D. W. Shaffer. 2005. Augmented by reality: The pedagogical praxis of urban planning as a pathway to ecological thinking. *Journal of Educational Computing Research* 33(1): 31-52.

Bereiter, C., and M. Scardamalia. 1993. *Surpassing ourselves: An inquiry into the nature and implications of expertise*. Chicago: Open Court.

Bransford, J., A. L. Brown, and R. R. Cocking. 2000. *How people learn: Brain, mind, experience, and school. Expanded edition*. Washington, DC: National Academy Press.

Brown, J. S., A. Collins, and P. Dugid. 1989. Situated cognition and the culture of learning. *Educational Researcher* 18(1): 32-42.

Clark, A. 1989. *Microcognition: Philosophy, cognitive science, and parallel distributed processing*. Cambridge, MA: MIT Press.

—. 1997. *Being there: Putting brain, body, and world together again*. Cambridge, MA: MIT Press.

Damasio, A. R. 1994. *Descartes' error: Emotion, reason, and the human brain*. New York: Avon.

diSessa, A. A. 2000. *Changing minds: Computers, learning, and literacy*. Cambridge, MA: MIT Press.

Gardner, H. 1991. *The unschooled mind: How children think and how schools should teach*. New York: Basic Books.

Gee, J. P. 1992. *The social mind: Language, ideology, and social practice*. New York: Bergin and Garvey.

—. 1996. *Social linguistics and literacies: Ideology in discourses*. Second Edition. London: Routledge/Taylor and Francis.

—. 2003. *What video games have to teach us about learning and literacy*. New York: Palgrave/Macmillan.

—. 2004. *Situated language and learning: A critique of traditional schooling*. London: Routledge.

—. 2005. *Why video games are good for your soul: Pleasure and learning*. Melbourne: Common Ground.

Gee, J. P., G. Hull, and C. Lankshear. 1996. *The new work order: Behind the language of the new capitalism*. Boulder, CO: Westview.

Gibson, J. J. 1979. *The ecological approach to visual perception*. Boston: Houghton Mifflin.

Glenberg, A. M. 1997. What is memory for. *Behavioral and Brain Sciences* 20(1): 1-55.

Glenberg, A. M., and D. A. Robertson. 1999. Indexical understanding of instructions. *Discourse Processes* 28(1): 1-26.

Greenfield, P. 1984. *Media and the mind of the child: From print to television, video games and computers*. Cambridge, MA: Harvard University Press.

Halverson, R. 2005. What can K-12 school leaders learn from video games and gaming? *Innovate 1.6*, http://www.innovateonline.info/index.php?view=article&id=81 (retrieved February 27, 2008).

Hawisher, G. E., and C. L. Selfe. 2007. *Gaming lives in the twenty-first century: Literate connections*. New York: Palgrave/Macmillan.

Jenkins, H. 2006. *Convergence culture: Where old and new media collide*. New York: New York University Press.

Johnson, S. 2005. *Everything bad for you is good for you: How today's popular culture is actually making us smarter*. New York: Riverhead.

Juul, J. 2005. *Half-real: Video games between real rules and fictional worlds*. Cambridge, MA: MIT Press.

Koster, R. 2004. *A theory of fun for game design*. Scottsdale, AZ: Paraglyph Press.

Klopfer, E., and K. Squire. (in press). Developing a platform for augmented reality gaming. *Educational Technology Research and Development.*

Newell, A., and H. A. Simon. 1972. *Human problem solving*. Englewood Cliffs, NJ: Prentice-Hall

Ochs, E., P. Gonzales, and S. Jacoby. 1996. When I come down I'm in the domain state. In *Interaction and Grammar*, ed. E. Ochs, E. Schegloff, and S. A. Thompson, 328-369. Cambridge: Cambridge University Press.

Reeves, B., and C. Nass. 1999. *The media equation: How people treat computers, television, and new media like real people and places*. New York: Cambridge University Press.

Salin, K., and E. Zimmerman. 2003. *Rules of play: Game design fundamentals*. Cambridge, MA: MIT Press.

Sawyer, R. K., ed. 2006. *The Cambridge handbook of the learning sciences*. Cambridge: Cambridge University Press.

Shaffer, D. W. 2004. Pedagogical praxis: The professions as models for post-industrial education. *Teachers College Record* 10(7): 1401-1421.

—. 2005. "Epistemic games". *Innovate 1.6,* http://www.innovateonline.info/index.php?view=article&id=81 (retrieved February 22, 2008).

Shaffer, D. W., K. Squire, R. Halverson, and J. P. Gee. 2005. Video games and the future of learning. *Phi Delta Kappan* 87(2): 104-111.

Shaffer, D. 2007. *How computer games help children learn*. New York: Palgrave/Macmillan.

Steinkuehler, C. A. 2006. Massively multiplayer online videogaming as participation in a discourse. *Mind, Culture, and Activity* 13(1): 38-52.

—. 2005. *Cognition and learning in massively multiplayer online games: A critical approach*. Doctoral diss., University of Wisconsin-Madison.

Sternheimer, K. 2003. *It's not the media: The truth about pop culture's influence on children*. Cambridge, MA: Westview Press.

Squire, K.D. 2005. Changing the game: What happens when videogames enter the classroom? *Innovate 1.6.* http://www.innovateonline.info/index.php?view=article&id=81(retrieved Feb. 22, 2008).

Squire, K., and H. Jenkins. 2004. Harnessing the power of games in education. *Insight* 3(1): 5-33.

Taylor, T. L. 2006. *Play between worlds: Exploring online game culture*. Cambridge, MA: MIT Press.

THQ (nd). *Full spectrum warrior: Instruction manual.* Callabbasas Hills, CA: THQ, Inc.

Tomasello, M. 1999. *The cultural origins of human cognition*. Cambridge, MA: Harvard University Press.

CHAPTER NINE

LITERACY ON A SOCIAL NETWORKING SITE

HÅVARD SKAAR

Some ethnographic studies use "culture" as the key concept for investigation of children's use of media and technology in and out of school (Schofield 1995). In this ethnographic study literacy is the key concept. An ethnographic approach implies that literacy is understood as a social practice, not as a set of autonomous skills (Street 1999, Barton and Hamilton 1998). The social practice investigated in this case is a group of children's ways of communicating and expressing themselves on a social networking site.

While carrying out field work in a 6th year primary school class (aged 11-12) in Oslo, I observed the pupils' use of computers and web-based learning resources. During my observations I also learned that 11 of the 22 pupils in the class had created, or were about to create, their own web pages on a social networking site called Piczo. Piczo. Inc. hosts web pages for children and adolescents world wide. On their individual sites, the users present their profile and a list of links to the Piczo-sites of their friends. In this way a social network is established online.

On Piczo pages, the pupils digitalize their social life on the computer screen. They transcend real life time and space limitations in ways that make the context of their interaction harder to determine (Jones 2004). In the actual situation, social networking sites like Piczo engage millions of children and adolescents in literacy activities worldwide. At the same time schools have experienced that social networking sites generate problems such as cyber harassment, cyber stalking and cyber bullying (Barrett 2006, Tonn 2006). For these reasons the use of social networking sites has been banned on many school servers. Nevertheless, ubiquitous online connection blurs the boundaries between pupils' social life in and out of school. Despite the social problems they create in schools, social networking sites have become an important part of pupils' literacy out of school. It has been argued, and also documented, that digital technology can help us bridge the gap between children's life world in and out of school (Hull and Schultz 2002, Østerud 2004). How does the pupils' use of Piczo fit into this picture? Is it possible to transfer pupils' out of school literacy on social networking sites like Piczo to classroom literacy learning? Does this make the lessons learnt at Piczo.com relevant for the literacy curriculum in school? These are important questions in a situation where the use of social networking sites is spreading like wildfire among school children. Ethnographic research aimed at exploring their use has yet to be carried out. This study is meant as an initial step.

Social networking-sites

Figure 9-1. Pupil's opening Piczo page

Piczo is presented on the net like this: "Piczo allows its users to create fully customizable personal websites that do not require any understanding of html code. Users share their life stories with friends by designing their sites with multiple pages featuring photos, graphics, guest books, comment boards, music, and more." Net sites based on the same commercial principles as Piczo provide the codes to these more or less complex semiotic resources for free. By a simple copy and paste technique, the users' own texts and pictures can be accompanied by games, music and video clips. On this basis Piczo hosts web pages containing the user's personal profile (typically including name, age, gender, interests etc.), and a list of links to the pages of the user's friends or contacts within the networking site.

Online sites with many similarities to social networking sites have been on the web for nearly twenty years, but the types that are most popular today, like Friendster, Facebook, Myspace, Bobo and Piczo, have only existed for the last two to three years.

Piczo was launched in 2004. It is primarily used by teens and preteens. The largest Piczo user group is girls under 18 years of age. According to its own figures, Piczo had 10.2 million unique visitors in August 2006, and was the most popular social networking site in Canada this year. Social networking sites generate income for the owners through promotion and advertising. In 2005 Piczo was the fastest growing online brand in the UK (9669 per cent growth).

The person who sets up a Piczo site has normally also allowed the intervention of others on the pages. Visitors can add comments, codes and links. This deprives the site holder of full control over what might be exposed on the pages.

Figure 9-2. Use of commercial brands on a Piczo page

It is important for Piczo Inc. not to be held responsible for exposing adolescents to sexual predators and other dangers on the net. Piczo cannot keep its 10.2 million visitors a week under effective surveillance. Instead the company has supplied the site with an online guide about "the risks that exist in any public network" (www.info.piczo.com/wiredSafety). This guide is provided by "the world's largest Internet safety and help group". But when Piczo users socialize, there is more than security at stake for Piczo Inc. Piczo makes semiotic resources containing brands, trademarks and different kinds of promotion available to Piczo users, and consequently has a financial interest in their use of these resources on their individual Piczo pages.

Literacy as social practice in and out of school

Classical sociological variables such as ethnicity, gender and class have been defined as pivotal for pupils' acquisition of literacy in numerous studies (e.g. Heath 1983). Moreover, anthropological and ethnographic approaches have turned the significance of literacy into a cultural question in a more general sense. Within the recently conceptualized field of "new literacy studies" the mutual constitution of text and context is a shared basic assumption, whether the point of departure is traditional ethnography (Barton and Hamilton 1998, Street 1998, 2003), or discourse analytic methodologies (Gee 1999, 2004).

On this theoretical basis, research carried out under the presupposition that literacy consists of autonomous cognitive skills has been accused of covering up for social and political injustice (Taylor 1998). Problems related to reading and writing are explained as due to deficient pedagogical techniques instead of cultural and economical inequalities. In opposition to this, the ethnographic approaches that describe literacy as a cultural or social practice have been criticised for providing only local perspectives on literacy. Some critics have claimed that these studies' fine-tuned descriptions of the ways in which literacy is embedded in local cultures undermine the acknowledgement of a general and global need for basic literacy skills (Gough 1995, Jones 1997). Within the field of "new literacy studies" the local problem is met by the development of concepts with global applicability. Ideology, power and identity can be made relevant for the findings in any context (Collins and Blot 2003). But basically the local/global problem is not a conceptual question. Theoretically one cannot make the local globally relevant without returning to an autonomous understanding of literacy. Methodologically, the local constraints of ethnography are inescapable, but this does not make ethnography inappropriate for the provision of in-depth knowledge of literacy both in and out of school.

Literacy understood as a social practice makes writing and design dependent on a cultural context to be experienced as meaningful. For pupils, presenting, shaping, developing, exploring and confirming themselves socially on Piczo *is* meaningful. The fact that schools do not allow their pupils to use social networking sites on their servers makes the conflict with school norms and ideology obvious. Nevertheless, social networking is a social practice that influences children's and adolescents' experiences and understandings of literacy in their life realms in and out of school. This study sets out to describe the typical features of social networking, writing and design on the pupils' Piczo pages. The presentation and discussion of these features are necessarily based on normative questions and assumptions. One basic assumption is that literacy on Piczo pages is not defined uniquely by their users.

Following Freire (1970), critical literacy studies have approached school literacy as institutionalized suppression of pupils belonging to underprivileged groups in society (Luke and Freebody 1997). It makes sense to argue that making these pupils' own culture relevant in school also means empowering them and giving them a chance to flourish like pupils from more privileged groups. In the actual situation, computers and online access are relevant for children's literacy both in and out of school. In a perspective of equity it also seems reasonable to ask how digital technology can contribute to bridging the gap between pupils' literacy practices in and out of school (Hull and Nelson 2005). But we must keep in mind that children and adolescents do not invent their out of school cultures all by themselves. Commercial actors like Piczo are also contributing to this cultural production. Further knowledge of how Piczo contributes, and how this contribution influences pupils' online literacy in this particular case, can enrich our understanding of the relation between school literacy and the literacy pupils engage in out of school.

Literacy as digital design

In the digital era, literacy is intertwined with technology in ways that makes it difficult to distinguish the one from the other. In the article "New media can never change learning", Richard Clark concludes that as long as new media do not offer new pedagogical possibilities but simply replicate existing ones, the media in itself cannot have any specific pedagogical consequences (Clark 1994). This position is based on a cognitive approach that distinguishes literacy from learning. The use of signs is not theorised. On the contrary, in a social semiotic perspective the use of signs in itself implies a learning process (Hodge and Kress 1988), and the notion of literacy is understood in accordance with this (Jewitt and Kress 2003).

The move from page to screen (Snyder 1997) implied in online communication makes certain ways of expressing oneself more appropriate than others. Kress and van Leeuwen have coined the term multimodal discourse in describing the semiotic consequences of our access to digital technology and communication channels such as the Internet. They have also stated that today the image is taking over the territory that was primarily held by written text (Kress and van Leeuwen 1996, 2001). In recent years, the research literature has produced numerous suggestions for more expanded definitions of the term than the ability to read and write (Lankshear and Knobel 2003). In this I will follow Günther Kress' line of thought. Although he thinks the notion of literacy should still be restricted to reading and writing, he does not think the content of the term is the same as before. In his view, new media and technology have embedded reading and writing in a multimodal discourse and thus altered the meaning of being literate (Kress 2003).

When the pupils in the study present themselves on Piczo pages, their writing is embedded in a simultaneous use of other semiotic recourses. This means that the skills required are not restricted to the use of alphabetic letters. This makes the term "multimodal discourse" relevant for the description of the ways the pupils express themselves online. Kress (along with other members of the so-called London group) uses the term "design" to distinguish this semiotic practice from alphabetic writing. The notion "digital literacy" has similarly been used to notify the ability to produce written text digitally (Lewis and Fabos 2005). In line with this, in this chapter "digital design" will be used to denote the digital production of multimodal texts.

Method

The study is based on data gathered during two periods of observations of computer use in a primary school classroom in Oslo. The class I observed had 23 (later 22) pupils, nine girls and 14 boys, most typically from middle class and lower middle class homes. Around one half of the pupils are ethnic Norwegians, the other half have mixed or immigrant backgrounds.

The first period of observation took place at the end of the 5th grade, the second half a year later. I observed the pupils' activities, once a week, during a three-month period. In addition to observations of quotidian classroom life, I conducted a series of short interviews aimed at charting the pupils' use of computers out of school. The pupils told me about their use of interactive games, their chatting on MSN, and also about their use of Piczo pages.

After my initial interviews (with all the pupils in the class but two) had revealed that 11 pupils had made their own Piczo pages, I started focusing on the differences between these 11 pupils' use of Piczo. The pupils' use of their Piczo pages was documented consecutively on the net. This made their literacy in peer interaction out of school, which is often hidden from parents and teachers, accessible for close observation over time. After the first round of interviews I downloaded the pupils' Piczo pages weekly for a period of six months in order to track the changes they made. This observation showed that the correctness of the answers already given in the interviews often was questionable. This generated additional interviews. To fill in the picture I also interviewed one of the class teachers about the pupils' Piczo use. The interviews varied in length from two or three to 25 minutes.

The Piczo users in the class can be divided into three groups. A brief description of a pupil in each group is given to clarify these three typical patterns of use.

Social networking

Online access of some sort was available to all but one of the 22 pupils in the class. Some had Internet access in their private rooms; others had to share access to the computer or computers available at home with parents and siblings. The level of interest and time spent showed great differentiation, but nearly all of the pupils reported that they had played games and chatted on MSN at home. Although research has pointed out the significance of such differences (Hutchby and Moran-Ellis 2001), it is reasonable to assume that participation in the class' social life online was technically possible for the great majority of the pupils.

11 of the 22 pupils in the class (five girls and six boys) had made their own Piczo pages. Although Piczo offers a digital network structure that is basically open to everyone, the persons in the network were primarily recruited from the pupils' social network offline. The 11 pupils in the class with their own Piczo sites had all been introduced to online networking by older friends or siblings, and they were primarily linking their pages to offline friends, most typically classmates. In this way the pupils' social preferences became explicit. The names and links to friends in the class also made it clear who was left out.

In the interviews, all the Piczo users in the class judge use of the Piczo website to be more interesting, engaging and exciting than school-based writing and interaction. The pupils themselves explain this with the richer possibilities for digital design on Piczo, but also with the fact that "Piczo has nothing to do with school". On Piczo they "can do what they want". The regulations Piczo imposes formally (e.g. that the users are required to be 13 years of age or that pornography or other kinds of inappropriate material are not allowed) do not regulate the pupils' actual use of the site.

Although Piczo's "Wired Safety Guide" informs users that "most webmasters won't tolerate cyber bullying, identity theft, online harassment, or anything else that hurts other members", I found all of these on the pupils' Piczo pages. This is not more surprising than the general existence of pupil behaviour at odds with school rules and regulations. But although "disembodiment" is established as an inescapable feature for online identity building (Slater 2002), the urgent request not to post any "personally identifiable information" on the Piczo pages must be a striking paradox for a networking-site based on self-presentations. Despite the warnings, all of the pupils presented their first name, school and neighbourhood on their Pico sites. Three of them also added their family name, and all but two presented pictures of themselves. All the Piczo users in the class were also MSN-users, and seven of them also gave out their email and/or msn-address on their pages. It is a common trait for the Piczo users in the class that they actively sought to transcend their preteen status by relating to an adolescent culture that in reality was unfamiliar to most of them. Still the pupils' online social life at the Piczo site functions more like an extension than an alteration to their social life offline. All the pupils built their networks to interact off- and online with children of about the same age as themselves. None of them stated in the interviews that they had been approached by adults on their pages.

The sociolinguist Dell Hymes gives his notion of "voice" a social dimension related to power in talking about "narrative inequality" (Hymes 1996). Some researchers assume that this inequality can be diminished by offering the pupils digital communication channels in addition to the face-to-face communication that takes place in the classroom. The findings in this study do not support this claim. My observations in the classroom revealed that the pupils who repeatedly took the floor to tell their classmates and teachers stories from their own lives were the same pupils who were setting up Piczo pages in their leisure time. About half of them belonged to the "cool" and trendsetting group of pupils in the class. The other half was generally of the outspoken kind that took any opportunity offered to make both teachers and classmates aware of their presence in the classroom.

The use of social networking sites has been compared to hanging out (boyd 2007). The pupils in this study establish their Piczo networks on a local basis, but these interactive channels are still open to everyone. Apart from their friends, they are never quite sure who they are going to meet.

Interaction on Piczo pages takes place in guest books, shout boxes, by polls and through links to external email or instant messaging. The most common way to interact on Piczo pages is by posting messages. The posts often contain a request for visits to the commenter's own Piczo site. The site holder can respond directly to the posts added by visitors. A topic for discussion can be described in a headline, which is very often left open.

Class- and schoolmates most frequently added posts on the Piczo pages monitored in this study. Their comments are mostly positive, but can also be teasing or insulting. Anonymous visitors, and visitors not included in the local network, tend to contribute the most hostile, unkind or insulting comments. When that happens, classmates often get involved and defend the person under attack:

> Very nice site. HELoo ALL YOU SCUMBAGS, WHAT'S THE POINT IN WRITING CRAP ON HIS PAGE, eh??? PISS OFF IF YOU JUST HAVE JERKY STUFF TO TELL, OK!! Hugggg <3

Among the messengers who did not identify themselves with a full name, a substantial number adopted an aggressive style. One of the pupils identified this example as an exchange between a girl in the class and a girl from her former school, apparently discussing football:

> ~I ~: You are a failed abortion
> ~I~: And…? Lesbian! Whore! Didn't you read this?
> Evelyn: I dont really like any (football)teams… I don't like any of them…
> ~~I~~: Fucking lesbian! You are ruining people's lives by showing your ugly face to the world (…) Do me a favour kill you self so I don't have to do it.

When the pupils in interviews were asked whether verbal attacks meant the same online as offline (for instance in the schoolyard), they seemed to lack concepts for an elaborated answer. When prompted they confirmed that aggressive and insulting use of language was tried out in a far more direct way online than offline. Also positive statements are amplified online. Many of the girls seem to try out growing psychosexual emotions by declaring their love rather casually in replies to whoever of their class- or schoolmates has left a post in their shout box: "luv yah.." (Jennifer). The hyperlinked structure combined with the offering of commercial and readymade signs stimulates ratings of commodities like pizza or trainers. Piczo's invitation to network by linking and listing up friends makes it tempting to rate them the same way. Some of the pupils made polls over brands and merchandise. Others added pictures of classmates and friends.

The current poll results were made available on the pages. One of the teachers reported that some of the pupils in the class had been hurt by this kind of poll. For this reason the teacher had informed the parents of the pupils involved about the problem, and the class had decided to abandon such practices. Despite this the ratings still existed on the pupils' Piczo pages at the time the study was conducted.

The practice had been taken even further by some of the pupils. In a sly use of polls, two pupils who shared a Piczo page gave the unidentifiable visitors the responsibility for their own harassment of a schoolmate. Under the heading "Guess who we hate" they first gave some alternatives on name, sex and interests. Then the visitors are asked to vote for this person being "Good looking", "dumb" or "disgusting". By looking at the poll results we can find out that an identified male person at school is disgusting.

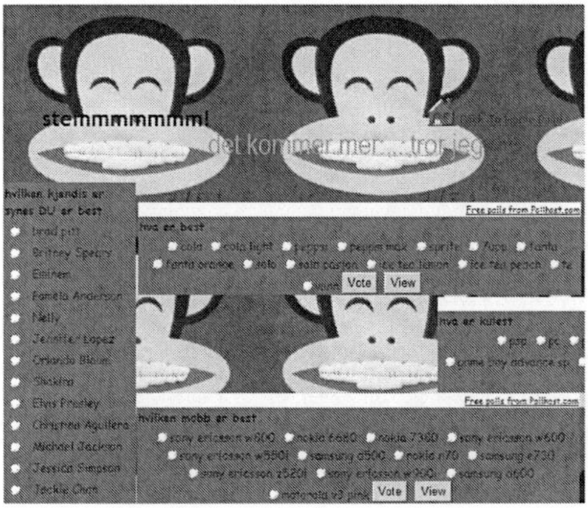

Figure 9-3. Voteeeeee! Pop artists and merchandise

Ironically, the two pupils had also made a page with the sole purpose of condemning bullying. When one of them was confronted with this contradiction in an interview, the final comment was that "Everybody can make a mistake".

Pizco replicates the schoolyard virtually in a way that exposes aspects of the pupils' social life not easily detectable offline. By making a club for "Best friends", and restricting access with a password, pupils use yet another strategy to transfer the inclusion/exclusion dynamics from the schoolyard to the net.

The most engaged pupils were those who allowed the Piczo pages to play a part in their social interaction both online and offline. In contrast to many other social networking sites, Piczo allows its users to sign up for as many Piczo pages as they want. The network is mostly links to school- and classmates. Some users reinforce this offline/online connection by joint making of Piczo pages with friends and classmates. They use their common pages to confirm their privileged relationship to each other:

> Hi Hi! We are two girls who is veeeeery good bestfriends :p
> We have been bestfriends since first grade and are really close. So this is our homepage. Pleas write in our guestbook!!!
> HUGZ

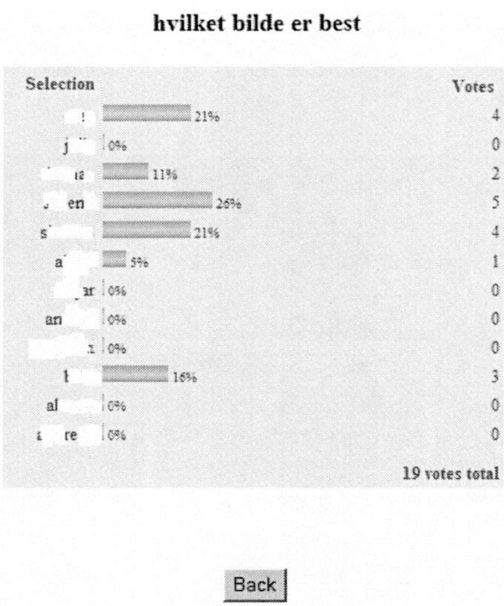

Figure 9-4. Poll results: Which photo (of pupils in the class) is the best? (names erased)

The pupils who shared Piczo pages with classmates used the interactive possibilities on their pages more persistently than those who just gave out their email and msn-addresses with a general call for response. The latter kind of online interaction tended to die out quite soon.

Writing and design

A central finding in this study is that skilful writing and skilful design correlate. In my own valuation, the most skilful design is made by pupils who are good writers. Accordingly, those who find it difficult to write do not compensate for this by the construction of skilful design.

My judgements are supported by the class teacher's valuation of the individual pupils' writing skills. My valuations of the pupils' design are in fact also confirmed by comments given by peer visitors to the actual pages. In the eyes of an 11 year old, being a good copycat can bring much more impressive results than meticulous construction of personal writing. Nevertheless the study shows that most pupils experience skilful design as much more than just being a good copycat. Hostile and insulting comments flourish in any shout box, but at the same time good design systematically gets credit for it:

> Nice site, Kim; P you have worked really well with this one!!!! Keep on :-D
> Hugzy from Vera :p
> Nice site :-P (Actually one of the best I have visited).

The ones not succeeding with their design are also made aware of this:

> Delete this site, you use Piczo`s memory
> Fuck, You should delete this shit.

Although the study exhibits a clear correlation between the mastering of writing and the mastering of design, skilful making of Piczo pages also requires practice. This practice is stimulated by interaction with the persons visiting the pages. Persistent redesigning is tied to an interest in the feedback visitors give on the elements presented on the pages.

Many 11-year-olds strive to be like teens, and Piczo gives them access to a semiotic space that can push them into the realm of adolescence. One way to enter is by presenting (randomly chosen) photos of teens as friends and adding video clips of rap and hip hop artists sending out "cool" and highly eroticised messages both visually and verbally. But a hasty presentation of make-believe, grotesquery, and sexualised content is not enough to establish a viable communicational structure on a social networking site. Over time it is primarily a strong interest in the possibilities for interactive communication that makes redesign of the pages relevant for the pupils.

The observation of the pupils' Piczo pages revealed differences that made it possible to roughly subdivide them into three groups (an internal analytic generalization, see Schrøder et al. 2003, 148). Arin, Safdar and Tom are typically members of each of these categories. A brief description of their respective use of Piczo pages can clarify and contextualise the characteristics of the three types of users.

Arin: Piczo literacy as a school literacy replicate

In Arin's opinion he has learned more about computer use from his father than from his teachers. Arin was the first in the class to make Piczo pages. His older sister taught him how to do it, and subsequently he has brought this knowledge to several of his classmates.

Arin designs and uses his Piczo pages in accordance with the guidelines for appropriate behaviour given at the Piczo site. He presents himself with a picture taken in the schoolyard after he has been playing in the snow. In the written text he emphasizes sports and training as his interests. Generally speaking, his literacy on Pizco is not in opposition to the literacy he presents at school – a literacy that is highly valued both by schoolmates and teachers.

His writing on the pages is correct and informative, while the semiotic resources copied from other pages and from commercial sign providers are mainly of the humorous kind. He presents pictures of his classmates and friends along with basically respectful and positive comments. His polls and rating lists are about the music and design he has chosen for his own site. In the interviews, he expresses agreement with the class decision not to rate classmates or friends. In the shoutboxes on his pages he gets positive and encouraging comments, and he says that it has not been necessary to delete unpleasant posts. He writes back on request, but not very eagerly. The interactive possibilities seem to interest him less than the actual construction of the pages. In the final interviews he says that he has not lost interest in his Piczo pages, but that his activities have slowed down lately, which is also confirmed by the surveillance of his pages.

Safdar: Make believe Piczo literacy

Unlike Arin, Safdar uses his Piczo pages to present a different literacy from the one he presents in the classroom. In his Piczo self presentation he is basically pushing himself into the realm of adolescence. Video clips of rap and hip hop artists present "cool" and highly eroticised messages, both visually and verbally. The friends he presents are mainly not from the class, and many of the girls look older than he does (although heavy make-up makes it rather hard to tell). In his comments he drops hints whichin an innocent way give his relationship to these girls a romantic/erotic dimension.

Safdar does not write much on Piczo, and most of his sentences are grammatically incorrect. He prefers bullet-point and lists of words, and seems to avoid syntactic constructions. Safdar counts his visitors on the opening page, and he is proud to tell that the number is rising all the time. During the interview he also (understandably enough) seems embarrassed when asked about the eroticized content on his page. He claims that he likes the male, not the female, dancers in the video clips. He says that he prefers the Piczo pages to the school use of computers, but at the same time he states that he now finds the Piczo site boring. He does not know why this is so.

Tom: Dynamic integration of Piczo and school literacy

Tom started with a number of different Piczo sites by himself, but then took more interest in setting up the sites together with friends. In this way he operates on several pages simultaneously: his solo site, two different sites with three of the girls from the class, and a site with a friend from the 7th grade. Eventually this site occupies him the most. The site is under constant reconstruction, and especially the interactive possibilities are investigated. Typically, while Arin announces his romantic attachments with great caution and Safdar is more ostentatious, Tom uses Piczo to take the role as matchmaker. Under the heading "Are you single?" he announces:

> Hi! If you are single this is perfect for you. May be you always have wished a sweetheart at you own age. Here you can tell what kind of sweetheart you want and I will fix it for you. You can also write who you like.

Through the formulation "at your own age" Tom is hedging against sexual predators. When I ask him about his offer to be a fixer he tells me that he has not had any response yet. It seems as if the matchmaker role serves more as a pretext for the last sentence in the invitation. At any rate, this sentence covers the actual use of the page. Everybody uses nicknames in a discussion of the social worth of their schoolmates. Some comments on other pupils are positive, but a great many are rather insulting. Tom and his friend are themselves very explicit in their likes and dislikes. In an early version of their page it opened like this:

> Hi folx! Hi this page is not for you that like ***! He has got a big ****, just so you know.(…) We love Paul Frank and summer, fruit, clothing and Louis Vuitton.

This quotation shows a mixing of persons, objects and brands typical for the way Tom and his friend give themselves an identity on their Piczo pages. In the later versions of their pages Tom and his friend call themselves “The crew”. They do not only advise their visitors on which types of clothes to wear or body lotion to use, but also who they should include or exclude from their social life at school. Their use of commercial semiotic resources in advanced combinations (music, video-clips, pictures, writing etc.) shows awareness of how brands and other commercial semiotic resources can be made socially significant in their local group of peers. Trademarks (e.g. Nike, see Elliot and Leonard 2004) have a symbolic value that is freely available to any Piczo user. Buying the trainers is not necessary. On the other hand, a material confirmation of the Nike-affinity might very well be requested offline, which implies that the interrelation between online and offline networking depends on more than just a successful use of the free access to the reservoir of signs and symbols on the net. Tom and his friend know how to make the link. Typically, visitors are offered to test their social status in polls measuring preference for e.g. Adidas or Puma. Likewise, visitors are invited to measure the status of their social background by answering how they pronounce “Adidas” (the different forms of pronunciation in Norwegian imply social stratification).

Tom is one of the most enthusiastic users of Piczo in the class. He tells me that he keeps on because he feels that he is “getting better and better at making homepages and making them look nice.”

Social networking

The threefold typology indicates that pupils exploit the perceived freedom to “do what they want” on their Piczo pages in different ways. For the first group of pupils, Piczo can stimulate literacy in accordance with the social demands from the school community and at the same time bring the pupils’ designing skills to a higher level. For the second group, pupils’ designing skills are much less developed, and the use of Piczo pages is also at odds with social norms in the school community. For the third group, the semiotic possibilities offered on Piczo are taken to a very advanced level, but still in a way that is socially unacceptable to the school. Altogether quite a nuanced picture, but in sum producing overall problems that explain why so many schools have chosen to ban social networking sites on their servers.

Schools and teachers use power to impose institutional norms on pupils, and this is reflected in the way pupils are allowed to express themselves in the classroom, and also in school-based online communication. As mentioned in the introduction, many studies on literacy have pointed to schools' cultural expectations and demands as unfair and excluding for many pupils. This has led to the belief that greater equity can be obtained if pupils' reading, writing and design out of school are made relevant on the same terms in school. But the pupils' Piczo pages did not give them an alternative "voice" in relation to their classmates in this case. The online networking and interaction rather confirmed and emphasized networks and patterns of interaction already established offline.

The study indicates that the pupils use their Piczo pages to confirm their preferences as consumers rather than to express something about themselves they are otherwise denied. Instead of solely being consumers, the pupils also became active distributors of promotion and advertising. In the social interaction, rating of products sometimes merged with the ratings of friends. Generally popular culture was not reshaped and personalized in the kind of inventive activities that have been described as preferable in the research literature on children, youth and media (Hodge and Kress 1988, Haas Dyson 2003, Willis 2003, Buckingham 2003). Some of the pupils used the commercially infused semiotic resources in a skilful way that clearly liberated their own creativity, but hardly in a way that subverted the providers' intentions at the same time. On the contrary, the Piczo pages were used, in full accordance with the Piczo company's interests, as a meeting place where consumption in itself was celebrated. Generally speaking, the most eager users of Piczo were the greatest consumers of fun and entertainment and, by the redistribution of these resources on their own pages, also the most eager promoters, marketers and advertisers. Understandably, Piczo has no interest in their users' critical awareness of this. Schools should have.

Writing and design

The most engaged pupils showed a clear interest in developing their Piczo-design in ways that gave them attention and credit among their peers. The study indicates that skilful writing on Piczo pages makes the design follow suit, but not the other way around. In other words: design skills do not compensate for lack of writing skills for the pupils in this study. Writing, design and interaction are mutually intensified in their use of Piczo pages.

On the Piczo site, the pupils express themselves through the use of written text and more complex semiotic resources. The first kind can be coded by the pupils themselves, whereas the latter kind is copied or uploaded either from the user's own hard disk, from commercial sites, or from the pages of other Piczo users. Theoretically the pupils themselves could have coded any of the resources they used on their pages. In practice, written text was the only mode they were actually able to code. In this sense the tools offered by Piczo create an inverse proportionality between the multimodal complexity of semiotic resources and the effort it takes to use them. A youngster who wants to get a message across might very well find it easier to upload a readymade video clip than to write a meaningful sentence.

High	Video clips, games, animations, music
Low	Written text

Table 9-1. Multimodal complexity of the semiotic resources used

High	Written text
Low	Video clips, games, animations , music

Table 9-2. The knowledge and skills invested in the use of semiotic resources

In a study of 5th grade pupils' story telling in front of computers (Skaar 2007), I related digitally provided multimodality and coding of signs to a theoretical argument launched by Jewitt and Kress:

> In making a representation a person is making a new sign out of what they want to signify, with existing signifying materials. The sign-maker chooses the signifier that is most apt for being the vehicle to represent that which they wish to signify. However, there is never an exact fit, but it is the best possible fit of meaning and form. In the gap between what they meant to mean and what they have to use to mean it exists the possibility of a new sign that not only had not been made before, but a sign that wrenches their meanings in unpredictable directions. That lack of fit, and that wrenching, change not only the externally made sign, but also the inwardly made sign in its relations to other signs inwardly held. The new state of all signs now marks the effect of sign-making as meaning (Jewitt and Kress, 2003, 13).

This social semiotic approach gives a theoretical basis for an understanding of how the use of digitally provided ready made signs, in contrast to signs coded by the pupils themselves, influences their literacy in this case. The use of ready made signs (e.g. a video clip) demands fewer semiotic choices than the use of signs the pupils code themselves (in this case only written text). Fewer semiotic choices give pupils less experience of the lack of fit between what they "meant to mean" and what they "have to use to mean". This implies less learning for the group of pupils just filling up their pages with readymade signs, than for the group of pupils who are also engaged writers. This indicates that the design of Piczo pages basically requires a willingness to submit to norms of the same kind that regulate the production of written text. In other words, writing stands out as the most crucial competence for success as a Piczo designer.

In discussing the hypertextual multimodality that wired computers make accessible for us, Lemke concludes that:

> Visual communication is at its most powerful, not when it retreats into the splendid isolation of an imaginary semiotic autonomy, but when it confronts verbal language head-on and challenges its hegemony, when it takes its place as an equal (…) partner in multimodal communication. The medium in which both confrontation and partnership, both subversion and empowerment, is most fully afforded today is that of hypertext. Traveling together in hypermodality, we can make meanings that will let people see and speak in new and more thoughtfully critical ways (Lemke 2002, 323).

A celebration of the empowering and critical thoughtfulness of hypermodality can also be found in Hull and Nelson (2005). The points made are not irrelevant or wrong, but the authors underplay the fact that pupils' literacy, whether hypermodal or not, always takes place within a context. Lemke also shows awareness of this in his work, claiming that the context of "commercial transmedia" requires a "critical multimedia literacy" (Lemke 2006). In this study the context is a commercial sphere of entertainment provided by Piczo. Piczo's financial interest lies in users' consumption of commercially saturated ready made signs, not in the coding of their own writing.

This reflects the critical difference between the use of these kinds of multimodal signs offline and online. Using scissors to cut pictures and text out of a newspaper or a magazine that are then hung up on the classroom wall is not profitable for anybody. Doing the same on Piczo pages means money for the site-provider. When children enter the Piczo site, they are immediately under the influence of a pre-scripted structure (Fagerjord 2005) aimed at making their texts and utterances as profitable as possible. Literacy learning in classroom must make this clear to children and adolescents. The meaning of communication in a structure that makes your self-presentation and social interaction profitable for those who offer you space and semiotic resources to do it is not evident to 11 year olds. It can be learnt in literacy hour at school.

In the actual situation, pupils' own writing often takes place in commercial contexts that are not easily seen through. Schools must give pupils a chance to understand the commercial interests involved in their use of writing and other semiotic resources online. Perhaps rather paradoxically, if the agenda is to empower pupils' literacy in a media-saturated and digitalized era, their actual Piczo literacy indicates that the mode of writing is the place to start. Learning to read and write in accordance with norms established in school communities, not on commercial net sites, gives pupils the opportunity to establish a genuine and personal voice that can resist commercial colonization.

Writing skills put pupils in a stronger position to resist commercial pressure and manipulation than the use of other semiotic modes, for two reasons. Firstly, alphabetic writing is a digital code that is hard to colonize in itself. You might offer children branded fonts, but you cannot control the way they are used. Secondly, written language gives an opportunity to mobilize a critical thoughtfulness on the use of other kinds of semiotic resources.

Conclusion

Viewing literacy as a social practice makes both the social and the semiotic relevant in analyzing pupils' Piczo use. Although this study does not allow external generalisations, it illustrates that transfer of pupils' Piczo literacy to the classroom setting is not possible without some kind of value judgement. Pupils are sent to school not only to improve their literacy, but also to learn how to participate in the school community in constructive ways. This knowledge is acquired through a socialization process that naturally brings school culture into opposition to the culture the children create for themselves. The implication of this is that classroom writing and designing will inevitably meet tough competition from Piczo when it comes to popularity. The institutionally imposed norms will always make school-based literacy duller than the literacy entangled in commercial entertainment, at least in the eyes of some of the pupils. On a technical level, we might also add that the pupils' interest and engagement in the use of digital design in school always have a potential for enhancement through a closing of the gap between the computerised possibilities experienced in and out of school. Faster processors and more updated programs are stimulating for everybody. This makes investments in new equipment reasonable, although it is tempting to add that in this race schools are always doomed to lag behind the commercial spearheads.

The battle for empowerment of pupils' literacy must be fought on other fronts as well. Banning of social networking sites on school servers does not make the commercial penetration of pupils' online literacy disappear. The study indicates that in the use of ready-made or pre-coded semiotic resources on their Piczo pages, pupils run the risk of losing control over their own textual production. They inevitably speak on behalf of Piczo as well as on behalf of themselves. As pointed out by a growing number of researchers, a central part of literacy should be a critical awareness of the commercial interests involved in the use of new media such as the Internet (Willett 2007, Buckingham 2006, Fabos 2004). Schools are not likely to exceed commercially provided online entertainment and fun, but are still in a privileged position to empower children with knowledge about the powers at play in various forms of communication in the new digitalized landscape of media and communication. In this way, schools can help children and adolescents to build the competencies that critical and thoughtful digital design actually requires.

References

Barrett, J. 2006. Social networking: A new tech tool and a new security concern for teens and schools. *MultiMedia and Internet@ Schools* 13(3): 8-11.

Barton, D., and M. Hamilton. 1998. *Local literacies: Reading and writing in one community*. London: Routledge.

boyd, d. 2007. Why youth ♥ social network sites: The role of networked publics in teenage
social life. In *Youth, Identity and Digital Media*, ed. David Buckingham, 119-142. Cambridge, MA: MIT Press.

Buckingham, D. 2003. *Media education: Literacy, learning and contemporary culture*. Cambridge: Polity Press.

—. 2006. Defining digital literacy: What do young people need to know about digital media? *Digital kompetanse* 1(4): 263-276.

Clark, R. E. 1994. Media will never influence learning. *Educational Technology Research and Development* 42(2): 21-29.

Collins, J., and K. Richard. 2003. *Literacy and literacies: Texts, power and identity*. Cambridge: Cambridge University Press.

Cope, B., and M. Kalantzis, ed. 2000. *Multiliteracies: Literacy learning and the design of social futures*. London: Routledge.

Dyson, A. H. 2003. "Welcome to the jam:" Popular culture, school literacy, and the making of childhoods. *Harvard Educational Review* 73(3): 328-361.

Elliott, R., and C. Leonard. 2004. Peer pressure and poverty: Exploring fashion brands and consumption symbolism among children of the "British poor." *Journal of Consumer Behavior* 3(4): 347-359.

Fabos, B. 2004. *Wrong turn on the information superhighway: Education and the commercialization of the internet*. New York: Teachers College Press.

Fagerjord, A. 2005. Prescripts: Authoring with templates. *Kairos* 10(1), http://english.ttu.edu/kairos/10.1/binder2.html?coverweb/fagerjord/index.html (retrieved June 2006).

Freire, P. 1970. *Pedagogy of the oppressed*. New York: Seabury Press.

Gee, J. P. 2004. *Situated language and learning: A critique of traditional schooling*. London: Routledge.

—. 1999. *Introduction to discourse analysis: Theory and method*. London: Routledge.

Gough, P. B. 1995. The new literacy: caveat emptor. *Journal of Research in Reading* 18(2): 79-86.

Heath, S. B. 1983. *Ways with words: Language, life, and work in communities and classrooms*. Cambridge: Cambridge University Press.

Hodge, R., and G. Kress. 1988. *Social semiotics*. Cambridge: Polity Press.

Hull, G. A., and M. E. Nelson. 2005. Locating the semiotic power of multimodality. *Written Communication* 22(2): 224-261.

Hull, G. A., and K. Schultz, eds. 2002. *School's out: Bridging out-of-school literacies with classroom practices*. New York: Teachers College Press.

Hutchby, I., and J. Moran-Ellis. 2001. Introduction: Relating children, technology and culture. In *Children, technology and culture: The impacts of technologies in children's everyday lives*, ed. Ian Hutchby and Jo Moran-Ellis, 1-10. London: Routledge.

Hymes, D. 1996. *Ethnography, linguistics, narrative inequality: Toward an understanding of voice*. London: Taylor and Francis.

Jones, R. H. 2004. The problem of context in computer-mediated communication. In *Discourse and technology: Multimodal discourse analysis*, ed. Philip.Levine and Ron Scollon, 20-33. Washington D.C.: Georgetown University Press.

Jones, S. 1997. Ending the myth of the "Literacy myth." *Literacy across the Curriculum* 12(4): 10-17.

Jewitt, C., and G. Kress. 2003. *Multimodal literacy*. New York: Peter Lang.

Kress, G. 2003. *Literacy in the new media age*. London: Routledge.
Kress, G., and T. van Leeuween. 2001. *Multimodal discourse: The modes and media of contemporary communication*. London: Arnold.
Kress, G., and T. van Leeuwen. 1996. *Reading images: The grammar of visual design*. London: Routledge.
Lankshear, C., and M. Knobel. 2003. *New literacies: Changing knowledge and classroom learning*. Berkshire: Open University Press.
Lemke, J. 2002. Travels in hypermodality. *Visual communication* 1(3): 299-325.
Lemke, J. 2006. Transmedia traversals: Marketing meaning and identity. Paper presented at the Third International Conference on Multimodality, Pavia: Italy, http://wwwpersonal.umich.edu/~jaylemke/papers/transmedia_traversals.htm (retrieved July 2007)
Lewis, C., and B. Fabos. 2005. Instant messaging, literacies, and social identities. *Reading Research Quarterly* 40(4): 470-501.
Luke, A., and P. Freebody. 1997. Critical literacy and the question of normativity: An introduction. In *Constructing critical literacies: Teaching, learning and textual practice*, ed. Sandy Muspratt, Allan Luke and Peter Freebody, 1-18. Cresskill, NJ: Hampton Press.
Schofield, J. W. 1995. *Computers and classroom culture*. New York: Cambridge University Press.
Schrøder, K., K. Drotner, C. Murray, and S. Kline. 2003. *Researching audiences*. London: Arnold.
Skaar, H. 2007. Digitalized story making in the classroom: A social semiotic perspective on gender, multimodality and learning. *Seminar.net. Journal for Media, Technology and Lifelong Learning* 3(1), http://www.seminar.net (retrieved July 2007).
Slater, D. 2002. Social relationships and identity online and offline. In *Handbook of new media*, ed. Leah Lievrouw and Sonia Livingstone, 533-546. London: Sage.
Snyder, I., ed. 1997. *Page to screen*. London: Routledge.
Street, B. 1998. New literacies in theory and practice: What are the implications for language in education? *Linguistics and Education* 10(1): 1-24.
—. 2003. What's "new" in new literacy studies? Critical approaches to literacy in theory and practice. *Current Issues in Comparative Education* 5(2): 1-14.
Taylor, D. 1998. *Beginning to read and the spin doctors of science*. Illinois: National Council of Teachers of English.

Tonn, J. L. 2006. Expert sees need for school staff to access social-networking sites. *Education Week* 25(33): 16.

Willett, R. 2007. Consumer citizens online: Structure, agency and gender in online participation. In *Youth, Identity and Digital Media*, ed. David Buckingham, 49-70.Cambridge, Mass.: MIT Press.

Willis, P. 2003. Foot soldiers of modernity: The dialectics of cultural consumption and the 21st-century school. *Harvard Educational Review* 73(3): 390-415.

Østerud, S. 2004. *Utdanning for informasjonssamfunnet: Den tredje vei* [Education for the information society: The third way]. Oslo: Universitetsforlaget.

CHAPTER TEN

COPY AND PASTE LITERACY? LITERACY PRACTICES IN THE PRODUCTION OF A MYSPACE PROFILE [1]

DAN PERKEL

Over the past several years, educators, the media, policy makers, law enforcement officials, advertisers, venture capitalists, academics, kids, teenagers, and parents—a large segment of American society as a whole—have all turned their attention to a website called MySpace.[2] With respect to teenagers, much of the public debate has been concerned with issues of privacy and safety. However, in this chapter my interest is in teenagers' production and use of their MySpace profiles as a part of their everyday communication.

MySpace is a site where millions of members[3] create personal profiles and take part in a variety of social activities. For the teenagers who actively use MySpace, it is one of their primary means of communicating with each other and is an environment in which they can participate in many facets of American culture, especially in entertainment sectors such as music, television, and movies (boyd 2006a). Many put significant time and effort into creating and maintaining their MySpace profiles. In what ways can the production of a MySpace profile represent a locus of new digital literacies?

The answer depends on what is meant by "literacy." Here, I first analyze the creation of a MySpace profile with respect to a framework of literacy that integrates prior social and technical perspectives, focusing on the use of code. Then, I argue that while MySpace is not an ideal environment for learning some of the languages of web production, the expressive power found in the creation of a MySpace profile concerns a technically simple but socially complex practice: the copying and pasting of code as a way to appropriate and reuse other people's media products. Finally, I contend that this practice calls into question the dichotomies used when describing the processes of "consumption" and "production" and the activities of "reading" and "writing". By integrating recent work in media and cultural studies with research on literacy, concepts such as "participation" and "remix" provide a useful way of describing this new literacy practice.

Studying MySpace in use

My understanding of MySpace use has been informed by prior research (Marwick 2005, boyd 2006a, 2006b), my own use of the site, and participant observation with teenagers. One of the methodological problems of studying the internet, especially when trying to use methods often associated with ethnography, is locating the "site" of research (Lyman and Wakeford 1999, Hine 2000). I have explored MySpace and the profile production process in order to gain a better understanding of how the site works; this has included following links to external resources, such as tutorial sites, blogs, and third-party resources. However, MySpace, as of this writing, is not a significant part of my routine communication, and I am also not a teenager. Therefore, inspired by research on literacy that emphasizes studying how tools and technologies are taken up and used in everyday life (e.g. Scribner and Cole 1981, Street 1995), I have been conducting participant observation at a community-based arts and technology center (hereafter "the Center") in order to understand more about how teenagers use MySpace in a "natural" environment, meaning a place where it would be used whether or not I was present.[4]

The Center runs classes for youth on a wide variety of media production skills. The Center has a high bandwidth Internet connection and ten Macintosh computers that the students use for class projects. However, before class, during breaks, after class, and even sometime during the small gaps between activities, many of the students (aged 13-17) use the computers to log in to their MySpace accounts. While I have no way of knowing if the students use MySpace differently at the Center than they do in other places, they do not exhibit many inhibitions while using it. In summary, the students have appropriated the Center as a place where they use MySpace as a part of everyday communication with their friends and family.

The MySpace profile: A social production

A MySpace profile is an often colorful and media-intensive web page, where members describe themselves, list their interests, and link to friends. Many teenagers' MySpace pages consist of a mish-mash of text, pictures, animated graphics, bright colors, and sound, leading a popular American business magazine to label them as "design anarchy" (James 2006). They look much different than the default page with which every member starts.

There are a number of factors that account for why different members' MySpace pages can look (and sound) radically different from one another.[5] First, members can override the parameters that control the basic "look and feel" of a page, including background colors, font sizes, font colors, borders, and background images (see Figure 10-1). MySpace members typically use one of many third-party sites and either choose from a wide variety of "layouts" or use a "code generator" that presents choices of colors, fonts, font-sizes, and so forth for each aspect of the page.[6]

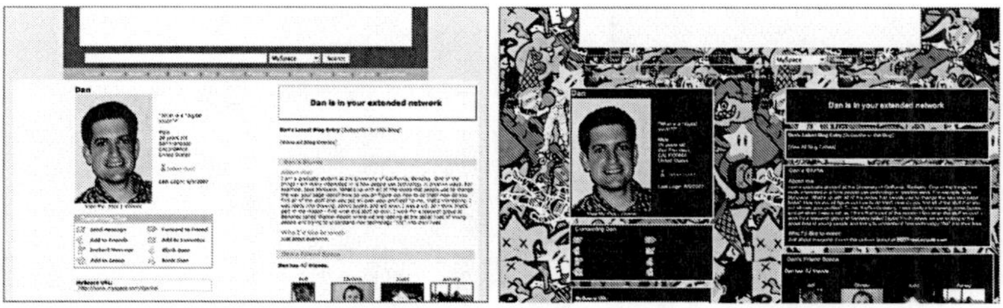

Figure 10-1. Two versions of the author's MySpace profile. The one on the left uses the default layout and colors. The one on the right uses different styles and graphics to change visual elements

After finding a layout or using a code generator, the person has to copy a block of HTML and CSS (Cascading Style Sheets) code from the site and paste it into one of the free-text form fields provided by MySpace for entering profile information (see Figure 10-2).[7]

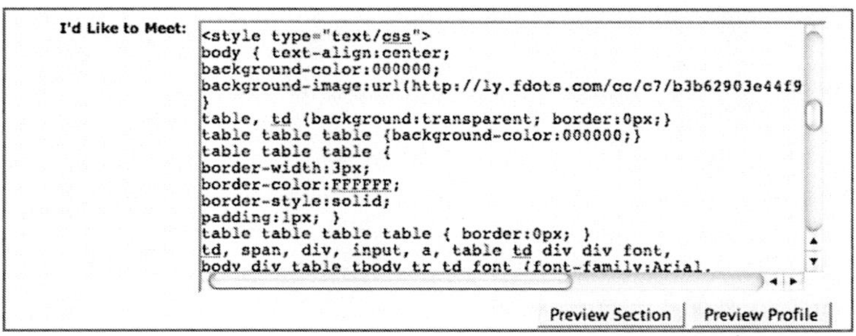

Figure 10-2. Changing the page theme requires putting code into a profile form

Customizing through a themed layout often involves using media and graphics that come with the templates, also hosted by other third party websites, as a byproduct of using that layout. However, members can also explicitly "embed" media in their pages by pasting code that links to images, video, audio, and even games (see Figure 10-3). This reuse and appropriation of media, account for much of the color, sound, and animation found on a page and also dictates the way other elements appear by taking up horizontal and vertical space. In linking to media in this way, either implicitly through the layouts or through explicit embedding, members give up much control of what appears on their profile and how it might change over time as the media often exists on someone or some company's servers.[8]

Figure 10-3. Embedded images and other media in a profile

Finally, people can often include media in their comments on other people's pages that come with the same aesthetic effects (see Figure 10-4). Therefore, even if a member carefully selects or manipulates media in an effort to wield more aesthetic and editorial control, friends' comments can work against those efforts.

The embedding of code with links to media, whether by a profile's "owner" or her friends, means that each profile is the product of many people, not just the work of the individual MySpace member. Continued control of how a profile is put together is distributed amongst many people and resources. Therefore, in looking at how profiles come to look the way they do, it is difficult to isolate the technical practices from social ones. A view of literacy that fails to account for the social dimensions of what is also a technical practice will not suffice. Yet ignoring the technical dimensions would not reveal the potential importance of new media, such as code, in these social practices. In the next section, I present a socio-technical perspective of literacy and analyze the production of a MySpace profile in relation to it.

Figure 10-4. Comments can include embedded media as well as textual messages

The MySpace profile as a site of new literacies

Different theories of literacy present different notions of what it means to be "literate" in society. Some have focused on what a technology (or medium) enables and what social and cognitive consequences come as a result of it (e.g. Goody and Watt 1968, Goody 1977, Olson 1977, Ong 1982). Arguing against many of the premises and conclusions of this work, Scribner and Cole introduced the notion of a "literacy practice," the situated use of a "combination of technology, knowledge, and skills" and the application of this knowledge "for specific purposes in specific contexts of use" (Scribner and Cole 1981, 235). Similarly, the "ideological model" of literacy (Street 1984) and the "New Literacy Studies" movement, which sees literacies as social practices (Street 1995, Gee 1996), shifts the focus from the medium of expression to the social practices in which the media use is embedded and in the ideologies implicit in those practices. Recently, research on digital or media literacies (Hobbs 2004, Livingstone 2004) show that there is a range of perspectives as to which aspects of the use of media are essential to notions of literacy, ranging from a critical consumption to being able to use the tools of production.

One perspective that seeks to integrate these different understandings of literacy is that of Andrea diSessa (2000, in press) who defines literacy as "the convergence of a large number of genres and social niches on a common representational form" (diSessa 2000, 24). His definition pulls together three theoretical influences from those outlined above. First, uses of particular media must be considered within their social context. Second, these uses take on specific patterns, or genres. Finally, the medium-dependent properties of those representational forms matter. This definition of literacy overlaps in important ways with Scribner and Cole's (1981) notion of "literacy practice," namely that understanding literacy means understanding how people use technologies, skills, and knowledge in specific social contexts. However, diSessa's goal is to see how the uses of a particular form bridge different social contexts.

In this chapter, I use this perspective to analyze the production of a MySpace profile because of the balance it strikes between social and technical views of literacy, and also because it provides a lens through which to view prior debate. In this section and the next, I argue that diSessa's theoretical framing of is a useful way of understanding the possibility of new literacies in the production of a MySpace profile.

MySpace profiles and social niches

According to diSessa a social niche represents the "complex web of dependencies" in communities that allow (or do not allow) various competencies to thrive (2000, 24). diSessa's emphasis on social niches demands a look at the range of uses of MySpace and how they are supported by values, beliefs and practices (see also Gee 1996).

The features and uses of MySpace demonstrate a convergence of many web predecessors and the uses that accompany them. MySpace can be seen as a more interactive alternative to personal homepages for many of its teenage users (Chandler and Robert-Young 1995). It is a "social networking" service that lets people expose and navigate their networks of "friends" (or contacts) and meet people through others (Marwick 2005, boyd 2006a). It also has features to support blogging, bulletin boards, synchronous instant messaging (IM), asynchronous messaging (like e-mail), online-dating, and photo sharing. Some of these features, as I saw at the Center, are used in concert to support teenage relationship-building between new friends within the Center and between.

MySpace is also a site where entertainment production and consumption converge. The MySpace music and video services allow professional and amateur artists to disseminate their music by making it publicly available for use on other people's profiles. Some of the teenagers at the Center are a part of this emerging practice using MySpace to promote videos created at the Center or on their own. On the consumption side, MySpace is also a site to find and share music and videos, something that seems to be a central feature for the teenagers at the Center. Grace, aged 14, for example, spends significant time finding music to embed in her profiles, as her "profile song." However, as a more complex example of consumption, she also uses MySpace as a source of ring-tones for her mobile phone. In one incident, I watched her navigate to several popular artist's MySpace profiles, choose a particular song, embed that song in her own profile, and then play the song while holding her mobile phone up to the computer's speakers to record.

The social niches in these examples could be said to include the variety of people and institutions that support and value how these teenagers use MySpace, such as the teachers and other students at the Center, the families and friends of the teenagers, and also the industries and institutions that also use MySpace for their own commercial interests. Understanding the diverse uses of profiles calls for further research of how these social niches and contexts overlap, which is beyond the scope of this chapter.

Genres in the production of MySpace profiles

The second component of diSessa's model is the concept of "genres" in the use of a medium. diSessa defines "genre" as "the specialized form in which we find literacy exercised in production and consumption" (diSessa 2000, 22). He adapts this term from Bakhtin, who discusses genres as patterns of language that gains stability through specific uses in a "sphere of activity" (Bakhtin 1986, 60). According to Bakhtin, generic forms shape how we choose our words and construct thoughts in communication. And, the generic forms we hear in others' speech shapes how we interpret and construct meaning. Finally, Bakhtin argues that, "genres must be fully mastered in order to be manipulated freely," implying a mastery of using generic forms, or generic competencies (Bakhtin 1986, 80).

Genre is the conceptual glue that binds social activity to technical activity. In order to understand literacies, one must pay attention to the particularities of social activity and also to the generic forms and competencies that groups share in their use of a media. The creation of a

MySpace profile involves an understanding of many generic forms and the use of generic competencies that cross spheres of activity.

Profiles and generic forms

With regard to generic forms of language, MySpace relies on a particular notion of "friend" that is common among social networking sites, but signals a particular definition of the word that is not necessarily the same as its use in everyday interaction (boyd 2006b). For example, in a discussion with three girls about MySpace, one of my colleagues listened to them contrast "associates" and "friends" in everyday language with how "friends" is used on MySpace. When I asked Gregory, aged 15, about becoming his friend on the site, he said "the more the better!" indicating that one of the aspects of MySpace use involves competition in collecting "friends." Amassing friends is not necessarily something just for online environments: it can be an indicator of status and popularity offline as well. Therefore, the use of the word *can* be similar to how it might be used in other contexts. Therefore, untangling the various meanings in order to use the word correctly requires a mastery of the genre.[9]

There are also generic forms of interaction within a MySpace profile. For example, the "Comments" on a page are forms in that they are a particular method of asynchronous, public interaction with a page's "owner," that is a standard aspect of blogging and other social networking sites. But, on MySpace, like similar features on other sites, comments are not in response to a particular piece of writing. Rather, they provide a way to "check in" with someone, coordinate plans, conduct a public "conversation," just to name a few observed practices. Similar to the competition to collect more friends, some of the teenagers repeatedly asked members of our research group to make a few comments on their pages so that they would have more comments than others, noting that numbers of comments also indicates status to some.

Generic competencies for profile customization

Beyond recognizing and using generic forms of language and interaction, there are also generic competencies required for mastering the creation and maintenance of the profile. Even though I am experienced with web programming languages, it took a great deal of effort for me to figure out how to use my knowledge on MySpace, despite claims by the MySpace FAQ that it is "easy" to customize a profile and "requires only a basic knowledge of HTML (MySpace FAQ 2006)."

The MySpace FAQ encourages members to go and "meet new people" in order to get help. This underscores how strange it might be that I had been trying to figure out how to customize my page on my own. At the Center, we have observed several situations in which teenagers faced a similar dilemma. New users of the site asked each other for help, and others in the class had no noticeable reservations about stopping what they were doing and trying to help them. When I have asked people how they learned how to customize their profile, the answer is usually "a friend," "a cousin," or some other family member showed them or even did it for them. Therefore, in reality, the "basic knowledge" is not just knowledge of HTML code, but also the skills necessary to use friends and one's networks on MySpace.

In my own search, I discovered member profiles that were collections of tutorials written by a number of different people. I also searched outside of MySpace and found a multitude of resources such as the layout sites and code generators described above. I found active discussion forums in which people discussed how to customize their pages, with experts providing tips and code snippets for making more complex changes. When I found code, I copied it, inspected it, and even modified it. My steps here match those I have taken to learn other programming languages (not just HTML and CSS) for other social purposes (not just customizing a MySpace page), and even those I have seen in other communities of software development.[10]

The role of the medium: From "coding" to "copy and paste"

Accounting for the "convergence" of social niches, generic forms, and generic competencies, have proven to be useful tools for analyzing the creation and use of MySpace profiles. However, diSessa claims that literacies are marked by this convergence on a particular medium. Different media have different expressive properties and facilitate new ways of thinking. How we think when we write can differ with how we think when we talk, draw, paint, or write software. Therefore, a particular use of a medium can lead to the development of a new "material intelligence," a way of thinking that "is achieved cooperatively with external materials" (diSessa 2000, 5). Thus, while rejecting "technological determinism," diSessa is critical of "socially oriented literacy studies that have backgrounded or dismissed the contributions of the 'props' of literacy, its technology" (diSessa in press, 21).

This aligns his work along with those that look at "multimodal literacies," which in part are dependent on the "affordances" of a mode and the "facilities" of a media (Kress and Jewitt 2003, Kress 2003: see also Hull and Nelson 2005). Similarly, Buckingham, in his call for a change in how researchers view child audiences of media, indicates that there is a need for research that looks at "constraints and possibilities embodied in media texts" (Buckingham 2000, 120). Livingstone (2004) agrees, noting that an emphasis on skills has left the question of technology and representation largely unaddressed.

In this section I evaluate the importance of two of the technical and medium-dependent practices involved in the creation of MySpace profiles. First I discuss the possibility of MySpace as promoting a digital literacy based on learning to code. Second, I explore the significance of the copying and pasting of code that links to media, a practice that it is an important, medium-dependent form of expression that I argue should not be subordinated to coding.

Learning to code HTML and CSS using MySpace

In speculative response to diSessa's notion of "material intelligence," my first focus is on the coding skills MySpace profile customization involves. From a technical perspective, one can think about any web page as having structure, content, and presentation (or style). HTML can be used to control all three, but over the past several years, Cascading Style Sheets (CSS) has become the standard way of separating content and structure from style.

An example helps clarify. Imagine I have a paragraph of text about myself. In my HTML code, rather than say that this text should be red, bold, and in 16pt font, I can indicate that that this paragraph of text should be "about me text." Then, I can create a style using CSS to indicate what "about me text" should look like. This separation in the code between what the text says from what the text looks like provides me with the ability to change a style in one place and apply the same style to multiple chunks of text throughout the document.

Therefore, HTML and CSS, like other programming scripts and languages, encourage a particular way of thinking about problems. Learning to use them requires learning how to think modularly, how to decompose problems in certain ways, in this case related to this notion of the separation of style, structure, and content. Learning the complex array of skills necessary to create dynamic, interactive Web pages *potentially* could meet diSessa's threshold of an "increase in expressiveness" or a new material intelligence, though this would require more research to prove. But even if this is true, how good of a learning environment is MySpace for mastering the representational form and technical competency of web programming?

Certainly, it provides an introduction to the medium, and some even may learn more about HTML and CSS as a part of trying to customize their profiles. However, the way in which the MySpace designers use CSS works completely against the intended purpose of style sheets. For example, the MySpace designers have defined "styles" for every font-color-size combination used. This results in members being forced to do some rather strange things to change properties like font colors (for example, making a style named "yellow" actually be red, and so forth). This might be fine for creating web pages, but eliminates many of the potential advantages and new ways of thinking that may come from separating form from content. Moreover, MySpace has constrained people into a way of using HTML and CSS that is not very flexible and does not inform ways of using the technologies that give them their potential power as expressive media outside of the context of MySpace.

The use of copy and paste on MySpace

Nevertheless, MySpace is an environment in which another practice has established a strong foothold, one that is also dependent on the nature of HTML and web technologies: copying and pasting blocks of code as an act of selection, manipulation, and appropriation of work done by others. Technically speaking, copying and pasting does not require much skill. It seems unremarkable, almost unworthy of consideration as a significant technical practice. However, the small act of copying and pasting blocks of code from many different sources is at the core of many teenagers' individual expression on MySpace. Furthermore, new companies have emerged (such as YouTube) that encourage people to copy and paste links to nearly every type of media object from one place to another on the Web, including a MySpace profile.

This activity resembles others: collage-making, quilting, pasting posters and magazine articles up on bedroom walls, and so forth. There are also connections to existing practices with digital media (e.g. Chandler and Roberts-Young 1998, Sefton-Green 2005). However, networked computational media changes the act copying and pasting in a number of distinct ways. First, a MySpace member can copy and paste links to almost any type of medium: images, personal photographs, music, home-movies, TV shows, cartoons, games, and even interactive applications.

Second, members can continuously update what their profiles looks like by swapping in and out different media or adding to what already exists. Third, copying and pasting on the web requires minimal effort; a staggering array of source material is available via the Web through the same browser interface.

Finally, people are not copying and pasting media. They are copying and pasting abstractions (code) that link to the sources of that media. This creates complex webs of dependency between people's creations. In other words, as Bakhtin argued about speech, members' pages are "filled with other's words, varying degree of otherness or vary degrees of 'our-own-ness'" which members "assimilate, rework, and re-accentuate" (Bakhtin 1986, 89). However, these pages are *materially* connected as well, through links. Through members' choices and those by their friends in comments, each person's form of expression is explicitly connected to others' expressions, which in turn are connected to others' and so on.[11]

The following example demonstrates copy and paste in practice, illustrating these aspects of the process. It is particular instructive because it highlights the network of resources, both social and technical, utilized for individual expression and also shows the sense that any one person's profile is created through distributed production. Taken from field notes, the following narrative describes a situation that came about while Janice, aged 15, and I were trying to make sure that the two of us were connected as "friends" on MySpace:

> After making sure that I was on her list of friends, I went to a second computer positioned to Janice's right to log in to my profile. Then, I heard her laugh out loud. I looked over and noticed that she was browsing a friend's page and was laughing at a particular image that someone had left her friend as a comment. Janice clicked on the image and it took her to another page, one of the many sites on the web that hosts images for the direct purpose of being used on MySpace or other sites. She scrolled down through the page of images that were on the site, which seemed to me to be like greeting cards. She saw one that was a take-off of one of the characters of the TV show "Family Guy." She clicked on that image, which took her to a page that had the image followed by a text box with the HTML code for the image…Janice copied the code.
>
> She scrolled through the pages of her friends and clicked on a friend. For a few seconds she scrolled up and down on that friend's profile, but then apparently changed her mind and returned to her browsing through her list of friends. Next, Janice said something out loud, but seemingly to herself, about "knowing" to whom she should "give" the picture (indicating a sudden realization). Janice clicked on one of her friends and went to her

> profile. She scrolled down to the comments and clicked on the "Add Comment" link. In the text box that appeared on the next page, she pasted in the block of code that she had previously copied. Janice then checked to see that the comment appeared, and noting that it did, returned to her "home" page.

In relation to my discussion of literacy, a number of points stand out as particularly interesting. First, it was an unplanned sequence of events. Janice's decision to comment on a friend's page arose spontaneously out of her interaction with someone else's comment on someone else's profile. The desire to comment stemmed from Janice's appreciation and enjoyment of a particular image, a representation from popular culture that had already been re-worked, and then searching for something to do with that image that was symbolically meaningful for her.

Second, the whole process was routine for her and took at most a few minutes. Each interaction with the browser, from knowing that she could click on the image to get to another site of images to copying the code from one site and then pasting into another was fairly insignificant. This was obviously something that she had done before and most likely fairly often.

Finally, it's important to note that the design of the code and media made the sequence possible and played critical roles. For example, the original image was also a link to another site. This site hosted many images and presented them specifically to be used on MySpace pages. Code and instructions for copying and pasting (though Janice didn't need the instructions) came with each image. Furthermore, all of this activity was possible within one application, the web browser.

This example also raises many questions and it is difficult to have a complete understanding of this situation without much more knowledge regarding the greater social context of Janice's use of the site. But the example should make it clear that copying pasting code for specific purposes is not trivial or meaningless simply because it appears to be simple in relation to programming.

Participation and remix: "New" terms for new literacies

Research on literacy practices in relation to the web has focused on the need to develop critical skills in analyzing and evaluating web content (e.g. Livingstone 2002) or on the use of HTML to "write" web pages (e.g. Chandler and Robert-Young 1998, Facer et al. 2003). In reaction to and anticipation of much of this debate regarding web literacies, diSessa is ambivalent:

> The World Wide Web is equally encouraging and discouraging regarding the practicality of new literacies. It is a big step in economics and distribution, but a small step in form. It is two-way and reaffirms the importance of two-way media in the enthusiasm in self-expression it has engendered, but it is only one-way with respect to new expressive possibilities offered by computational media: ordinary folks are limited to text and pictures; they can't create dynamic and interactive documents (diSessa 2000, 221-222).

But are there other ways to become literate in the interactive space of the web? Despite diSessa's dismissal of the web's potential for new forms of expression, I argue that that there are problems with framing potential literacy practices as "one-way" or "two-way" as important new social and technical practices, such as the copying and pasting of media, are easy to overlook.

Focusing on learning to use HTML and CSS coding in MySpace paints a picture that is consistent with diSessa's point of the Web as only "one-way with respect to new expressive possibilities." However, a focus on the act of creating networks of links to media clouds the picture. By stitching together media from a variety of sources, "ordinary folks" on MySpace can *easily* "create dynamic and interactive documents," to which diSessa refers. Millions of people, including teenagers are already doing it.

Part of the problem in seeing the potential importance of the "simple" act of copying and pasting maybe because of the fundamental terminology of the discussion. It calls into question the notion of "two-way" literacy and a focus on the consumption and production of media. The creation of a MySpace profile is neither strictly "reading" or "writing," yet is somehow both simultaneously.

Facer et al. (2003) point to examples of how kids "creatively copy" material and templates in order to learn, resembling some of the practices I have just outlined. The practices are neither "'simply reproduction' nor 'simply creative'" (Facer et al. 2003, 114). Nevertheless, they opt to recast the word "consumption" to describe kids' accumulation of "cultural resources" that enable them to produce and communicate their identities (Facer et al. 2003, 112). This type of redefinition of terms has led researchers in media and cultural theory to question the dichotomy between the "consumption" and "production" of media, with implications of how to consider copy and pasting as part of MySpace profile production.

In Jenkins' (1992) account of television fans he reveals that people traditionally viewed as "consumers" are also producers in two ways. First, people create meaning in products, such as toys or narratives, through their use. As French cultural theorist de Certeau previously argued, this meaning-making through reinvention is an act of production as well as consumption: the reader "invents in texts something different from what they 'intended'" (de Certeau 1984, 169). Second, deviating from de Certeau, Jenkins reveals how various fan groups produce tangible artifacts, such as fan fiction and "transform the experience of media consumption into the production of new texts, indeed of a new culture and new community" (Jenkins 1992, 46).

Ito builds on these arguments and other debate concerning active and passive media audiences[12] and argues that "new convergent media…require a reconfigured conceptual apparatus that takes productive and creative activity at the 'consumer' level as a given rather than as an addendum or an exception" (Ito 2008, 394). Building on the work of Jenkins (1992) and Lave and Wenger (1991), Ito uses the concept of "participation" as an alternative to consumption. A notion of "participation" assumes that engagement with media is "social and active," provides a way to consider issues of power and ideology, and takes into account both the relationships between individuals and media and between groups engaged with media. According to Ito, "the research question has been recast from the more individualized, 'How does a child interpret or localize a text?' to the collective question of 'How do people organize around and with media texts?'" (Ito 2008, 395).

If "participation" is a word that challenges the consumption/production dichotomy, then "remix" may be its counterpart to bridge the reading/writing dichotomy. The word "remix," originally used to describe a particular way of mixing music samples, has itself been appropriated to generally describe the mixing of a variety of media forms to create new products.[13] A recent study by the Pew Internet and American Life Project (Lenhart and Madden 2005) uses the word "remix" of teen content creation to imply the creation of new "artistic" content from prior media forms.[14] Jenkins et al. (2006) view artistic appropriation of content through remix as an essential aspect of new media literacies (see also Jenkins 2006, Manovich 2005).

But there is no reason to constrain "remixing" practices to the development of "artistic" creations as that study defines the term. These practices are similar to those described by Willis as "common culture," "symbolic creativity in everyday life, everyday activity and expression" not an elite notion of "art" (Willis 1990, 1). In exploring literacy, Dyson analyzes first graders' use of popular media in their classroom writing assignments as "remixing," explicitly connecting their work to musical sampling. She notes the "textual play" involved in the "appropriating, differentiating, translating, and reframing cultural material across communicative frames and social world" (Dyson 2002, 555). Here, my use of remixing presumes these types of symbolic and material appropriations and translations, what Erstad et al. (2007) describe as "re-mixing semiotic resources" in their study of high schoolers' media productions.[15] However, my emphasis is on the re-use of distributed media through the remixing of *code*, thus adding yet another material dimension to the process.

If "remixing" is used to describe the practices required to blend text, images, video, audio, and games in the creation and maintenance of a MySpace profile, the perception of "simple" technical feats of copying and pasting links to media, turn into socially complex chains of appropriations of media between people. Furthermore, the concept distinguishes itself from typical notions of "reading" and "writing." It parallels Ito's view that participation, "leads to a conceptualization of the imagination as collectively rather than individually experienced and produced" (Ito 2008, 395) in that remixing media by copying and pasting is a collective technical practice; people's creations are dependent on each other in many different ways. One could see remixing as a sign of a new, *networked material intelligence*, to adapt diSessa's concept, though it would take further research to demonstrate this. Nevertheless, through MySpace and sites like it, knowing, socially and technically, how to re-use media in this particular way has become foundational for communication and creative expression over the web.

Conclusion

In this chapter, I have laid out an argument that in light of theories of literacy concerning both "old" and "new" media, there is good reason to suspect that the work involved in the production of MySpace profiles involves new forms of literacy practices, and that those practices, to some extent, are dependent on a particular representational form, code, and the systems to manipulate it in a particular way. With diSessa's emphasis on the importance of the representational form as well as the social context of use, he calls into question accounts of new media literacy that treats computational media as a "text." Similarly, Livingstone argues that if using the Web represents something new, rather than an extension of textual practice, more research is necessary that will "investigate the emerging skills and practices of new media users as they meaningfully appropriate ICT into their lives" (Livingstone 2004, 10). Understanding teenagers' use of MySpace calls for a deeper look at the social practices and niches that shape how people create and maintain their profiles and also a look at the roles that code, the multiple forms of media found on the web, and the site itself play in enabling certain practices and constraining others.

A social perspective of literacy helps show that a part of problem in this framing of copying and pasting as a literacy practice is that it does not neatly fit within common educational practices. From the perspective of the social niche of traditional schooling, to copy and paste is to plagiarize, unless there is careful attribution of sources.[16] Therefore copying and pasting is antithetical to a literate practice. But, on the other hand, from the perspective of other social niches such as software development, copying and pasting is routine. Understanding when, why, and *how*—socially and technically—to re-use code are among core competencies. The question for future research is in what social niches might copying and pasting in the process of re-using a diverse array of media be considered the sign of a deep shift in how people engage with one another?

The teenagers who have created and are maintaining MySpace pages, are developing new technical and social skills that enable their participation in a variety of social activities using a new medium. They are learning to incorporate the Web in multiple overlapping facets of their lives. And, they are engaging in a networked discourse, one that many teenagers understand how to use, but not necessarily understand how to critically reflect upon (at least, not yet).

Reframing literacy in terms of both social and technical, or medium-dependent, practices helps us understand how these practices are embedded in existing social groups and niches, what they mean to the people who engage in them, and what properties of the media are that facilitate new expressive forms. Finally, considering "participation" and "remix" as the social and technical frames for understanding new media practices will help us recognize what new media literacies might be developed through them. Whether or not there are long term "consequences" of these practices is impossible to know now, but it's important to recognize them now as important and to consider what might be gained by having them accepted by society as an aspect of new "literacy," or lost by a failure to do so.

Notes

[1] The research for this paper was conducted as part of a grant funded by the MacArthur Foundation, "Kids' Informal Learning with Digital Media." I am indebted to Heather Horst, Peter Lyman, and Ryan Shaw for extensive comments and discussion on earlier drafts. Thanks are also due to the Center, its teachers, and students, and Judd Antin and Christo Sims for their role in the project. Also, thanks to inspiration, valuable suggestions, and advice from Andrea diSessa, danah boyd, Mimi Ito, Sarita Yardi, Øystein Gilje, Eli Chapman, Jessica Parker, the editors of this volume, and other members of the Digital Youth project.
[2] http://www.myspace.com. MySpace launched in 2003 and Rupert Murdoch's News Corp bought the site in 2005 for $580 million. Since its founding, MySpace has become one of the most visited web-sites each month. For an overview of the site and how some teenagers are using it, see boyd 2006a.
[3] It is quite difficult to accurately estimate the number of people who use MySpace. There is often a large discrepancy between the number of profiles, registered users, and active users. People may have multiple accounts and businesses and institutions have accounts on the site as well. In late 2006, the *San Francisco Chronicle* estimated the number as above 70 million (Fost 2006). Earlier in the year, a July 2006 estimate noted "membership approaching 100 million in total" (Olson 2006).
[4] Some of this research involved collaboration with two colleagues and my work here is informed by their observations as well. Therefore, sometimes in this chapter I will refer to "we."
[5] In this chapter, I do not consider the use of text on MySpace. MySpace, though, provides few limits on the amount of text one can enter, and the visual importance of large or small blocks of text as visual elements should not be disregarded. As Kress argues, "on the screen the textual entity is treated as a visual entity" (Kress 2003, 65).
[6] Two layout sites that I have encountered frequently from casual browsing of profiles: "Free Web Layouts" (http://www.freeweblayouts.net/) and "Pimp-My-Profile" (http://www.pimp-my-profile.com/). A generator that I have encountered frequently is "Thomas MySpace Editor" (http://www.strikefile.com/myspace/).
[7] MySpace, as of this writing, does not provide explicit "features" for profile customization. As it turns out, it is a case of an engineering "mistake" turned into a feature that occurred when engineers failed to strip out the HTML tags from the form-fields. Later, members and third party sites, exploited this feature to create the idea of "customization" (Carr 2007).
[8] Servers that host the media can go down. Media hosting services may limit bandwidth on a user account. Some of the teenagers I have talked to have profiles that contain "image not found" graphics where something else had previously appeared.
[9] See boyd 2006b for extensive discussion of friendship on MySpace and similar sites.
[10] As a demonstration of the generic nature of my process, my activities are quite similar to the ones that diSessa (2000) depicts in his examples of sixth graders

learning physics with another programming medium. The student-run "library" of projects allowed students to check out and learn from other students' projects. Students obtained help from an expert and then re-used and re-purposed code in order to develop a complex game. Finally students developed tutorials for each other.

[11] Livingstone (2002, 226-229) discusses the importance of the "routes model" of the web, where the link is the focus of critical analysis as opposed to the sites. Analyzing links to media in this way could prove useful. But, it's also important to note the difference between how links to media are different than links between sites or pages. The former type of link is referred to as "transclusion" where one document is partially included in another document. The difference may be important in considering the relationship between culture as "rooted in a locale" (by analyzing pages) vs. "routed" between spaces (by analyzing links and "surfing" behavior). Links that result in embedded media seem to fit somewhere in between.

[12] For two reviews of the debates concerning active versus passive audiences of television and other media, see Kinder 1991 and Buckingham 2000.

[13] Not only has the term remixing been used to describe audio, video, and image appropriation. It has also been used to describe the development of software applications that rely on the integration of multiple data sources and services from the Web. In his introduction to the Korean edition to *The Language of New Media*, Lev Manovich (2003) discussed three types of remixes with "new media" as "the remix between the interfaces of various cultural forms and the new software techniques – in short, the remix between culture and computers." He extends his discussion of the importance of this practice in Manovich 2005.

[14] 19 per cent of teenagers surveyed reported that they had participated in some form of remixing activity, but again, note that the definition indicated the creation of "artistic" content.

[15] See also Buckingham's (2007) introduction to the June 2007 issue of *Learning, Media, and Technology* in which he highlights the theme of remixing found across a number of the articles in the issue that also connects the concept to new media literacies. Unfortunately, I was making the final edits to this chapter just as the issue was released and could not incorporate a more detailed comparison between those perspectives and the one I outline here.

[16] See Gilje, this volume, for more on the tensions that can arise when out-of-school media use is brought into a school-based media production class and the possible ethical implications.

References

Bakhtin, M. M. 1986. The problem of speech genres. In *Speech genres and other late essays*, ed. C. Emerson, M. Holquist, and V. W. McGee, 60-102. Austin, TX: University of Texas Press.

boyd, d. 2006a. Identity production in a networked culture: Why Youth ♥ MySpace. Presentation given at the Annual Meeting of the American

Association for the Advancement of Science, February 19, 2006, in San Francisco, CA. http://www.danah.org/papers/AAAS2006.html (retrieved June 12, 2006)

—. 2006b. Friends, friendsters, and Top 8: Writing community into being on social network sites. *First Monday* 11(12), http://firstmonday.org/issues/issue11_12/boyd/index.html12/5/2006 (retrieved December 2006).

Buckingham, D. 2000. *After the death of childhood*. Oxford: Polity Press.

—. 2007. Media education goes digital: An introduction. *Learning, Media, and Technology* 32(2): 111-119.

Carr, D. 2007. User customization: Too much of a good thing? *Baseline* January 16. http://www.baselinemag.com/print_article2/0,1217,a=198615,00.asp (retrieved January 27, 2007).

Chandler, D, and D. Roberts-Young. 1998. The construction of identity in the personal homepages of adolescents, http://www.aber.ac.uk/media/Documents/short/strasbourg.html (retrieved September 12, 2006).

de Certeau, M. 1984. *The practice of everyday life*. Berkeley, CA: UC Berkeley Press.

diSessa, A. A. 2000. *Changing minds: Computers, learning, and literacy*. Cambridge, MA: MIT Press.

—. In press. Can students re-invent fundamental scientific principles? Evaluating the promise of new-media literacies. In *Children's learning in a digital world,* ed. T. Willoughby and E. Wood. Oxford: Blackwell.

Dyson, A. H. 2002. The drinking god factor: A writing development remix for "all" children. *Written Communication* 19: 545-577.

Erstad, O., Ø. Gilje, and T. de Lange. 2007. Re-mixing multimodal resources: Multiliteracies and digital production in Norwegian media education. *Learning, Media, and Technology* 32 (2): 183-198.

Facer, K., J. Furlong, R. Furlong, and R. Sutherland. 2003. *ScreenPlay: Children and computing in the home*. London: Routledge Farmer.

Finnegan, R. 2002. *Communicating: The multiple modes of human interconnections*. London: Routledge.

Fost, D. 2006. Key web 2.0 sites. *San Fransisco Chronicle,* November 5.

Garnett, J. 2006. MySpace: Design anarchy that works. *Business Week Online,* January 3, http://www.businessweek.com/innovate/content/dec2005/id20051230_570094.htm (retrieved January 4, 2006).

Gee, J. P. 1996. *Social linguistics and literacies: Ideology in discourses*. London: Taylor and Francis.

—. 2003. *What video games have to teach us about learning and literacy*. New York: Palgrave Macmillan.

Goody, J. 1977. *The domestication of the savage mind*. Cambridge: Cambridge University Press.

Goody, J., and I. Watt. 1968. The consequences of literacy. In *Literacy in traditional societies,* ed. J. Goody, 27-68. Cambridge: Cambridge University Press.

Hine, C. 2000. *Virtual ethnography*. London: Sage.

Hobbs, Rene. 2004. A review of school-based initiatives in media literacy education. *American Behavioral Scientist* 48(1): 42-59.

Hull, G., and M. E. Nelson. 2005. Locating the semiotic power of mulimodality. *Written Communication* 22(2): 1-38.

Ito, M. 2008. Mobilizing the imagination in everyday play: The case of Japanese media mixes. In The *international handbook of children, media, and culture,* ed. K. Drotner and S. Livingstone, 385-406. London: Sage.

Jenkins, H. 1992. *Textual poachers: Television fans and participatory culture*. London: Routledge.

—. 2006. Learning by Remixing, http://www.pbs.org/mediashift/2006/07/learning_by_remixing.html (retrieved July 20, 2006).

Jenkins, H., K. Clinton, R. Purushotma, A. J. Robinson, and M. Weigel. 2006. Confronting the challenges of participatory culture: Media education for the 21st century. An Occasional Paper written for the MacArthur Foundation. http://www.digitallearning.macfound.org/site/c.enJLKQNlFiG/b.2029291/k.97E5/Occasional_Papers.htm (retrieved October 20, 2006).

Kinder, M. 1991. *Playing with power*. Berkeley, CA: UC Berkeley Press.

Kress, G. 2003. *Literacy in the new media age*. London: Routledge.

Kress, Gunther, and C. Jewitt. 2003. Introduction. In *Multimodal literacy,* ed. C. Jewitt and G. Kress, 1-18. Bonn: Peter Lang.

Lave, J., and E. Wenger. 1991. *Situated learning: Legitimate peripheral participation*. New York: Cambridge University Press.

Lenhart, A., and M. Madden. 2005. *Teen content creators and consumers: Findings of the Pew Internet and American Life Project*. http://www.pewinternet.org/PPF/r/166/report_display.asp (retrieved November 2, 2005).

Livingstone, S. 2002. *Young people and new media: Childhood and the changing media environment*. London: Sage.

—. 2004. Media literacy and the challenge of new information and communication technologies. *The Communication Review* 7: 3-14.

Lyman, P., and N. Wakeford. 1999. Introduction: Going into the (virtual) field. *American Behavioral Scientist* 43: 359-376.

Manovich, L. 2003. Introduction to the Korean edition of *The Language of New Media*. http://www.manovich.net/DOCS/Introduction_Korea_2003.doc (retrieved July 25, 2006).

Manovich, L. 2005. Remixability and Modularity, http://www.manovich.net (retrieved July 25, 2006).

Marwick, A. 2005. "I'm a lot more interesting than a Friendster profile:" Identity presentation, authenticity and power in social networking services. Paper presented at conference of the Association of Internet Researchers 6.0: Internet Generations, October 5-9, in Chicago, IL.

MySpace. 2006. FAQ, http://collect.myspace.com/misc/faq.cfm?question=1 (retrieved March 24, 2006).

Olson, D. R. 1977. From utterance to text: The bias of language in speech and writing. *Harvard Educational Review* 47(3): 257-81.

Olson, S. 2006. MySpace blurs lines between frinds and flacks. CNET's News.com, July. http://news.com.com/MySpace+blurs+line+between+friends+and+flacks/2009-1025_3-6100176.html (retrieved August 1, 2006).

Ong, W. 1982. *Orality and literacy: The technologizing of the word*. New York, NY: Routledge.

Scribner, S., and M. Cole. 1981. *The psychology of literacy*. Cambridge, MA: Harvard University Press.

Sefton-Green, J. 2005. Timelines, timeframes, and special effects: Software and creative media production. *Education, Communication and Information* 5(1).

Street, B. 1984. *Literacy in theory and practice*. Cambridge: Cambridge University Press.

—. 1995. *Social literacies*. London: Longman.

Willis, P. 1990. *Common culture*: *Symbolic work at play in the everyday cultures of the young*. Boulder: Westview Press.

CHAPTER ELEVEN

CREATING MEDIA LITERACY IN JAPAN: INITIATIVES FOR NEW CITIZENSHIP[1]

YOSUKE MORIMOTO

Japan is one of the most digitized countries in the world, and young Japanese have access to and use a plethora of digital media. Yet Japanese students are often seen as passive and as not having confidence to express their opinion, even if they have digital tools at hand and the skills to use them. The main argument of this chapter, to be developed in the following, is that critical media literacy needs to be systematically integrated into Japanese schooling in order to facilitate that young Japanese develop the requisite resources so that they may fully partake as citizens exercising their own opinions and interests. Two studies of Japanese students' media literacy are analyzed in order to ground a subsequent report on a media literacy project carried out in an underserved area of Japan and showing a possible way forward for Japanese media literacy education.

Japanese media literacy education: The current situation

In Japan, the media researcher Midori Suzuki introduced media literacy in the 1980s. But like other countries, Japan has no commonly accepted definition of the term. Still, there is a common element in some definitions. For instance, Suzuki defines media literacy as "citizens' ability to critically analyze and evaluate media in a socio-cultural context, to access media, and to create communications in a wide variety of forms" (Suzuki 1997, 8). According to Suzuki's definition, media literacy includes both the critical analysis of media and the creative production of mediated communication.

The concepts of information literacy and computer literacy are similar to that of media literacy, and this similarity causes some confusion in Japan. Some people think computer literacy is the same as media literacy. Therefore, in the absence of a common definition and with the confusion of similar terms, Japanese media literacy education mainly incorporates production and it is carried out without the process of establishing students' critical independence. Newspapers and films have been used as teaching materials since the 1950s in the Japanese language curriculum, but few teachers know how to use these media as tools for education, so they are rarely put into practice (Inoue and Nakamura 2001, 20-22).

Between 1998 and 2006, 96 case studies on media literacy education in normal primary and secondary schools were reported in educational journals and research literature. About one third of these case studies relates to production. In another third of the studies analysis is the main focus of lessons. The reports on these cases demonstrate that the meaning of *critical* is a in itself a contested issue.

In many cases media literacy education is offered as part of a subject such as Japanese (38 cases), period for integrated study (11) and social studies (10), or as part of a special activity (10). The case studies also demonstrate that focus is on a variety of media such as television (29), newspapers (15), the internet and mobile phones. In some cases, classes are held over a year or one semester, but the average amount of time spent on media literacy is 4.5 hours. In either case, it is impossible to cover every aspect of media literacy education, so only one part is taken up. In addition, if a teacher takes up some media literacy education, he or she does not pursue it. It can be said that Japanese media literacy education is concluded after only one unit. For instance, if a teacher teaches advertising using tv, he or she does not teach forms of representation using tv, or does not teach internet after that time. Therefore, Japanese students are not introduced to media studies such as it is known from, for example, United Kingdom or Canada.

In most cases teachers only practice what they are personally interested in. The precarious position of Japanese media literacy education may be summed up as follows:

> The opportunity for learning media literacy is not provided in teacher training programmes, and teachers do not understand the theory of media literacy.
> There is no opportunity to create learning places based on discussion and dialogue for practical training.
> There is no view that teachers practice media literacy based on contextualised studies of young people's media uses.

A more systematic integration of media literacy as part of the school curriculum is in order, for example as part of social education and civil activities (Suzuki 1997, 8). A precondition for this integration is to map more systematically the trends in young people's media uses and to develop practice-based studies of ways in which media literacy education may be developed based on these trends.

Previous research on Japanese children's media uses and media literacies

In Japan, as well as in other countries, various organisations have conducted surveys demonstrating how much children use media and how children feel or think about for example tv programmes.

However, criteria for assessing media literacy understanding have not been specified. One example is Goto's study (Goto 2005). He classified media literacy understanding into three groups, namely children's understanding of the media's manipulation skills, children's critical thinking and autonomous attitudes. In particular, he examined the reliability and validity of the questionnaire he made which asked about critical thinking and autonomous attitudes. Since the background of respondents is not well-defined, and follow-up research was not performed, Goto could evaluate the object of the survey and the time period but he could not clearly state that his results were derived from media literacy education.

Conversely, Komaya (2000) did a pre-test and a post-test, and then evaluated her practice. However, her evaluation is about the understanding and knowledge of media rather than media literacy understanding. Certainly, understanding of and knowledge about media may lead students to an understanding of the key concepts of media literacy. However, Komaya focused on students' awareness of media (especially tv), their active interpretation of media and their ability to distinguish between factual and fictional genres on tv. It could be argued that such an approach fails to take into account an understanding of the concept of media literacy.

A new approach to studying children's media uses

In order to map more systematically Japanese children's media uses and media literacies, we conducted a pilot and a full survey. In more concrete terms, we focused on measuring what kind of media young Japanese people are currently using, how much they access these media and what their attitude towards media is. Both the pilot and the full survey fall into three parts. The first part asks about how much young people access media and what kind of media they usually use. The media included were newspapers, tv, magazines, comics, music, mobile phones, personal computers and video/DVDs. In particular, we asked young people how they used personal computers.

The second part of the survey focused on tv. We asked young people what they do when they watch tv, and we asked about their knowledge of tv organization and ratings. The aim of these questions was to ask how much respondents know about the reasons for the existence of tv commercials, how broadcasting stations are organized and how tv programmes are made.

The last part focused on students' understanding of the key concepts of media literacy. All the questions in this part related to the eight key concepts of media literacy as defined by Suzuki: 1. media construct reality, 2. media construct versions of reality, 3. audiences negotiate meaning, 4. media messages contain commercial implications, 5. media messages contain ideology and values, 6. media messages contain political and social messages, 7. each medium has a unique aesthetic form, 8. reading media critically enables people to create a variety of communications (Suzuki 2004, 18-21). Suzuki's eight key concepts are based on the definition of media literacy as defined by the Association for Media Literacy (AML) in Ontario, Canada. Suzuki's unique contribution to this definition is that she combined concept number seven and eight from the AML and added another eighth key concept which relates to creativity.

This kind of research has never been undertaken by Japanese researchers before, and it therefore offers a new entry point to understand and develop Japanese students' media literacies.

The pilot study

In June 2006, we conducted a pilot study with 34 of high-school students at the Tokushima prefecture high school (located in a rural area). 24 of the respondents are aged 17-18 and are in their third year media literacy class, and 10 students are aged 16-17 and in their second year information technology and expression class. For the third-year students, data collection took place in the class. The second-year students were surveyed by their teacher, who had observed the third year students' survey. Students answered the questionnaire at their own pace, and if they had questions they asked individually.

Results of the first part, focusing on access and types of media used, demonstrate that students use mostly tv, as was expected before the survey. However, we did not estimate the extent to which respondents use mobile phones. From other studies we know that almost 100 per cent of

Japanese students own a mobile phone, and this near-universal penetration has recently made some commentators argue that Japanese children need mobile phone literacy. In general, students in Japan have classes until 4 p.m. and then an upward of 70 per cent do a club activity; but in our survey many students do not attend an after-school club but go home straight away. This may be one reason that their media use extends that of other students. In addition, the percentage of students who use personal computers is 56 percent (19 people). Almost all of them use it as a hobby.

The second part of the survey, focusing on tv use, shows that the respondents have some knowledge of media, though their knowledge seems one-sided. In Japan, newspaper companies have founded broadcasting corporations, and mass media today are organised as huge conglomerates. Some students know about this, but many students do not. Because they tend to watch tv while doing other things, the survey demonstrates that they turn on the tv set rather than watch what is on. The fact that respondents use tv extensively give room for optimism about developing media literacy education that will enhance students' awareness of for example media ownership. On the other hand, their preferred programmes are animation, variety and drama. Our findings support a survey performed by the Japanese public-service broadcaster Nihon Hoso Kyokai (NHK) (NHK 2006) and demonstrating that only two per cent in the ageband 7-19 watch NHK news between 7 p.m. and 7:30 p.m. whereas 16 per cent in the ageband 7-12 and four per cent in the ageband 13-19 watch NHK animation programmes (these programmes are broadcast from 6 p.m. to about 6:30 p.m.). As a whole, children and teenagers do not watch NHK because sponsored broadcasting is much funnier than NHK. In our survey, only 2 NHK programmes (2.7 per cent) were listed amongst a total of 74 programmes that respondents listed. That is, more than 90 per cent of tv programmes that teenagers watch are sponsored broadcasting programmes. The variety programmes on sponsored channels tend to be funny and violent and this gets them higher ratings, and so those programmes may also be assumed to offer selective views on the world.

Young people talk more often about tv programmes with their friends than with their family, and these discussions tend to focus on interesting programmes and fashion trends, rather than on criticizing the contents of the programmes. Taken together, the ways in which favoured tv programmes address viewers and respondents' own everyday discussions of tv situate the young as consumers of media rather than as citizens participating in mediated discourses.

The third part of our pilot study focused on respondents' media literacy. Respondents tended not to understand the key concepts, and this was most notable in their answers to two sets of questions: questions about communicating and giving voice through the media and questions about the understanding of media literacy. In the questions about their wish to communicate through the media, students who answered both yes and no may have some doubts as to whether society will change or not, even if they are allowed a say. In other words, there are students who want to have a say even if things do not change, and there are those who do not want to have a say because they do not think anything will change anyway. The question "what do you want to say through the media" had the following options for answers: "abolish school system", "society is wrong" and "social gap". In their answers, some respondents made comments such as "this world is filled up with fools", and "comment on the customers who come to the shop where I'm working part time". None of the additions expressed optimism, and the answers seem to illustrate that students harbour pessimistic views about Japanese society in general and their own influence in particular. The fact that the overall majority (85 per cent) did not answer this question about having a voice through the media indicates a general sense of powerlessness among the respondents.

To acquire some form of media literacy would seem important for students who think their society is strange and who seem to surmise that they cannot do anything about it. Through media literacy they may learn how to express an opinion and debate through the media as active citizens. Despite the fact that 24 of the respondents in the pilot study are doing a media literacy course, 18 of them (53 per cent) answered that they "do not know" what media literacy is.

The results of part three of the pilot study illuminate a curious paradox facing young Japanese. They live in one of the world's most advanced societies in terms of technology and access to digital media, and yet few of the young use their access and knowledge of digital tools to express their opinion through the media. They tend to exercise their media skills for their entertainment, not as a public or for society. Our results also indicate that students may want to criticize their society but they do not know how to do so. This is why systematic media literacy education needs to be integrated into Japanese education.

Main survey and results

On the basis of our pilot study and adopting the same means of data collection, we conducted a main survey with 97 first grade students (aged 12-13) of junior high school in Takatsuki Forth Junior High School, Osaka prefecture. However, we undertook a number of revisions prior to our data collection: we focused on weekday media use only; we eliminated a question on the purpose of computer use and a question on sources for learning about incidents or accidents. Because the main survey also included first grade of junior high school students (aged 12-13), who are younger than the students involved in pilot survey, we also left out some questions that the pilot had revealed as ambiguous. Our main results are as follows:

Respondents watch television an average of 3.3 hours per day. They typically do other things while the tv is on (prepare going to school, having a meal and so on). Thus, television operates as a mechanism of adjustment to their everyday life pattern at home.

Personal ownership of media and ICT hardware varies considerably. Many of the students share media with younger or older siblings, and this situation widens their access to tv, computer and games machines.

Respondents' favourite tv genres are variety programmes, animation and drama. They hardly watch any news. Because of these genres, their favorite idol or celebrity character are related to these programmes. As for audiencing and its relation to consumerism, we may note that half of the respondents answered "often" or "sometimes" to whether they feel like buying something when they watch tv commercials, or when they see magazine or internet advertisements. The items they want to buy are mostly related to tv programmes like goods branding animation characters, sports products (baseball, football), idols' CD/DVD or many kinds of video game (not only hardware like Nintendo DS, Play Station Portable, but also software for these).

Contrary to most adults' standard perceptions, young respondents seem to have some knowledge of the concepts of funding and rating. For example, two thirds of our respondents claim they know the meaning of rating, and 82 out of a total of 97 respondents claim they know what is the purpose of rating.

As for respondents' knowledge about the key aspects of media literacy, answers are too diverse to merit clear trends, a result that may be due to our design of the question.

Most of the respondents find it important to be able to express oneself through the media, but few want to have a voice themselves. It seems that they tend to escape from such responsibility, or they think that media are used by authorities. In addition, two thirds of those who want to have a voice in the media still answer that they do not consider the society will change. As in our pilot, respondents express a pessimistic or negative attitude to any transformative possibilities of the media.

Of key importance to the main argument of this chapter is the respondents' claimed pessimism about their society. Across different age groups and schools, they do not think they have any part in changing Japanese society. Based on these findings, we argue that Japanese schools do not educate the young as citizens. If that was the case, we would find more respondents with confidence in their abilities to influence society through actions such as elections, demonstrations or other forms of civic engagement. Actually, the concepts of democracy and citizenship do not figure anywhere in the Japanese national curriculum, only concepts such as moral, public and "zest for living." That respondents do not know about media literacy and its key concepts makes sense because media literacy has hardly been taught in Japan. As noted by Shibata (2006, 4), Japanese schools only taught critical literacy immediately after World War II. Shibata mentions only textbooks and print media, but in advanced ICT countries such as Japan, we need critical literacy that encompasses all types of media, that is media literacy. However, Japanese educators lack the knowledge, teaching materials and teaching strategy when it comes to media literacy education, and researchers possessing those competences have very few opportunities to offer their competences through systematic interaction with practitioners. In this situation, local community projects may be a way forward. The Takatsuki Media Literacy Project is one such project whose results may become a touchstone for creating Japanese media literacy education.

The Tonda Youth Center and Takatsuki Media Literacy Project

The Tonda district in Takatsuki city, located in the east of Osaka prefecture, has historically been systematically segregated as a Buraku community. The Tonda Youth Center caters for young people and supports them through various kinds of educational activities connected to the problems caused by the discrimination against the Buraku people.

"Buraku" is a Japanese word referring to village or hamlet. But the word also means former "outcast" communities - where discriminated-against Buraku people reside.[2] They are not a racial or a national minority, but a caste-like minority among ethnic Japanese. Historically, they were placed at the bottom of society. In 1871, an edict to emancipate them was promulgated and this "lowest rank" in Japanese society was abolished. Nevertheless, there are still many incidents of discrimination, particularly in terms of marriage and employment, as well as discriminatory remarks and inquiries made by non-Buraku people, including public officials.[3]

A survey of junior high school students focusing on gender and discrimination against Buraku was carried out at the Fourth Junior High School in 1999 (Survey 1999). It indicated that the students of the district were inclined to be more affirmative and receptive to the traditional view of gender, and the way of life it is based on, than those living outside the district. Their views were influenced by the mainstream media.

These results made the staff of the centre and the teachers at the Fourth Junior High School aware of the necessity for each student in the district to acquire the ability to plan his or her own life and not accept such traditional gender perceptions. They thought that this would lead to an improvement in students' abilities. As part of this process, they found that fostering involvement and critical awareness of media was important. Furthermore, they assumed that students would be empowered by having social access to various kinds of communication and options to make their own productions. In the literacy classes that started in the 1970s, adults learned to read and write. Today, the kind of literacy education that adults in the district think is necessary is media literacy.

Gradually, the centre focused more on the importance of media literacy, and since 2000 the centre has conducted a series of courses in media literacy for citizens. In 2004, the teachers who had participated in the courses conducted media literacy classes as part of the Period for Integrated Studies[4] over the course of one year. However, it has not been practiced since then because the school could not reach a general consensus on the practice of media literacy education and provide a system to support it.

A new departure is now being made with the establishment of the "Takatsuki Media Literacy Project" which is a cooperation between Takatsuki Fourth Junior High School, Tonda Youth Center and researchers from Ritsumeikan University, including the author of this chapter. The overall aim of the project is to implement media literacy education and to empower junior high school students and young people in the area. So far, workshops and other activities on media literacy education have already commenced for teachers who can act as facilitators in later stages of the project. Here, media literacy will be taught as part of the curriculum and evaluations will be made by the researchers involved. Throughout the project, facilitators will learn about media and how to produce materials for analysis. These materials are vital for students in their media literacy learning. This project aims to encourage students to create communication as well as to cultivate the ability to analyze media critically. The project started in 2006, so it is still at a quite primitive stage. However, the notions of the junior high school students are gradually changing through this project, and media literacy classes began in 2007.

Conclusion and further development

Taken together, our surveys and the initial phases of the Takatsuki Media Literacy Project confirm that media literacy is key to the development of citizenship in advanced digital societies, not least to underserved communities. Since media literacy cannot be taught through the traditional Japanese teaching style which focuses on transmitting knowledge from teacher to students, we need to locate and develop frameworks of learning that facilitate media literacy. That is, media literacy classes must promote student dialogue, participation and self-reflection. Also, teachers need systematic training in media literacy in order to heighten their awareness of what it means to live in a media society and to provide tools for their teaching. For this reason, we need to acknowledge media literacy education as integral to continuing education and adult education.

The training of media literacy is particularly important to underserved children whose basic literacy skills are often lower than in other parts of the country, and who tend to be more affirmative in terms of media content (*Survey* 1999). And this importance holds true not only for Japan. For instance, aboriginal children in Australia (grades three, five and seven) are a bit superior to other children in terms of computer literacy (MCEETYA 1998), while their reading skills score 9-26 per cent lower than the average (MCEETYA 1998). Inuit children in Canada (grades 4-10) are 20 per cent lower in terms of literacy and numeracy, and in grade 12 the difference is 40 per cent (British Columbia Human Rights Commission 1999, 9-10). Such groups of children are in special need of developing tools so that they will be able to access and analyze media critically and be able to co-product on their own terms and with their own views on society and social change. Digital media offer a wide range of access options, but children need training if they are to also use these options for their own empowerment and critical awareness. Since children from underserved areas tend to be the most affirmative audiences, they will most likely benefit the most from developing and exercing digital tools for production, participation and collaboration (see also Livingstone 2005, 26).

Still, some scholars suggest that media literacy is difficult to promote in societies dominated by neo-conservative policies (Andersen et al. 2000,

13), and this label fits the current Japanese government, so it seems difficult to develop media literacy education as part of the national curriculum. Although some teachers or schools offer media literacy education as part of their own work, the lack of a long term perspective in media literacy education in Japan will probably not change any time soon. Therefore, local communities play a key role in developing innovative environments for students' media literacy learning. This is also demonstrated to some extent by the many projects carried out by the Canadian Association for Media Literacy. Naturally, learning resources, processes and results cannot simply be transferred across boundaries of culture, class and gender. Still, both scholars and practitioners can benefit from knowledge exchange and collaboration, not only to confirm obvious differences, but equally to detect unsuspected commonalities resulting from living in and handling everyday life in societies permeated by digital media.

Notes

[1] The author would like to acknowledge the participation of the following colleagues at the Ritsumeikan University in the preparation of and participation in the survey on which parts of the analyses in the present chapter are based: Midori Suzuki, the late Director of the Japan Media Literacy Research Institute; researcher and MA graduate student Hideyuki Yatake; researchers and ph.d. candidates Reiko Fuji, Sally McLaren and Hisaka Nishimura.

[2] A report prepared by the Dowa Measures Council in 1965 stated: "The Dowa Problem is Japan's most serious social problem since it constitutes discrimination against a special group of the nation's people based on the historically-developed social class structure. The people concerned are forced into an economically, socially and culturally inferior position, and face both grave violations or their basic human rights and complete ignorance of their civil rights and liberties, which are to be fully guaranteed to all Japan's people as a principle mechanism of modern society" (quoted in Buraku 2006, 8-37).

[3] See the home page of Buraku Liberation and Human Rights Research Institute: http://blhrri.org

[4] The Period for Integrated Studies is "essentially a 'free subject' to be designed by individual schools and teachers" (Ministry n.d.).

References

Andersen, N. et al. 1999. Media education in Canada: The second spring. In *Children and media: Image, education, participation. Yearbook 1999*, ed. Cecilia von Feilitzen and Ulla Carlsson. Gothenburg: Nordicom.

British Columbia Human Rights Commission. 2001. *Pathway to equality: Hearings on access to public education for aboriginal people.* Vancouwer: Education Resources Information Centre. http://www.eric.ed.gov/ERICDocs/data/ericdocs2sql/content_storage_01/0000019b/80/19/77/14.pdf.

Buraku liberation and Human Rights Research Institute. 2006. *Buraku liberation human rights instruments.* 3rd ed. http://homepage3.nifty.com/nagahumanrights/shiryo1/toshin.htm#dai1bu

Goto, Y. 2005. Conctruction of a scale for media literacy. *Bulletin of Japan Society for Educational Technology* 29: 77-80.

Inoue, N., and A. Nakamura. 2001. *O sodateru kokugo no jyugyo [Media literacy].* Tokyo: Meiji tosh.

Kikuzawa, M. et al. 2001. *Jyoho [Literacy].* Tokyo: Morikita shuppan.

Komaya, M. 2000. The practice of media literacy curriculum. *Audio-Visual Education* 54(12): 36-39.

Livingstone, S. et al. 2005. *Adult media literacy: A review of the research literature.* London: Ofcom. http://www.ofcom.org.uk/advice/media_literacy/medlitpub/medlitpubrss/aml.pdf

Ministerial Council on Education, Empolyment, Traning and Youth Affairs (MCEETYA). 1998. *National report on schooling in Australia 1998.* http://www.mceetya.edu.au/mceetya/anr_1998,12030.html#download.

Ministry of Education, Culture, Sports, Science and Technology. n.d. http://www.mext.go.jp/b_menu/shuppan/sonota/990301c/990301l.htm.

Mizukoshi, S., and S. Yoshimi, ed. 2003. *Media practice.* Tokyo: Serikashobo.

National Institute for Educational Research of Japan. 2004. *Heno shotai: Shougaigakushushakai o ikiru chikara [Media literacy].* Tokyo: Toyokan shuppan.

Nihon H. K. (NHK). 2006. hosobunkakenkyusho seronchosabu shichoritsu group [Research on television viewing and radio listening: From the rating survey June 2006], *The NHK monthly report on broadcast research* 664.

Nishioka, K. 2003. *Kyoka to sogo ni ikasu portfolio hyoka: Aratana kachikijyun no soshutsu ni mukete.* Tokyo: Toshobunkasha.

Shibata, Y. 2006. *Hihantekishikouryoku wo sodateru: Jyugyo to gakushushudan no jissen.* Tokyo: Nihon Hyojun.

Suzuki, M. 1997. *O manabu hito notameni [Media literacy].* Kyoto: Sekaishisosha.

—. 2001. *No genzai to mirai [Media literacy].* Kyoto: Sekaishisoha.

—. 2003. *Study guide Media Literacy gender hen*. Tokyo: Liberta shuppan.

—. 2004. *Shinpan nyumon hen [Study guide media literacy]*. Tokyo: Liberta shuppan.

Survey of junior high school students: Focusing on gender and discrimination. 1999. Tonda: Tonda Youth Community Center, Fourth Junior High School and Human Rights Research Institute.

Wakayama, H. 2001. *Gakusei no tameno jyoho [Literacy]*. Tokyo: Tokyodenki University Press.

Yamauchi, Y. 2003. *Shakai no: Manabi no o suru [Digital literacy: Community design]*. Tokyo: Iwanamishoten.

CHAPTER TWELVE

INFORMAL LEARNING: A SOLUTION IN SEARCH OF A PROBLEM?

JULIAN SEFTON-GREEN

This chapter offers an historical and discursive interpretation of the ways that the concept of informal learning has been deployed in relation to digital media (especially commercial leisure forms of media culture) in recent years in order to tease out some of the assumptions underpinning the yoking together of the two terms - digital media and informal learning. In effect I want to suggest that their coming together exemplifies a kind of mythologisation – almost in the Barthesian tradition – so that we now take an unconsidered and under-theorised notion of informal learning to explain the uses (and more problematically the alleged "benefits") of media use. My focus is primarily on digital media in relation to out-of-school commercial use by children and young people. I am not suggesting that informal learning is used to explain all possible uses of all digital media, but I am arguing that reflecting on how and why the two concepts have become connected reveals interesting ambitions about how we think about education and learning in current times. Indeed, I conclude by suggesting that informal learning has become a discursive strategy to lever the use of commercial media as part of an overall educational strategy for modern times in ways that paradoxically echo the use of the new literacies as ways of deconstructing the dominance of print culture.

My premise is that informal learning (not necessarily the phrase, but the idea) has become a bit of a buzzword as forms of media culture have become accommodated into the broad spectrum of educational technologies now comprising the media ecology for youth today. I am suggesting that participating in forms of media culture is now presumed to involve some kind of informal learning, and that therefore some of the benefits of the spread of commercial media cultures could be said to be a kind of "learning dividend". There are many examples of these popular "myths" and some of them are analysed and explored in this volume. Keri

Facer's opening salvo to an article, brought out by the British Futurelab, "Why do we think it's worth talking about computer games and learning in the same breath?" (Facer 2003) is good example of attempts to engage with a common-sense public agenda making a radical and radical transformative offer, utilising a kind of subversive learning going on counter, or in parallel, to schooling.

It is not that I do not support such ambitions. I do, and as I discuss later I have been involved in several projects that take a similar strategy and approach. But what I want to do here is investigate how informal learning has been used over quite a long period of time as a way of deconstructing the tight supposedly "closed" relationship between learning and schooling, of showing that learning does not "equal" schooling. The relationship between learning and schooling is, as Street (2003) would phrase it, an "ideological" construction anyway, it is the result of historical and discursive influences; so my argument is that making informal learning carry an alternative position, even an oppositional one, in the end only buys into the ideological construction closing off learning and schooling in the first place. Paradoxically, I suggest it reifies and mystifyies learning; and so, for all the strategic advantages of how we characterise informal and out-of-school learning, its radical potential can only remain locked in a dialectic struggle with schools: it does not offer a solution or synthesis.

My underlying question is thus to try to work out what this common-sensical yoking together of informal learning and digital media might mean in social or policy terms, and to do this we need to work out the relative truthfulness unpinning claims that the uses of digital media do of course encourage kinds of informal learning. The chapter is thus organised into three sections. I first explore definitions of informal learning, describing the history and uses of the term (or concept). Secondly I look at the connection of the idea (which of course pre-dates digital media) with contemporary forms of media culture and try to tease out why the idea is so dominant at the present time. This second section first looks at ICT in education and then at some examples of research into informal learning and digital media. The conclusion tries to answer the challenge I have set for myself: what difference might informal learning make and for whom?

The history of informal learning

Conceptions of informal Learning in some shape or form have been around for a long time. For example, *Jude the Obscure*, the novel by British author Thomas Hardy first published in 1895, tells the story of a young rural child desperate to learn and study but excluded from university – symbolised by the distant spires of Oxford – by class and poverty. The novel does make a great case for the virtues of informal learning and describes the early years of Jude hunched over books, reading surreptitiously and subversively as he delivers milk, for example. Later in the book, this autodidactism leads to the tragic end of Jude's family, and it may be that this vengeful moralism still underscores ambitions for self-teaching.

However, the book exemplifies some key themes for our purposes and implicitly sets up a contrast between out-of-school learning as characterised over a hundred years ago and contemporary processes. Jude is a good example of a motivated, engaged learner. He learns outside formal schooling structures and systems (albeit obviously aping them at a deeper level, as shown in descriptions of him learning bits of the classics he does not "understand"). If *Jude* described a young boy playing his PSP under a desk we would, I suggest, categorise it as a subversive, transformative experience - which is what Hardy does. Indeed, the way Jude's learning mimics forms of inclusion (reading the classics exemplifies the way that the possession of knowledge creates status, for example) is also a very contemporary educational concern. Yet, paradoxically, learning for Jude only reinforces his exclusion just as it appears to open doors for him, and in the narrative of this novel such aspirations lead to tragic consequences – which is not, I think, what I am saying about informal learning in digital culture.

In the United Kingdom, this tradition of self help book learning – of the entry into literacy as a coming to consciousness, is strongly represented in the literature of the working class labour movement (Rose 2001). Indeed, as Rose shows, institutions like Ruskin College at Oxford and several Working Man's Colleges throughout the United Kingdom were all created as a way of making visible the informal study group or the self help kinds of experiences represented fictionally by Jude. As can be seen in the current manifestations of these traditions, like the web resource <www.infed.org>, writing and policy interventions supporting the creation of community based education institutions have eventually become incorporated into mainstream provision and I will return to this process of recuperation later.

This deliberately "alien" reference to informal learning emphasises that in and of itself it is not a new concept. Indeed, prior to the digital age informal learning had been a key theme in educational discourse and associated with key values. It has been particularly associated with what we would now call social capital acquisition.[1] Indeed, throughout the 20th century there has been a strong tradition in Scandinavia as well as in the

United Kingdom and the USA about the value of out-of-school learning and in particular the role of this domain for traditionally excluded groups as well as a strong (frequently religious) belief in the rounded nature of informal learning.

Of course, what is beginning to emerge here is the nature of the difference, explicit or implicit, political or structural, between informal and formal learning. Interestingly, the title of this volume is not simply “learning” and digital media’ but informal learning and digital media. On one level this distinguishes its field of interest from pure educational technology drivers, but on the other hand it begs the question what is the difference between formal and informal learning; or indeed in what ways is informal learning a sub-set of learning in general.

Defining informal learning

One of the earliest academic attempts to theorise informal learning beyond simply asserting its value, is the 1973 paper by Scribner and Cole. This begins a tradition of work in the socio-cultural tradition and makes a clear case:

> Our thesis is that school represents a specialized site of educational experiences which are discontinuous from those encountered in everyday life and that it requires and proposes ways of learning and thinking which often run counter to those nurtured in practical daily activities. In making this argument we will accentuate the contrasting features of school learning and everyday learning, although, in fact, the two are constantly intermingled (Scribner and Cole 1973, 553).

In what now seems a prescient move, Scriber and Cole started from the assumption that most research on learning derived from non-socio-cultural approaches looking at school based systems of learning and argued that if we just accept the fact that the social organisation of learning differs from site to site, then learning occurring in the non-formal domain is crucially important. This approach opened the door to a huge range of research of which language learning and literacy acquisition are the most prominent examples (see Baynham 2004). Implicitly, this work explored the complexity, the structured nature and the embedded social nature of informal learning, although learning language or literacy was the object of this study rather than the notion of informal learning in its own right. The more ethnographic and anthropological accounts of literacy and language acquisition also inscribed the study of informal learning as in some ways an adventure into the unknown.

Although right from the beginning scholars in the socio-cultural tradition accepted that they had to over-exaggerate the differences between both domains (formal and informal), and that features of both kinds of processes could be found in both domains, this work has spawned a huge range of learning and social theory, in particular leading to theories of learning as participation associated with Lave and Wenger (1991) which have become especially useful in characterising the values of communities of learners in the digital age.

Once it had become accepted that informal learning could be theorised in this way, that it offered a legitimate object for study, the key (and oft repeated question) becomes how we distinguish between formal and informal learning. Scribner and Cole focus on the social organisation of knowledge. In doing so, they also touch on the idea (followed up by later scholars) that debates about the nature of learning via this informal route is indistinguishable from the politics of education.

Because schools occupy such a central role in the organisation, transmission, and regulation of knowledge and accepted forms of pedagogy it is obvious that a discussion about informal learning becomes more than simply a disinterested account of socio-cultural (or even cognitive) processes. The critique of schooling as social reproduction, the analysis of the status of knowledge developed by Bernstein (1990) and the power of pedagogy developed by Bourdieu and Passeron (1990) are all examples of how discussion about the nature of formal learning becomes a discussion about power in society. In other words, socio-cultural discussion cannot separate claims for the impact and significance of school learning from notions of how individuals are subjected to, identify with and "behave" according to its process, and this affects the nature of the claims that can or are made for informal learning. In particular it become very difficult to isolate pure cognitive claims for informal learning if the socio-cultural approach aims to explore how context constructs the nature of the learning process. Most writers and researchers are sensitive to this problem and in fact have circled round this problem of the distinctiveness of informal learning from formal learning. Implicitly and explicitly, then, discussion of informal learning thus become a lens through which to interrogate some of these political questions about formal learning.

There is a substantial literature about informal learning (e.g. Bekerman et al. 2005) and much of it does try to distinguish the unique and distinguishing characteristics of informal learning as a distinct mode; although it is also true that many writers do not at the end of the day generally hold onto extremely hard and fast distinctions between informal and formal learning, or between modes of informal learning and learning in general. In general, much of the recent study of informal learning derives from workplace studies and/or cultural anthropology and does not focus on young people. Taking these caveats into consideration, the literature on informal learning can be broken down along the following key axes (see Colley et al. 2003 for an extended and more detailed taxonomy):

1. Location. Where the learning takes place - how and if context is a determinant of processes
2. Processes. How the learning is organised, whether there are forms of accreditation and assessment: what kind of style or pedagogic relationship is used. How the learning is supported and whether it is collective, collaborative or individual
3. Purposes. Why the learning occurs, in whose interests ?
4. Content. Whether the knowledge has disciplinary provenance, how it is applied theoretically and in practice.

In very general terms these elements underpin all attempts to characterise and describe formal and informal learning.

Finally, and as a way of summing up this overview of the pre-digital uses of informal learning I want to refer to a chronology of the use of informal learning in policy over the longer term (see also Drotner, this volume). Again, I suggest that this historical perspective is useful in trying to evaluate the meaning of current interests in informal learning in respect of digital media. Indeed, as I suggested in my reference to *Jude the Obscure*, the ways that formal institutions have responded to or been influenced by the practices of informal learning are also instructive. Colley et al. (2003) identify five key moments of institutional practice, and I want to outline some of these to complete my framing of the concept.

The period prior to the 1970s saw an incorporation of informal networks and a growth of state sponsorship for bottom-up initiatives. It also saw the growth of youth clubs and adult education programmes, especially in the emerging nation states of the post-colonial world. Secondly, and post the 1970s there was a move to validate and describe kinds of informal learning in ways that could not be incorporated by the disciplinary organisation of knowledge represented by the formal education system. This was in response to a variety of theoretical challenges to academic conventions. Thirdly, in the 1980s Colley et al. (2003) argue that we can see the processes of recuperation whereby non formal education was brought under the state‘s changing remit by changing forms of assessment and validation as well as by changing control of funding for voluntary and non-institutional education systems.

The final era, it is suggested, can be characterised by a re-evaluation of current non-formal learning. Informal learning and the non-formal education sector have become much more visible in policy and focus particularly on strategies to promote social cohesion and economic competitiveness. In effect, I am suggesting that current attention to the role of digital media and commercial culture in young people's lives is being constructed by the same criteria; that, for some, the spaces of commercial media culture offer a form of recuperation of what has been often regarded as "dangerous pleasures", although the mainstream rejection of media culture as an educational site means that this remains a contentious strategy.

In summary, this brief review of the definition and uses of the idea of informal learning exhibits two key themes:

1. There is a history of the processes of recuperation, that is how kinds of informal learning, which started outside of schools and state-funded education, have developed in respect to each other.
2. The increasing visibility of informal learning as part of the rhetoric around learning strategies and, in particular, how the moves towards an interest in the knowledge economy as part of neo-liberal economic governance have continued to emphasise types of informal learning as a key component of this shift.

The idea and practice of informal learning predates digital media, but obviously current interest in the concept is co-terminus with the growth and penetration of digital media into the home and into all forms of leisure use; and it is to a more precise discussion of this relationship that and I now want to turn with my second organising question: what is the connection of informal learning to digital media, and why now?

Informal learning and digital media I: The ICT approach

For this section, I want to begin by referring to the distinction between information and communication technologies (commonly known as ICT within English discourse) and digital media in general. ICT is the name given to computers, often in conjunction with the internet, but usually found in discourse of a more explicitly educational nature than the cultural uses of digital media (which relate to forms of commercial media culture). In the United Kingdom, the ICT term is used in virtually all policy and curriculum documents relating to digital media in education and is really a kind of shorthand. However, I want to introduce it because there is a substantial literature about informal learning with ICT – but the literature dealing with learning and media culture is less oriented towards educationalists and education readers (see Sefton-Green 2006).

There is no doubt that intertwined with the current re-evaluation of informal learning, as suggested in the model put forward by Colley et al. (2003) in the previous section, is the fact that access to the resources presumed to be necessary for learning are now more widespread and available. Indeed, the relationship between scarcity of resources and social access runs through this whole discussion (right back to the exclusion experienced by Jude and the other working class autodidacts), and it is likely that a political economy approach to this subject would prove fruitful, but there is not space to discuss that here. The wider business of education has moved very clearly away from the narrow market of the school into family life, and it is clear that pursuing ICT into the home has been a key feature of this shift (Nixon 1998, Kenway and Bullen 2001, Buckingham and Scanlon 2002). It would be intriguing to speculate whether it is the growth of ICT that has galvanised this interest in informal learning or vice versa, but we do know that the collision of interests has received a considerable amount of policy attention in the last decade.

There is a critique which argues that the first generation of what we might call "ICT-isation" into the home deliberately and explicitly used notions of informal learning (amongst others) as part of its strategy to place computers in the home. I do not especially want to concentrate on that here but rather draw your attention to Helen Nixon's case study of the discourse around learning and ICT which accompanied the selling of computers into Australian homes in the 1990's (Nixon 1998). That study clearly showed how learning was positioned as a necessary good in the acquisition of ICT in the home and how a national economic strategy - Australia's smart society - was intertwined with this kind of individualised expenditure. Nixon shows very well how ICT was associated with an "educational" benefit. The kind of educational benefit she explored was significantly related to achievement in the formal domain – how ICT could be shown to support school based achievement; and to a great extent much of the study of informal uses of ICT have been oriented to this argument - to supplement formal learning and/or to offer different opportunities to learn at the learners' own time and pace (for a review, see Sefton-Green 2004b).

It is well known that ICT has thus played a key role in broadly based educational strategies of the United Kingdom, Europe and the USA over the last 10-15 years. The UK Online centres (UK Online n.d.) and the initiatives formed as part of the Clinton-Gore administration to cross the digital divide are good examples the uses of ICT to increase participation in learning (Warschauer 2004). There has been a huge spate of ICT based initiatives to remediate the inequalities of social access and to use the advantages of "own time/own space" learning allegedly offered by ICT as a way of addressing low skilled workers and those who were deemed to have failed (or been failed by) mainstream education. Although this approach to the uses of ICT and informal education is usually taken for granted and seen as a general public good, there is now an emerging body of research which is actually showing that ICT is not quite the solution to the problems of low skilled workforces and that despite its appeal and assumed accessibility it is not closing the education gap.

Evidence here, especially the work of Neil Selwyn, shows that the persistent policy interest in ICT is leading to a narrowing of provision, that the so called benefits of learning at your own time and in your space can actually lead to closure and conflict with formal education institutions. An over-reliance on ICT as *the* key way of breaking down barriers mean that people have taken their eye off other social issues relating to participation and continuation in learning by fixating on the technological solution. Finally, it has been argued that whatever the pedagogical benefits of learning with ICT it does not necessarily offer a single, simple solution to successful learning (Selwyn 2006).

Both Nixon's and Selwyn's approaches thus point to the limitations of ICT as a key mechanism to facilitate informal learning for two reasons:

1. They implicitly argue that bandwagon effects – about ICT as the solution to learning – exaggerate claims at the expense of analysis and
2. They underscore how differentiating between formal and informal learning is an artificial process and that we need to pay attention to the structure of formal learning more than imagining that attention to the informal route resolves challenges already extant within the education system. Informal learning may be important as a supplement but it cannot replace formal systems.

As I noted above, ICT is not quite the same thing as digital media (it obviously is for technical or theoretical purposes but not in respect of the discursive frames used to characterise different social domains). But unlike the field of digital media studies there is consistent research in the ICT tradition about its impact on informal learning in the way there is not about media culture or digital media in general. But the analysis of the limits of that bridging or cross-over are also instructive.

Informal learning and digital media II: The media culture approach

By contrast, study of the informal learning attendant on the consumption of digital media in the home or in media culture is by definition much less clear about impact and significance. I am referring here to the study of any learning that may or may not be going on as part of the consumption and use of digital media produced for commercial purposes and usually consumed as forms of popular youth culture. Obviously, learning is not the stated primary aim of digital media culture (unlike, it should be noted, the ICT uses of digital media), and therefore it is much more complicated trying to work out what role learning might play in the consumption process.

In addition, the recent development in participatory communities deriving from Web 2.0 technologies as a part of active consumption has given new impetus to what learning might mean. Although statistics about the exact nature of participation on social networking sites and in other forms of expressive culture are notoriously difficult to prove, it is suggested that access to the means of production now allow young people hitherto undreamt of opportunities to make, share and create forms of media culture (for an extended discussion of these arguments, see Sefton-Green 2004b). Importantly, and in tune with the point of view of this chapter, these developments appear to be underpinned by the argument that participation in new forms of media culture offers young people a different kind of agency which in turn allows them access to different kinds of learning. Here, how the young person is positioned in response to local or global audiences as a social actor is at odds with the conventional roles usually accorded youth and, it is argued, is central to the different nature of the learning that is attendant on consumption (e.g. Prensky 2006, Gee 2004).

The kinds of informal learning investigated in this area are many and varied and several examples have been covered in this volume. To give a brief characterisation of the kind of arguments developed here I will reprise two examples from my own work, not because they are particularly original but because they illustrate the range of and scope of the analytic field; and, I would now argue, point to some of the limitations inherent in the strategic aspirations about the uses of informal learning.

My first example comes from a study I co-authored in 2004 (O'Hear and Sefton-Green 2004). This is case study of a young man (Tom, aged 14 at the time) and how his leisure-time enthusiasm for a particular band, "Interpol", transferred into his participation on an online web-site, and thence to his growth and development as a young artist. We described Tom's online interactions on the forum, or bulletin board, dedicated to the band - on a site initially set up by the recording company - and showed how one strand of the bulletin board became, through user pressure, dedicated to artwork about or for the band. Tom became a lead member of this group, and, in stark contrast to his experiences of formal schooling, we showed a series of interactions with other group members, including a detailed study of how his semi-anonymous participation led to peer critiques (of his art work) and a real sense of engaging with critical support groups. We analysed how Tom used his experience (looking at a succession of pictures he worked on and through reflective interviews) as a way of finding and relating to an audience for his work and how he developed a position within the social network of the forum; and finally how he could use hobby-style activities as a way of progressing his art work – which he thought at the time led directly to his getting into art school. We were interested in how the structural features of the forum (both social and technological) supported Tom's growth as a young artist and how social experiences like these offer a different model of a "learning community" – a model, we suggested, which has profound implications for education and the creative industries.

The chapter was clearly interested in the nature of the learning underpinning all of these transactions, and we itemised the uses of anonymous identity, the construction of a learner identity, the directness and focus on the critical discussion and the agency afforded to a young man who would not usually be as confident in acting in this way. These features were all important because of the way they offered forms of supplement to Tom's characterisation of failure in his mainstream formal learning experiences. Of course, much of the learning interactions taking place were not informal at all, especially the way that Tom learnt from critiques provided by the board's moderator and accepted "guru". However, the learning is voluntary and took place in relation to the space of youth culture which is not normally assumed to be "educational".

Being able to analyse how and why learning takes place in sites that are not usually conceptualised as such is important. It suggests a number of policy shifts, mainly in terms of focusing on what people know and do, rather than most educational policy which tends to be oriented towards service provision. Here we can see how this idea of informal learning works in concert with changing models of the education market, in that such studies suggest a more demand driven rather than supply focused approach. They also show how part of the value of this sort of study is to challenge assumptions about learning perhaps more than to re-invent new kinds of learning in the first place.

The same problems of delineating the boundaries between informal and formal modes of learning and formal and informal forms of knowledge disciplines runs through my second example. This study tried to log my then six-year-old's engagement with Pokemon as he learnt to play the gameboy version of the game and became absorbed in Pokemon culture (Sefton-Green 2004a). In the face of considerable public opprobrium especially by schools across the United Kingdom, the study argues that that engaging in Pokemon was a profoundly complicated learning experience. Indeed, the more the study described how the child modelled himself as a learner, how he absorbed information, how he deployed, reflected on and calculated on the ins and outs of Pokemon, and indeed how he learnt to engage with new media forms, to transfer understanding across modalities, the more strange it seemed that such process were proscribed by schools. So, the reception of Pokemon at that time (2000) exemplified all the classic features of a moral panic.

The study showed how the child's use of trial and error was "disciplined" through iterative and recursive experiences into a more "scientific" process of enquiry and game-strategy, and how his entry into formal literacy (reading and writing) and numeracy was not only co-terminus with these experiences but complemented and supported skills in both the game and the school domain. It also showed how a range of cross media experiences (playing the game across a range of media platforms in what the Japanese media scholar Mizuko Ito (2005) calls the contemporary "media-mix") developed a range of other literacy competencies (reading maps, icons and interpreting story and narrative genres) in ways that clearly support and embed the acquisition of formal literacies.

In many ways I suggested that these experiences paradoxically construct the child as a "pedagogic subject" (Bernstein 2000) in more effective ways than schooling. Pokemon itself uses several pedagogic strategies which mimic forms of schooling like rote learning and forms of testing. Despite being in a domain excluded from formal schooling and totally commercially driven, the experience of the game, learnt informally, had resonance for the child's formal learning in ways that *de facto* put the formal and informal domains into a kind of market competition. And yet, of course the knowledge of Pokemon is entirely fictitious and only has meaning within its game parameters.

I am not suggesting that either of these two examples are extraordinary, but they do show that in paying attention to the processes and meaning of creative consumption we can see young learners involved in atypical acts of agency, and how they take control of their learning in interesting and dynamic ways. Furthermore, although both examples are rooted in studies of informal culture both studies tried to show the links between informal and formal learning.

If we use these examples to reflect back on the issues of what defines informal learning in general, we can see that the four issues of process, purpose, context and content (see section one above) are all at stake here, as are the ways in which these case studies of informal learning circle their relationship with modes of formal learning - from Pokemon rote learning and testing with its mock natural world to Tom's use of the bulletin board as a way of preparing entry to employment.

I suspect that the attention to agency in these and other contemporary studies is a new feature of the interest in informal learning (compared with older models of informal learning). Moreover, the changing power relations (as in the example of Tom) and between young person, media participation and authority (as in the Pokemon study) may well add something new to the debate, especially as, unlike the working class tradition identified at the beginning of this paper, questions of status and the regulation of knowledge seem to have become more permeable than in past times – although this is not to say that they disappeared altogether.

The power of "informal learning"?

This final section aims to reflect back on our key question here which is what difference might the idea of informal learning make and for whom? And, to recapitulate, I am asking this question because I have suggested that informal learning has been used with greater intensity as a form of educational polemic in conjunction with a host of other social developments, especially around the spread of new technologies and changes in the "communications order", a use which suggests that this confluence of ideas is in some way connected.

Not taking the common sense attractiveness of informal learning at face value is important because of the sense in which digital media (and by this I mean popular forms of media culture produced and circulated by the marketplace) have become ideologically incorporated as a kind of "educational technology". Scholars have identified ways in which learning has become a kind of contemporary moral imperative, almost the hallmark of a "good citizen" as part of the move to a "knowledge economy" (see Coffield 2000a, 2000b, 2000c). A key issue in the larger shift is the issue of credentialising forms of learning (Edwards 1997) in the push to re-frame all kinds of intellectual work as educational in some sense or other. My challenge is to ask whether the current discourse of informal learning now found in studies of media culture, deriving from the more explicitly ICT oriented educational language, is in some ways incorporated into this aspiration; and if it is, would it be a good or a bad thing?

I and others have been involved in a number of initiatives to reconcile learning in the informal domain with the formal domain. If young people are involved in all sorts of exciting learning outside school how could or should the curriculum or pedagogic relationship be re-worked to accommodate this? Of course school is not a neutral space, so this challenge becomes one of negotiation, resistance and/or setting aside by both young people and adults. Moreover, I admit to being quite entranced by the romance of informal learning. In the face of its denial, as in the Pokemon study, I feel a great sense of frustration about how such learning is ignored; but in arguing for the recognition of informal learning we should not overstate its impact or effectiveness.

One way of entering into this discussion about informal learning is to locate it as part of a debate about the status of knowledge in general, and this relates to anxiety about the curriculum, the meaning of high culture and so-forth – all of which we can find within the formal domain. The desire to validate informal learning and to emphasise its role in young people's lives derives partly from a desire to question and unsettle conventional assumptions about what counts as learning in the first place.

Just as I re-visited *Jude* at the opening of this chapter I also re-examined Jon Katz's emblematic text *Geeks* as a way into this argument (Katz 2000) This book created a great deal of controversy in its elevation of the geek, a controversy which is not germane to my discussion here. My interest is in the contradictions of its narrative. Following the story of two IT autodidacts from Idaho, Katz tells the story of how the young men came to Chicago and earned a good living in the new digital economy of that time. What is interesting about this story is that on the one hand informal learning (albeit of newly constituted forms of formal knowledge) get these young men into well-paid jobs. It validates informal learning as a new democratising mode of access into previously excluded occupations. On the other hand, Katz spends a lot of the "story" (it is journalism) trying to get the young men into university as a way of safeguarding their future. The issue here is how to invest what they know in ways they can recoup in later life and also, it should acknowledged, giving them ways to reflect on their learning in deeper and more structured ways. The contradiction emerges from Katz's attachment to the liberal values of a university education in the face of his thesis: that digital media is changing traditional routes to learning, achievement and employment. Like my arguments above, Katz acknowledges that the informal route is exciting and challenging, but ultimately he is unwilling to use it to supplant formal learning. It become a strategy for broadening access, not for challenging the status of learning in the first place.

Katz suggests that you cannot escape the structure of formal learning, that however good these young people are at IT, however employable they become, they still benefit from going to university. But is this a moral or a value judgement or an assessment of the role of credentials in defining the value of learning?

Here, I suggest that the uses of informal learning have come to echo the strategies of what has become known as the New Literacy Studies (NLS) which has been developing over the last twenty years (Street 2003). This approach argues that literacy is an ideological construction rather than an organic, universal process and that it depends on local, contingent definitions. The NLS suggests a host of ways to re-consider literacy practices as a way of validating unrecognised and un-acknowledged forms of understanding, expression and communication. A recent example might be the collection edited by Mahiri identifying and celebrating informal learning in and of itself (Mahiri 2003). That volume brought together a number of studies about non-traditional literate practices and, in the same way I have argued here for informal learning attendant on the consumption of commercially produced media, made the case for the need to recognise and acknowledge the marginalised, excluded and unrecognised.

I have deliberately concluded with this reference to the new literacy studies because for all its intellectual coherence and acceptance, NLS have made very little inroad into most formal curricula governing literacy across the developed world. Indeed, in the United Kingdom and the USA, for example, literacy has become even more defined as a closed narrow practice emphasising the mastery of print literacy quite the opposite of the NLS with its understanding of multimodality and multiple literacies. By analogy, I am thus suggesting that informal learning has been as useful as new literacies as unsettling what we take for granted but possibly of limited effect in impacting on core definitions of the value in learning in society at large.

As a conclusion I would repeat that whilst I do not think there is anything substantive about the role of digital media in the construction of informal learning, there are plenty of important accidental issues to consider. It is important to value kinds of informal learning if only to continue to push away at the definitions and regulatory controls of formal learning; although it is equally important not to be distracted by the medium and let digital technology take the credit for that. I am genuinely agnostic whether this remains a rhetorical strategy - that in redefining learning (by allowing for all kinds of informality), it becomes so elastic that it disappears. Above all, we need to know more about the differences we are claiming from informal learning. Do they remain at a local level? Can young people transfer this understanding beyond immediate experiences to other domains? Or, like the young people in Katz's book, do they need university? And finally, we need to tease out a little more who exactly is participating in these new learning regimes? My own studies did not deal with young people who are socially excluded, they were both middle-class subjects who were best positioned to utilise and exploit these informal experiences. Are we changing the franchise for learning in general, or has informal learning become another way of validating those already on "the inside"? There are not sufficient studies of the new creative class to know this as yet, and that is where future studies should be directed.

Notes

[1] See, for example, descriptions of the Germanic tradition of social pedagogy and accounts of philosophy of camping and how it underpins the power of association and sociality. http://www.infed.org/i-intro.htm

References

Baynham, J. 2004. Ethnographies of literacy: An introduction. *Language and Education* 18(4): 285-290.

Bekerman, Z., N. C. Burbules, D. S. Keller, and D. Silberman-Keller. 2005. *Learning in places: The informal education reader*. New York: Peter Lang.

Bernstein, B. 1990. *Class, codes and control: The structuring of pedagogic discourse. Vol 4*. London: Routledge.

—. 2000. *Pedagogy, symbolic control and identity*. Rev. ed. Lanham, MD: Rowman and Littlefield.

Bourdieu, P., and J.-C. Passeron. 1990. *Reproduction in education, society and culture.* London: Sage.

Buckingham, D., and M. Scanlon. 2002. *Education, entertainment and learning in the home*. Maidenhead: Open University Press.

Coffield, F. 2000a. *The necessity of informal learning*. Bristol: The Policy Press.

—. 2000b. *Differing visions of a learning society: Research findings*. Bristol: The Policy Press.

—. 2000c. *Research findings: Differing visions of a learning society*. Bristol: The Policy Press.

Colley, H., P. Hodkinson, and J. Malcom. 2003. *Informality and formality in learning: A report for the Learning and Skills Research Centre*. Leeds: University of Leeds.

Edwards, R. 1997. *Changing places? Flexibility, lifelong learning and a learning society*. London: Routledge.

Facer, K. 2003. *Computer games and learning.* Bristol: FutureLab. http://www.futurelab.org.uk/resources/documents/discussion_papers/Computer_Games_and_Learning_discpaper.pdf (retrieved May 31, 2007).

Gee, J. P. 2004. *What video games have to teach us about learning and literacy*. Basingstoke: Palgrave Macmillan.

Ito, M. 2005. Technologies of the childhood imagination: Yugioh, media mixes, and everyday cultural production. In *Structures of participation in digital culture,* ed. J. Karaganis and N. Jeremijenko. Durham: Duke University Press.

Kalantzis, M., and B. Cope. 1999. *Multiliteracies: Literacy learning and the design of social futures*. London: Routledge.

Katz, J. 2000. *Geeks: How two lost boys rode the internet out of Idaho*. New York: Villard Books.

Kenway, J., and E. Bullen. 2001. *Consuming children: Education, entertainment, advertising*. Buckingham: Open University Press.

Lave, J., and E. Wenger. 1991. *Situated learning: Legitimate peripheral participation*. Cambridge: Cambridge University Press.

Mahiri, J. 2003. *What they don't learn in school: Literacy in the lives of urban youth*. New York: Peter Lang.

Nixon, H. 1998. Fun and games are serious business. In *Digital Diversions: Youth Culture in the age of multimedia,* ed. J. Sefton-Green. London: Routledge.

O'Hear, S., and J. Sefton-Green. 2004. Creative "Communities:" How technology mediates social worlds. In *Collaborative creativity: Contemporary perspectives,* ed. D. Miell and K. Littleton. London: Free Association Press.

Rose, J. 2001. *The intellectual life of the British working classes*. Yale, CT: Yale University Press.

Scribner, S., and M. Cole. 1973. Cognitive consequences of formal and informal education. *Science* 182: 553-559.

Sefton-Green, J. 2004a. Initiation rites: A small boy in a Poke-world. In *Pikachu's global adventure: The rise and fall of Pokemon*, ed. J. Tobin, pp. 141-64. Durham: Duke University Press.

—. 2004b. *Literature review in informal learning with technology outside school. Report 7.* Bristol: FutureLab.

—. 2006. Youth, technology and media cultures. *Review of Research in Education* 30: 279-306.

Selwyn, N. 2006. *ICT in adult education: Defining the territory. ICT and Learning: Supporting out-of-school youth and adults*. Paris: OECD.

Street, B. 2003. What's "new" in new literacy studies? Critical approaches to literacy in theory and practice. *Current Issues in Comparative Education* 5(2): 77-91.

UK Online Centres. (n.d.). http://www.ukonlinecentres.com/consumer (accessed 31 May, 2007).

Warschauer, M. 2004. *Technology and social inclusion: Rethinking the digital divide*. Cambridge, MA: MIT Press.

CONTRIBUTORS

Kirsten Drotner is Professor of media studies at the Institute of Literature, Culture and Media at the University of Southern Denmark and founding director of DREAM (Danish Research Centre on Education and Advanced Media Materials). Her 15 books include *English children and their magazines, 1751-1945* (Yale UP, 1988), *Researching audiences* (Arnold, 2003; with Kim C. Schrøder, Steve Kline and Catherine Murray), *The international handbook of children, media and culture* (Sage, 2008, co-editor Sonia Livingstone). Currently, she serves on the editorial board of *International Journal of Cultural Studies, International Journal of Learning and Media, Journal of Feminist Media Studies, Journal of Children and Media* and on the editorial advisory board of *Young: Nordic Journal of Youth Research.*

Nelly Elias (Ph.D), Lecturer at the Department of Communication Studies (Ben-Gurion University, Israel), specialises in audience studies of immigrants and their children. She has various academic publications in the field of mass media and immigrants integration, including a book entitled *Coming Home: Media and Returning Diaspora in Israel and Germany* (SUNY Press, 2008) and several peer-reviewed articles in journals such as *Israeli Sociology, International Communication Gazette, Journal of International Communication* and *Journal of Advertising Research.*

James Paul Gee is the Mary Lou Fulton Presidential Professor of Literacy Studies at Arizona State University, USA. His wide-ranging publications include *Sociolinguistics and literacies* (Falmer, 1990) *An introduction to discourse analysis* (Routledge, 1999), *What video games have to teach us about learning and literacy* (Palgrave MacMillan, 2003), *Situated language and learning* (Routledge, 2004) and *Why video games are good for your soul* (Common Ground Publishing, 2005).

Øystein Gilje is PhD student at the Institute for Educational Research, Faculty of Education, University of Oslo, Norway. With a background as a journalist, teacher and consultant to the Norwegian Film Institute, his current research explores how the digitization of visual media has democratized the creative process of making multi-media digital texts, such as films and digital stories.

Glynda A. Hull is Professor of Language, Literacy, and Culture in the Graduate School of Education at UC Berkeley, USA. Her books include *Changing work, changing workers: Critical perspectives on language, literacy, and skill* (SUNY Press, 1997), *The new work order: Education and literacy in the new capitalism* (Allen and Unwin, 1996; with James Gee and Colin Lankshear), and *School's out! Bridging out-of-school literacies with classroom practice* (Teachers College Press, 2002; with Katherine Schultz). The winner of UC Berkeley's Distinguished Teaching Award, Hull offers undergraduate and graduate courses on literacy teaching learning in and out of school.

Hans Siggaard Jensen is Research director and professor at Learning Lab Denmark, University of Aarhus, Denmark. He has worked across the traditional scientific disciplines for many years, with a focus on the field of knowledge and theory of science, especially questions connected to applied sciences, ICT and education. His books in Danish include *The history of western technology* (co-author, Technical Press, 1990), *The power of the mind? The history of ideas in western civilization* (co-editor, Lindhardt and Ringhof 2006).

Sisse Siggaard Jensen is Associate Professor at the Dept. of Communication, Business and Information Technologies at Roskilde University, Denmark. With a professional interest in social interaction and communication through digital media, she has mangaged and collaborated on several interdisciplinary research projects in Denmarks as well as within the European Union's framework programmes, just as she has designed and developed distance learning for more than 15 years.

Nora L. Kenney is a Graduate student who is completing her Ph.D. in the Language and Literacy, Society and Culture program at the University of California, Berkeley Graduate School of Education. She has studied how computer-mediated communication and composition impacts urban youth identities, relationships, and literacy practices. Her dissertation research focuses on urban youth, especially African American boys, and aims to uncover patterns of resilience that enables them to succeed in school and life. Prior to entering graduate school, Kenney worked in the high-tech corporate sector as a writer.

Graeme Kirkpatrick is Senior Lecturer in Sociology at the University of Manchester, UK. His research is on the philosophy and sociology of technology and the political aesthetics of video games. His *Critical technology* (Ashgate 2004) won the 2005 Philip Abrams Memorial Prize from the British Sociological Association. He has published articles in several internationally reviewed journals, including *Thesis Eleven*, *Max Weber Studies* and the *Journal of Cultural Research.*

Guy Lancaster is Web Project Manager at the Humanities Law and Social Sciences Faculty of Manchester Metropolitan University. He has a BSc in Maths and Computing from the Open University and has worked in IT systems development for 25 years in the health, construction, finance, and telephony industries. He has worked in ten different computer languages and on mainframe, server and single user platforms. He is currently developing web-based database-linked systems at MMU, including e-learning, research and student management applications.

Dafna Lemish is Professor of Communication at the Dept. of Communication, Tel Aviv University, and a member of the Board of Directors, International Communication Association. Her research interests include children and media and global communication. She is founding editor of *Journal of Children and Media* (Routledge) and has published widely in internationally reviewed journals such as *Journal of Broadcasting and Electronic Media, New Media and Society* and *Journal of Communication,* and her book publications include *Media education around the globe: Policies and practices* (Hampton Press, 2003, co-editors B. Tufte and T. Lavender), *Media and the make-believe worlds of children: When Harry Potter meets Pokemon in Disneyland* (Erlbaum, 2005, co-authors M. Gotz, D. Aidman and H. Moon), and *Children and television: A global perspective* (Blackwell, 2006).

Yosuke Morimoto is PhD. student at the Graduate School of Education, Kyoto University. He is currently Research Fellow at the Japan Media Literacy Research Institute where he conducts research on young people's media uses.

Dan Perkel is PhD. student at UC Berkeley's School of Information. His research is in how young people produce and use media in their everyday lives and how they influence and shape the technologies they use in this process.

Kim Christian Schrøder is Professor in Communication Studies at Roskilde University, Denmark. His books include *The language of* *advertising* (co-author, Blackwell 1985), *Media cultures: Reappraising transnational media* (co-editor and contributor, Routledge 1992), and *Researching audiences* (co-author, Arnold 2003). His current research deals with news consumption in the media landscape of the digital age, and with methodological issues around the quantitative/qualitative divide.

Julian Sefton-Green is an independent consultant and researcher working in education and the cultural and creative Industries in addition to being an Associate Research Professor at the Hawke Research Institute, University of South Australia. His publications include *Evaluating creativity: Making and learning by young people* (co-editor R. Sinker, Routledge, 2000), *Creativity, young people and new technologies: The challenge of digital arts* (editor, Routledge, 1999), *Digital diversions: Youth culture in the age of multimedia* (editor, UCL Press, 1998), *Making media: Practical production in media education* (with David Buckingham and J. Grahame, English and Media Centre, 1995), *Cultural studies goes to school: Reading and teaching popular culture* (with David Buckingham, Taylor and Francis, 1994).

Håvard Skaar is Research fellow at Oslo University College, Norway. His current research explores how the use of computers and the Internet influences pupils' literacy in and out of school.

John Wilson is an independent scholar working in the fields of game studies and philosophy of technology. He has a BA in Literae Humaniores (Ancient History and Philosophy) from the University of Oxford and an MA in Computer Games Studies from the University of Northumbria.

Sarita Yardi holds a Master degree in Information Management and Systems from UC Berkeley and is currently a Phd. student at the Human-Centered Computing Program, Georgia Institute of Technology, where she specialises in Design of online social networking communities.